CONTEXTUALIZING PSYCHOLOGY

Much contemporary psychology is characterized by a natural science epistemology that overlooks the richness of human experience. This book offers a timely and necessary critique and emphasizes a conception of human beings as persons embedded in relationships, cultural groups, and historical contexts. Eva Magnusson and Jeanne Marecek provide strategies for critical reflective scrutiny of contemporary psychological theories and practices. Using "styles of thinking" as one of their conceptual tools, they investigate whether, and how, theories, research methods, and debates across subfields such as cognition, language, and psychopathology take people's situatedness into account. The book gives readers practical guidance for conceptual analysis, and a set of questions for scrutinizing other subfields and practices. It also describes research methods and projects based on a view of humans as situated persons. The book offers both a philosophical foundation and a hands-on guide to a psychology with persons at its center.

EVA MAGNUSSON is Professor Emerita of Psychology, Umeå University, Sweden, and former Head of Research at the Nordic Institute for Gender Research in Oslo. Eva has published on qualitative research and the psychology of gender, and has served on the editorial board of *Feminism & Psychology* and *NORA (Nordic Journal of Gender Research)*.

JEANNE MARECEK is Professor Emerita of Psychology at Swarthmore College, USA. A cultural psychologist trained in clinical psychology, Jeanne has served on the editorial team of *Feminism & Psychology* since 2007. The American Psychological Association has awarded her the Carolyn Wood Sherif Award (2017) and the Theodore Sarbin Award (2022).

CONTEXTUALIZING PSYCHOLOGY

Critical Perspectives and Person-Oriented Approaches

EVA MAGNUSSON

Umeå Universitet, Sweden

JEANNE MARECEK

Swarthmore College, Pennsylvania

CAMBRIDGE
UNIVERSITY PRESS

Shaftesbury Road, Cambridge CB2 8EA, United Kingdom

One Liberty Plaza, 20th Floor, New York, NY 10006, USA

477 Williamstown Road, Port Melbourne, VIC 3207, Australia

314–321, 3rd Floor, Plot 3, Splendor Forum, Jasola District Centre, New Delhi – 110025, India

Cambridge University Press is part of Cambridge University Press & Assessment, a department of the University of Cambridge.

We share the University's mission to contribute to society through the pursuit of education, learning and research at the highest international levels of excellence.

www.cambridge.org
Information on this title: www.cambridge.org/9781009374101

DOI: 10.1017/9781009374071

First published 2026

Cover image: lasagnaforone / DigitalVision Vectors / Getty Images

A catalogue record for this publication is available from the British Library

A Cataloging-in-Publication data record for this book is available from the Library of Congress

ISBN 978-1-009-37410-1 Hardback
ISBN 978-1-009-37412-5 Paperback

Contents

CHAPTER I

Finding One's Way around Psychology

In this book, we explore research, theory, and practices in psychology with the purpose of identifying ways of doing psychology that are based on a view of human beings as socially and culturally situated *persons*. The book builds on ideas and strategies that we, together with many colleagues, have developed for navigating the wealth of psychological information and knowledge that is available in modern societies today. Such strategies for navigation are helpful because finding one's way around contemporary psychology can otherwise be a daunting task: first, because of the sheer number of theories, research studies, and practices, and second, because there are very few unshakeable and universal truths about human psychology. In this, psychology differs from the natural sciences, where many discoveries and theories are universally valid. Psychological theories and practices, to the contrary, have varied across historical time, and they vary today across cultural settings in different parts of the world. A reason for this is that people vary, over time and across the world, because their living conditions and cultural settings vary. Furthermore, psychologists – researchers as well as clinicians – are also people who live and work in a variety of social and cultural contexts. Their lives in these different contexts provide them with different experiences and assumptions about humans which will inevitably influence how they approach and think about those they study or treat. One should therefore not expect to find any single view of humans, or any one fact about psychological properties, to be always and everywhere valid.

What we have just written means that there are no neutral positions for psychologists to write from. Psychologists are always doing their research and carrying out their psychological practice while situated in some cultural, political, and organizational settings, and belonging to some social, sexual, and ethnic categories. There is no neutral position from which to observe and work. And there are no universal humans to study and draw universal conclusions about. The psychology discipline and, therefore, psychologists as a profession have been increasingly criticized for ignoring these facts and writing from an unacknowledged "Western" platform as if it were neutral and universal. Psychologists have also been criticized for misrepresenting some categories of people, whether consciously or not. This critique is currently doing much to reform many ingrained "Western" ideas and practices in psychology internationally. But, of course, we should remember that the critics are just as culturally and politically, and so on, situated as those they criticize. The critics bring in new essential perspectives, but those perspectives are also partial. This is also true of us who have written this book.

We are clinically and academically trained psychologists and have spent most of our working lives in the academy, doing research and teaching psychology undergraduates, master's students, and doctoral candidates. One of us (Eva) is Swedish and has worked mainly in Sweden and the Nordic countries. The other (Jeanne) is American and has worked mainly in the USA and Southern Asia. One of our common interests as psychologists and researchers has been the psychology of women and gender, which both of us began studying, writing about, and teaching in the 1970s. This interest brought us together in the early 1990s, and since then, we have collaborated on several writing projects. Our interest in questions about gender also very soon and very naturally led to a deepening engagement with more general questions of culture in psychology: the inevitable sociocultural situatedness of individuals and the impact of this situatedness on individual psychology. This is what inspired us to write this book.

In this book, we take seriously what we wrote already about the influence of different cultural contexts on psychologists' assumptions about humans as psychological beings. Strategies for informed reflection upon these assumptions and ways to identify their consequences had high priority for us when we wrote the book. Just as important was the view of human beings as *persons* (more about this soon). We therefore have two main ambitions with the book:

- We want to convey strategies and tools for scrutinizing and navigating among psychological theories and practices (research practices and/or clinical practices). The purpose is to give our readers tools with which to judge whether a theory or practice makes it possible to take people's social and cultural situatedness into account. This is the first ambition.

- The strategies for scrutiny that we describe are based on a perspective on psychology that brings into focus the social and cultural contexts in which persons are embedded. The second ambition is for the book to serve as an introduction to such psychologies.

In the rest of this chapter, we first briefly describe our view of culture and of persons. We then introduce our strategies for informed reflection on psychological theories, methods, and practices. This is followed by the roadmap for the rest of the book.

Culture and Cultural Contexts

In our view, culture is one of the foundational conditions for there to emerge and exist something like what one means by words such as "person," "humans," or "humanity." But at the same time, of course, culture is something that humans have created. This means that there is a kind of circularity regarding culture that might seem confusing: put briefly, culture is both human-created and human-creating. One way of thinking about culture is, therefore, first, as a human-created web of meanings that exists outside of the individual and is part of collective ways of thinking about the world. Secondly, an individual who is a member of a cultural community is, therefore, by definition, as it were, suspended in this local web of meanings (Geertz, 1973). It is this cultural web that provides the conventions, habits, and norms that this individual will encounter from early in life and therefore likely will live by. This, then, means that this cultural web of meanings will be integrated into that individual's psychological life, as the individual becomes integrated into the community. These webs of meanings differ among communities across the world, and they change with changing circumstances.

However, and this is just as important as what we have just said about webs of meaning: human individuals are no cultural dopes. A human individual is always something more than the surrounding cultural context and rules, just as a human individual is always something more than their biological functions. Human individuals are *persons*.

Persons

The concept of *a person* is central to this book. A person is, by definition, part of a sociocultural milieu and is regarded as having certain rights there, as well as certain duties and obligations. Persons can reason, decide on goals, and make choices, and they can reflect on their goals and choices, take actions consonant with them, and change their goals if necessary. And persons are held morally accountable for their choices and actions. However, there is no unanimity, either among psychologists or in other disciplines, about what the word "person" should mean. So, for instance, several understandings of "person" are evoked or implied in contemporary debates on questions about "mind," "self," and "consciousness," as well as debates about the relations between brains, bodies, and individuals. We take up such questions in the book. For instance, in Chapter 4, we consider the many vexed debates about what "mind" is and what its relation is to the person, and what this might mean for psychology. And in Chapter 5, we discuss the equally vexed and long-debated questions about the relations between brains, bodies, and persons, including what can be learned about brain functions in real life from studies done under typically very restricted experimental conditions.

When writing this book, we settled on a definition of "person" that is congenial with the view of culture that we sketched previously and with a view of human beings as socially and culturally situated. The British philosopher Peter Hacker has offered a definition of *person* that captures what we mean:

> While *human being* is a biological category, *person* is a moral, legal and social one. To be a person is, among other things, to be a subject of moral rights and duties. It is to be not only an agent, like other animals, but also a moral agent, standing in reciprocal moral relations to others, with a capacity to know and to do good and evil. Since moral agents can act for reasons, and can justify their actions by reference to their reasons, they are also answerable for their deeds. To be a human being is to be a creature whose nature it is to acquire such capacities in the course of normal maturation in a community of like-natured beings. (Hacker, 2007, p. 4)

In our reading, the crucial elements in Hacker's definition are as follows: *Person* is a moral, legal, and social category. A person stands in reciprocal moral relations to other persons. A person has the capacity to know and do good and evil, to act for reasons, and to be answerable for their deeds in a community of like-natured beings. To be a person is therefore (at least potentially) to have certain physical and psychological capacities (the individual aspect). It is also to take part in certain kinds of activities and interactions (the interactional aspect). And it is to belong to a social and cultural infrastructure that enables personhood (the social and cultural aspect) (Schechtman, 2014).

If one wants to understand a particular person and that person's life, it is therefore not enough to limit one's studies to the person's physical and psychological capacities. Neither is it enough to settle for the person's activities and interactions. One must also take into account the background structures, practices, institutions, and local and general norms that make the other aspects possible; that is, the social and cultural aspects.

Different background structures and practices will enable different kinds of personhood; therefore, these structures and practices are as essential as the individual's physiological and psychological capacities for there to be persons at all. Just as the existence of the social infrastructure depends on the capacities of the humans who built it and keep it going, the capacities of those humans depend on the social infrastructure. The sophisticated cognitive and agential capacities of humans could exist and be developed only within some organized social-cultural setting (Schechtman, 2014).

Now we should ask who qualifies as a person. A fairly common criterion of personhood is the possession of the sophisticated cognitive and agential capacities that we just mentioned (Wagner, 2019). However, applying this criterion strictly would exclude a substantial number of human beings from being considered persons: very young children, those with dementia, and perhaps also comatose individuals on life support. In our experience, most people do not actually apply this stringent criterion in practice. Therefore, we have chosen other criteria of personhood.

Inspired by Marya Schechtman (2014), a US philosopher, and Nils-Frederic Wagner (2019), a German philosopher, we argue that social embeddedness is the key aspect of personhood. Naturally, this embeddedness could not at the start of a human life be based on any higher-order or sophisticated cognition. Human infants have a long period of dependence on caretakers, and it is through interactions with these caretakers that the infant's basic cognitive capacities are gradually developed into the capacities associated with full personhood. This means that social embeddedness precedes – and is a prerequisite for – the development of higher-order cognition. Now, as developmental psychologists have shown in recent decades, human babies from birth engage in social interaction; they are social. This sociality is a constant in humans, and it is an essential part of what it means to be a person. Sociality and social embeddedness are therefore unavoidable parts of a person's life before, and independent of, higher-order cognition (Schechtman, 2014; Wagner, 2019).

In this view, a baby would qualify as a person, although not as a person who, on their own, could make all the necessary decisions about life. The baby would qualify as a person who is enmeshed with others – its caretakers – who are prepared to act as the baby's scaffoldings while supporting them in developing increasingly complex cognitive and moral capacities. What about those with dementia or comatose individuals on life support? Should we see them as persons, or have they ceased to be persons? In the view we suggest here, they are still persons. Again, as with babies, think about the attitudes of the people on whom they depend: The loved ones of someone struck by dementia certainly still think about them as a person. It will necessarily be as a person with limited capacities, but still a person. The same is true of someone struck by long-term coma and medical life support. Just as with young children, the person with dementia and the person on life support are scaffolded by others in their social networks. But they are scaffolded while being seen as, and treated as, persons.

This quote from the British psychologist and historian Roger Smith nicely summarizes our view of persons:

> . . .a human mind, whatever its architecture, has concrete existence only in the life and language of a particular time and place – in a particular culture. Whatever the biological arguments, understanding the psychology of a person, from this viewpoint, requires knowledge of what a "'person" signifies within a language or symbol system. People exist as living social realities not as abstract biological entities. (2013, p. 255)

We share the view of humans as socially situated persons with many others. This view can be found, for instance, in the fields of the psychologies of gender, of racial issues, and of queer theory, in some parts of social psychology, and in the increased interest in decolonial movements among many psychologists, as well as in the recovery movements among and for sufferers of psychiatric disorders. All these fields and movements share the view of human beings as socially and culturally located persons, and they are developing psychological theories and practices that integrate this view in both research and practical psychological work (Allesøe et al., 2025). One tool that enhances this development is the practice of informed reflections on psychology.

Reflecting on Psychology: From the Inside and from the Outside

One of our starting points when writing this book was the insight that to really know psychology as a discipline and as a set of practices, it is necessary to reflect on psychology not just from the inside of the discipline but also, and especially, from its outside. The "inside" is what is provided by textbooks written by psychologists about common psychological topics. Reading such literature is, of course, a good way to learn about psychology. But this insider learning does not reach far enough for our purposes here. One also needs to look in on psychology from the outside. One then asks questions based, for instance, on the philosophy of science, the history of psychology and science, and cultural studies. These questions enable one to find out from where psychological theories and practices emanate, historically and socially, and what have been the social and historical consequences of the theories and practices. For us, one overarching purpose of asking such questions is to help in finding out about the conceptions of human beings that prevail in different parts of psychology and to aid in determining whether or not a theory or practice is compatible with a view of humans as socially and culturally situated persons.

In the book, we offer strategies and tools for informed reflections on, and scrutiny of, subfields, topics, and contested issues in contemporary psychology. Our aim is to help readers choose between existing schools and theories, including research, theory, and practice, by considering how well they fit with a view of persons as socially and culturally situated beings.

It Is Essential That Psychologists Be Prepared to Criticize Their Discipline

We have directed our scrutiny at the kinds of psychologies that are taught and practiced in the "Western" parts of the world. We have done this because these theories and practices have dominated large parts of the world scene of psychology for several decades. Some of them have, on the assumption of universal validity, been exported to very different cultural settings from those in which they were developed. In recent decades, these assumptions of universal validity have come under increasing pressure and critique, and several efforts to move beyond such assumptions have been made. We see this book as part of these efforts. Such developments will inevitably lead to tension and debate – and this is a good thing.

We agree with an increasing number of colleagues in many countries in the world that large parts of contemporary psychology have long been riddled with problematic research practices and theories. At a minimum, by failing to account for the diversity of the world's peoples, such problematic practices and theories risk making the discipline as well as the profession of psychology less than relevant for most of the world's population. At worst, such theories and practices risk imposing the psychological measuring sticks, values, and norms of middle-class people in rich "Western" industrialized countries on people who are not "Western."[1] However, and just as bad, they also risk imposing the same norms on people in "Western" countries who are not middle class or who do not

---

[1] A well-known example of such critique was summarized by the acronym "WEIRD." It was minted by Henrich et al. (2010) and stands for Western, Educated, Industrialized, Rich, and Democratic countries. They focus especially on the narrow "Western" samples of research participants typically used in much of psychology.

belong to the dominant ethnic group (Apicella, Norenzayan, & Henrich, 2020; Ibanez, 2022; Sanches de Oliveira & Baggs, 2023). Further, we should not imagine that all "Western" countries share the same values, norms, and measuring sticks. This means that if most psychological research and theory are produced in a very small number of Western countries, all of this research may not be applicable, or accepted as valid, in the other Western countries. While writing this book, we became increasingly aware of these issues and discrepancies. We therefore decided that, in order to give a sense of the origins of the ideas that we incorporate and discuss in our book, we provide the localities (usually countries of origin) of those whose ideas we have found especially interesting and inspiring.

Moreover, beyond these critiques of cultural myopia, several critics have also argued that many ways of doing psychology have long been riddled with logical and conceptual problems, such that they lack conceptual clarity in their uses of central scientific concepts, and thereby also in their research practices. These critics delve into the discipline's foundational assumptions about humans and about science and question several taken-for-granted practices and ideas (cf. Slaney & Maraun, 2007; Slaney, 2023). The works of critics like these have been an important inspiration to us while writing, and the questions that they have posed appear in several places in the book.

The Roadmap of the Book

Part I: Resources for Investigating Psychology

In Chapter 2, *Thinking Styles in Psychology*, we present a way to reflect upon and scrutinize psychological theories and practices. We use the framework of thinking styles (or thought styles), which was developed by the microbiologist and philosopher of science Ludwik Fleck in the 1930s. A thinking style is the preparedness to see, act, and think in a particular way that characterizes members of cohesive work groups, such as colleagues in a clinic or a research setting. In this view, thinking, acting, and seeing are thoroughly social phenomena that cannot be fully understood without taking context into account. Thus, thinking styles are, by definition, the property of some community of people: a thought collective. Becoming skilled in a field of knowledge includes becoming increasingly socialized into the ways of seeing, acting, and thinking that characterize the thinking style of one's thought collective. In the chapters that follow, we use this framework as a tool when we describe and critically reflect on subfields, topics, and practices in the psychology discipline.

In Chapter 3, *Culture, Communities, and Persons*, we present different views of "culture" in the social sciences. We also present several examples that illustrate how cultural habits and life patterns, and even understandings of what it is to be human, vary across the world. And we point to examples of how psychologists in high-income countries have sometimes, without grounds, assumed the universal validity of theories developed by such psychologists, and suffused by Western (usually middle-class) cultural values. On the contrary, these theories may be inapplicable outside Western contexts, as well as in Western contexts outside the well-educated middle classes and dominant ethnic groups. We draw conclusions about the need for psychologists to be aware of how their own locations and national and other identities may shape what they can see and say.

Part II: Exploring Psychological Subfields, Topics, and Techniques

In Chapter 4, *Minds in Psychology*, the topic is the concept of "mind" and its uses in psychology and philosophy throughout history and today. A reason why it is important to investigate how "mind" is understood in psychology is that, in order to evaluate psychological research, one needs a clear image of the conception of mind that underpins that research. We describe the historical background of the concept itself, as well as changes over time in how the word "mind" has been used, and some differences across languages and cultures today. We identify four historical and contemporary thinking styles – that is, different ways of conceiving of "mind." We discuss the issues and problems connected with each of these styles.

In Chapter 5, *Human Brains and Psychology*, we first describe important attributes of human brains such as their complexity, flexibility, and plasticity. We also consider how cultural habits and traditions influence how brains come to be understood. We look at the many metaphors that have been used, and are still being used, to make sense of the brain. Especially interesting is the computer metaphor, which has developed over time but has accrued increasing debate and critique in recent years. Further, we scrutinize how psychologists and neuroscientists talk and write about brains; for instance, we look closely at ideas about what people's brains are doing when people are doing things: Should brains be seen as active agents that "think," "feel," and so on, or should such agency be reserved for humans? We also discuss the use of brain-focused reductionist explanations of human behavior. Finally, we identify and discuss contemporary styles of thinking about brains.

Chapter 6, *Thinking Persons*, begins by reviewing how thinking has been conceptualized throughout history. We then present two contemporary ideas of how to think about thinking. According to the first idea, thinking takes place in the brain, which is seen as a computational and representational system, often in analogy to how digital computers function. Connected to this view are debates about how thoughts and other mental activities and properties can be represented in people's minds or brains. According to the second idea, thinking takes place in an interactive and dynamic system that includes the individual's body and surroundings. These two ideas are based on different definitions of what "thinking" is: Is it something that could only occur inside a person's brain, or something that may include tools, other people, and other things outside the person? The chapter ends by comparing how different thinking styles about thinking fit with a view of human beings as socially contextualized persons.

Chapter 7, *Language and Psychology*, begins with a review of theories about the evolution of human language, focusing on biolinguistic and usage-based theories. The body of the chapter is devoted to the study of contemporary language use: How people use words to do things, usually things that involve other people. Such study is often based in the so-called action tradition in language studies. It focuses on language use as arising in people's joint activities, including how meaning is typically negotiated and determined through both linguistic and nonlinguistic social interactions. Central concepts in these studies are joint activities, coordination, interactive repair, common ground, and social accountability. The chapter also contains a discussion of two ways of conceiving of how words get their meanings: the classical view and the anthropological view. After a discussion of different styles of thinking about language, we end the chapter by presenting suggestions for the psychological study of people's talk and language use in social situations.

In Chapter 8, *Social and Historical Perspectives on Psychological Suffering*, we consider people's experiences of psychological distress and dysfunction. The forms they take, the meanings they are given, the remedies available, and ultimately, the prognosis for recovery all vary widely. We first turn our attention to questions of diagnosis and categorizations of psychological suffering, focusing on the 75-year endeavor to produce a satisfactory version of the DSM – the *Diagnostic and Statistical Manual of Mental Disorders*, and some of the conceptual and practical problems it has engendered. We also examine the manifold ways in which mental health diagnoses have permeated everyday conversations, and how they are utilized by many social institutions. The next part of the chapter offers a chronology of treatments, not a few of which would now be regarded as dangerous and destructive. We conclude by describing contemporary consumer-centered approaches that support persons coping with severe psychological distress and their families.

In Chapter 9, *Critical Perspectives on Psychologists' Research Practices*, the topic is psychology as a research discipline and what can be learned from intra-disciplinary debates about its research methods. As an example, we use the debates about the recent failures to replicate a number of research findings in psychology. These debates can be seen as a sign of psychologists' commitment to establish and maintain secure foundations for their research methods. Some suggested explanations for the replication failures are: "p-hacking" and other questionable research practices (QRPs); unreflective and misguided uses of conventional methods, especially statistics; and a lack of conceptual and epistemological knowledge among psychologists. We then look closely at the assumptions that form the basis of the psychological research practices implicated in the replication debates and discuss whether some of those assumptions are problematic.

Part III: Exploring Debates in and about Psychology

Chapter 10, *Disagreements and Debates in Psychology's History*, elucidates how theories and practices in psychology are influenced by historical and cultural circumstances and modes of thought. First, we look back to the nineteenth century, when some psychologists were influenced by evolutionary theory and adopted the eugenic framework, with ideas of selective breeding of "good" types of humans. We then give a brief account of psychology and evolutionary theory today. This is followed by a discussion of the history of psychological measurement, and of how, eventually, a wide-ranging imperative to use quantitative methods was established in the discipline. Next is the history of operational definitions. We then take a short tour of the histories of psychology's words – where they come from, how they change, and the importance of being aware of these changes. In the final subsection, the topic is the history of psychological theories and practices regarding women and gender, and the debates about them.

Chapter 11, *Contemporary Debates among Psychologists*, covers some issues that are currently being debated in psychology. One message of the chapter is that psychologists should debate foundational issues –

debates are necessary in a scholarly endeavor. The first section describes methodological circles: when a research method has built-in assumptions about that which is studied, and therefore always produces data that confirm these assumptions. We then discuss the logical problems of research that uses group averages as a basis for formulating theories about individuals. Then we look into the uses of "variables" in psychology and discuss problems accompanying some of these uses. The widespread practice of statistical significance testing is the next issue we discuss. It has been increasingly criticized over several decades but has remained in place. We end by discussing two ways of understanding and using the concept "concept" in psychology and recommend one of these ways.

Chapter 12, *Explanations in Psychology*. We begin the chapter with a description of psychological phenomena and the temptations to think of them as "things." We then discuss whether psychological categories should be seen as natural or human-made. Next, we look at psychological explanations of people's behavior and experiences and describe contextualized explanations focusing on reasons and interpretations, causal explanations, and abduction, sometimes called inference to the best explanation. We describe and discuss the most important features of these explanatory strategies. We examine some of the limitations of causal explanations built on reductionist assumptions and the seemingly almost inevitable consequence of assuming determinism when using such explanations. We also discuss explanatory strategies that tempt psychologists to reify psychological phenomena such as behaviors or experiences. This means imagining that such phenomena are "entities" inside people's minds or brains, even though one only has access to the observed behaviors or recounted experiences.

Part IV: Taking Persons Seriously

Chapter 13, *Being a Discerning Reader of Psychology*. In this chapter, we present ways to scrutinize psychological theory, research, and practice in order to identify those theories and practices that work well and those that are problematic in one or more ways. We first describe conceptual analysis, an investigative strategy borrowed from philosophy. Conceptual analysis enables one to examine the conceptual bases of theories and practices, focusing on logical inconsistencies in the uses of words and concepts. Such analysis is essential because inconsistencies in a theory must be resolved before one begins empirical work. If unresolved, such problems will eventually hamper scientific progress. The second part offers ten questions that are based on the principles of conceptual analysis and aimed at supporting beginners in psychology. Reflecting on these questions is helpful when reading to get acquainted with a field of knowledge and also when planning a study.

In Chapter 14, *Studying the Psychology of Persons: Methods, Assumptions, and Commitments*, we describe the general characteristics of research methods that are based on a view of people as socially situated persons. These methods go by different names, such as interpretative research, qualitative research, and, in some cases, ethnographic research. We describe the steps in such research: developing a knowledge interest and useful, researchable questions; selecting participants and composing a group to study; deciding how to gather data; and choosing methods for analysis. We discuss common assumptions and commitments in these approaches, such as an interest in what is specific and contextualized in human life, and an interest in people's language use. The final part of the chapter contains a discussion of what it would mean for psychologists to change their theoretical thinking to such a degree that they need to change their thinking styles, as well as suggestions for how to initiate such changes.

CHAPTER 2

Thinking Styles in Psychology

In this chapter, we provide a framework for reflecting on and scrutinizing the practices that psychologists have devised to produce knowledge and to verify that knowledge. We have chosen to use the ideas of Ludwik Fleck, a Polish microbiologist and philosopher of science, as our main basis for these reflections. Fleck wrote his major works on the history and philosophy of science in the 1930s, and his ideas are having a renaissance in contemporary philosophy and history of science (see esp. Stuckey et al., 2015; also Abi-Rached & Rose, 2010; Binney, 2023; Goldman, 2021; Zittel, 2012).[1] One reason for Fleck's renaissance is that his writings offer insights about how the social elements in the life of researchers influence their research and the knowledge they produce. In his book *Genesis and Development of a Scientific Fact* (1935), he offered a set of concepts and a language for exploring the social practices that shape the process and outcome of scientific research in a field, while at the same time shaping the outlook of researchers in that field. Fleck's account directs our attention to the ways in which knowledge – including scientific and laboratory-based knowledge – is thoroughly enmeshed in, and dependent on, layers of social relations (Zittel, 2017).[2]

---

[1] Ludwik Fleck (1896–1961) was born in a Jewish family in Lvov, which was then part of Austria-Hungary. He trained as a physician and worked as a microbiologist. He soon also developed an interest in the philosophy of medicine and science and published several works on such questions in the 1920s and 1930s. When Nazi Germany in 1941 occupied the area where Fleck and his family lived, they escaped the fate of being executed which befell a large number of Polish intellectuals and scientists. It was probably the efforts of Rudolf Weigl, an influential local senior biologist, which protected Fleck and other Jewish intellectuals. After forcibly recruiting Fleck to work for German medical companies, the Nazis deported him and his family to the Auschwitz concentration camp. There, and later in the Buchenwald concentration camp, he worked with other medically educated prisoners to produce a vaccine against typhus. After the war, Fleck became a professor at the Marie Curie-Skłodowska University in Lublin, Poland, where he conducted microbiological research and published prolifically about this work.

[2] We should note here that we do not presume to give a complete presentation of Fleck's philosophy of science. We are making use only of those aspects of his philosophy that provide a framework for

Fleck began by considering what happens when one enters a new field of knowledge. It is only through training and the gradual growth in understanding that one becomes fully adept in the new field. Becoming adept includes gaining knowledge of the terms and forms that experienced workers in the field use, as well as the prevailing theories and methods. Equally important, becoming adept involves mastering the expert methods of observation that are part of one's new field of knowledge. For this, the novice needs practical work experience, because formal education rarely provides all the everyday knowledge and experience required to achieve this level of practical expertise. Such work experience is often gained by working as an apprentice alongside a mentor or supervisor who is a seasoned professional.[3] As the US historian of science Lorraine Daston has put it,

> . . .scientific perception . . . is disciplined in every sense of the word: instilled by education and practice, checked and cross-checked both by other observers and with other instruments, communicated in forms – text, image, table – designed by and for a scientific collective over decades and sometimes centuries. (2008, p. 102)

Through such work experience, the apprentice eventually becomes adept at making the correct observations and distinctions and drawing the proper conclusions from them. During this period, the apprentice typically also gains entry into the social networks of their field and learns how to navigate its social terrain.

As a beginner gradually becomes proficient, several transformations take place. While studying and beginning to practice a profession or embarking on an academic career, one does more than learn facts, theories, and the methods needed to observe and measure in the proper ways. One is also steeped in the *ways* of thinking, the *ways* of putting knowledge to use, and the *ways* of being a skilled professional that are customary in the workplace. Those ways of being and working are based on the accepted knowledge and practices in the field or profession, but they go beyond the formal knowledge base. They may include local traditions and variations in methods and theories, distinctive forms of interaction, collegiality, hierarchy, and loyalty in the workplace, as well as tacit, though pervasive, standards of

---

scrutiny of psychological theory, research and practice. For more about the further philosophical aspects, and applications, of his ideas, see, for instance, Binney (2023).

[3] The supervised training needed to become a licensed psychotherapist is an example. Being a graduate student working with a supervisor is another example.

ethical conduct. Such practices and habits are usually conveyed during daily interactions in the workplace and not through explicit instructions.

Inspired by the writings of Ludwik Fleck, we call the totality of such "ways" in a profession and/or workplace *a thinking style*. In what follows, we describe Fleck's theory of thinking styles, including their functions and consequences.[4]

Thinking Styles Defined

Ludwik Fleck defined a thinking style as *"the entirety of intellectual preparedness or readiness for one particular way of seeing and acting"* (1935/1979, p. 64). We can think of a workplace, such as a laboratory, a workshop, a university department, or a clinic, where the apprentices are taught how to use the equipment in the specific ways that are necessary for their tasks. Note that Fleck used the term "intellectual preparedness" to include acting and seeing, as well as thinking. This means being prepared to use certain methods (the "acting") and theories (the "seeing" and the thinking). To become an expert, an apprentice needs to become thoroughly knowledgeable and practiced in a thinking style.

Fleck argued that this preparedness for seeing and acting in certain ways will be accompanied by a certain attunement to one another by the members of a work group. A thinking style, therefore, is not limited to knowledge, thinking, and acting. Equally important, it also encompasses the shared experiences, feelings, and ways of acting of the people who work together in a particular setting. This means that a thinking style is a *social* phenomenon as well as a *scientific* one.

A thinking style is always the property of a community of people; it is not something that a single individual can establish. That is, if one individual develops an idiosyncratic way of thinking about and acting on some issue, this does not constitute a thinking style. If that individual convinces others (such as coworkers) to think and act in the way he or she does, then the totality of these workers might develop a thinking style. However, because of the cumulative effects of the ensuing social

---

[4] We follow the German philosopher Claus Zittel (2012) and use the expression *thinking style* instead of "thought style." "Thinking style" is a more exact translation of the original German word, which is *"Denkstil."* "Denken" is a verb and translates into English as the verb "to think." Therefore, "Denkstil" is correctly translated as "thinking style." Another reason to prefer "thinking style" to "thought style" is that the expression "thought style" is used in psychiatry to denote certain unhelpful (for instance, ruminating) ways of thinking connected with certain psychiatric diagnostic categories.

interactions within the work group, chances are that the group's style will not be identical to the first worker's original way of thinking.

In sum, two key features of thinking styles are that they are collective phenomena and that they are not hewn in stone – they evolve and change through interactions.

Thinking Styles Are Constraining

Now we turn to another key feature of thinking styles. Think back to our first quote from Fleck's writings: a thinking style is "*the entirety of intellectual preparedness or readiness for one particular way of seeing and acting.*" The sentence continues: "*. . . and no other*" (p. 64). This constraining quality of thinking styles will be in focus here.

Fleck claimed that a thinking style exerts a powerful constraint on one's thinking. This is so because the training and education that transform a novice into an expert at the same time cause the budding professional to "*lose the ability to see something that contradicts the form*" (p. 92) that the thinking style acknowledges. Becoming skilled in a field of study means getting better at making certain distinctions and judgments, while the capacity to make other kinds of distinctions and judgments is not developed. This means that persons who are adept in different thinking styles may not be able to make the same distinctions, and therefore, in practice, they may not be able to see the same things. Let us consider a historical example as an illustration.

In the early seventeenth century, someone who thought of the Earth as the center of the universe (the geocentric view) saw the movements of the planets in a different way than someone who thought of the Sun as the center (the heliocentric view). This was so even though both had access to the same observations of planetary movements across the sky. The two individuals were looking at the same things (the charts of observations), but their differing thinking styles led them to interpret the observations differently. What caused these different interpretations was the chasm between the traditionalists' belief in the still-dominant geocentric view and the new thinkers' rejection of that worldview, along with their acceptance of the planetary observations as evidence for the heliocentric view. In other words, the same observations meant different things to the traditionalists and the new thinkers. The traditionalists were so enmeshed in the old worldview that, for them, its dogma of geocentrism overrode all other possible interpretations of the observations. Apart from the taken-for-granted nature of this worldview, there were also religious prohibitions against straying from the dogma, and those prohibitions served to reinforce the traditional thinking style. The new thinkers, by contrast, had rid themselves of the old worldview and argued for the value of *observation* over dogma. These new standpoints – both that of heliocentrism and perhaps especially that of valuing observation over dogma – were unacceptable to large parts of the world in the early seventeenth century. They could be dangerous to uphold.

Today, we know who was right and who was wrong about the solar system. Let us consider what changes led to the acceptance of the heliocentric model of the universe. One important development was the invention of the telescope, which enabled new observations of planetary movements. However, this technological development was far from the only factor. Sociocultural changes that diminished the force of church authority were also key. Until the middle of the seventeenth century, it could be dangerous to profess a heliocentric view of the universe. Galileo Galilei, for example, who wrote several publications built on this view, was put on trial for heresy in 1633. He was – under threat of corporal punishment and torture – forced by the papal court to formally recant his views and was forbidden to publish about heliocentrism. Furthermore, he was sentenced to house arrest for the rest of his life.

In spite of the punishment meted out to Galileo, it did not take very long for the heliocentric view to gain support, first among astronomers, and soon thereafter among other educated people. This change was partly due to an increase in astronomical observations. However, the interest aroused by the fate of Galileo sparked interest in previous books that put forward a heliocentric model of the universe, such as Nicolaus Copernicus's 1543 book and Johannes Kepler's 1609 book. By the mid seventeenth century, there was a Europe-wide network of astronomers and other scientists who were convinced that the heliocentric view was correct. Their activities contributed greatly to the seventeenth-century scientific revolution. The Catholic Church's pronouncements lost their force, and the heliocentric view soon gained followers in addition to the astronomers. Indeed, by the 1680s, books on popular science presented the heliocentric view as established.

The development of a new network, or collective, of thinkers was what was needed for the heliocentric view to gain credence and the geocentric view to be set aside. In Ludwik Fleck's words, we would say that the geocentric and heliocentric views belonged to two thinking styles that were distinct from each other and incompatible. We would also say, as would Ludwik Fleck, that these styles were the properties of different *thought collectives*. We now turn to Fleck's idea of thought collectives. As a preparation, we first introduce his ideas about human thinking as a social activity.

Thinking as a Social Activity

Ludwik Fleck saw thinking as a genuinely social activity, such that, "*...without social conditioning no cognition is even possible*" (1935/1979, p. 43). That is, an individual's thinking is always structured by that individual's location in a particular social environment. It is not the person in isolation who thinks, but the person as a part of, and informed by, their social community. This is so because the social community provides a store of knowledge – that is, things that were already known before a particular individual came along. For instance, an individual researcher's thinking is deeply influenced and directed by the accumulated store of knowledge in their field. Fleck therefore argued that thinking should not be seen as an individual process going on only within an individual's consciousness. On this basis, he argued against the individual-focused psychological theories of his time (the 1920s and 1930s), "*since the existing stock of knowledge exceeds the range available to any one individual*" (p. 38), and "*even the simplest observation is conditioned by thinking style and is thus tied to a community of thought*" (p. 98). Thinking, for Fleck, could not be completely localized within the confines of the individual:[5]

> ... cognition must not be construed as only a dual relationship between the knowing subject and the object to be known. The existing fund of knowledge must be a *third partner* in this relation as a basic factor of all new knowledge. It would otherwise remain beyond our understanding how a closed and style-permeated system of opinions could arise. (p. 38, italics added)

Fleck connected this "three-partner" view of cognition to his ideas about the force of thinking styles. For him, therefore, thinking, including thinking styles, can never be fully understood or explained without taking the context(s) of the thinker(s) into account. To use his own words:

> ...the statement, "Someone recognizes something," demands some such supplement as, "on the basis of a certain fund of knowledge," or, better, "as a member of a certain cultural environment," and, best, "in a particular thinking style, in a particular thought collective." (p. 39)

We now consider what such a "thought collective" entails.

---

[5] We return to the idea of thinking as a foundationally social activity in Chapter 6, *Thinking Persons*, where we discuss theories about situated cognition.

Thought Collectives

Thought collectives are the carriers of thinking styles. Fleck defined a thought collective as "*...a community of persons mutually exchanging ideas or maintaining intellectual interaction*" (Fleck, 1935/1979, p. 39). Thought collectives can be large or small; their size may range from two persons to a whole discipline or even a whole nation. They may be short-lived or enduring. Political parties, religious groups, and academic research groups are some examples of formal thought collectives. It is also possible for informal thought collectives to be established, such as very cohesive groups of friends. Once established, thought collectives develop a common language for their activities and common technologies and methods for these activities. Their members usually develop strong feelings of solidarity. In Fleck's words, a thought collective "*...has its special rules of behavior and its special psychological form*" (p. 44). And, as Lorraine Daston has pointed out, they could also, and perhaps at least as importantly, be described as "seeing collectives." Daston pointed to the training of novices in specific methods of observation and measurement: "*step by step, seminar by seminar, as apprentices learn to see like the masters ... [a] schooling of the senses. ... Novices must be taught to see things and to see the same things, a world held in common*" (2008, p. 107). Further, as Fleck noted in his historical studies of medical thought collectives, the longer a particular idea has circulated in a thought collective, the more certain that idea seems – and the more difficult it is to change. Another important characteristic, related to Fleck's ideas about thinking as a social activity, is that thought collectives have more constancy and longevity than the individual members. That is, thought collectives have histories, and it is important to know the history of one's thought collective.

Fleck, who was a medical scientist with a deep knowledge of the history of his field, studied the scientific thought collectives of his own time, as well as those of earlier times. In his view, a thought collective's history always lives on in some form within the collective. He therefore argued extensively for the necessity of knowing the history of one's own discipline or field if one wants to have any chance of understanding the discipline and its contemporary workings. In Chapter 10, *Disagreements and Debates in Psychology's History*, we provide some historical background for today's discipline of psychology as it has developed in "Western" countries since the end of the nineteenth century.

Established thought collectives typically have an inner circle of experienced members who are specialists and experts in the field, and an outer circle of less experienced members. The members of the innermost circle are usually the ones with the longest time in the collective, the highest formal status, and the most prestigious job positions. They tend to be the ones most tightly wedded to the prevailing thinking style; some of them may be its originators. Members of the outer circle share the thinking style of the collective but are not as knowledgeable about it as those in the inner circle. The members in the outer circle are guided by the members in the inner circle, while the members in the inner circle may not always pay much heed to the ideas and opinions of those in the outer circle.

Newcomers to a collective will usually be initiated into its thinking style through some kind of didactic introduction, such as a course, a study program, or supervision by a more experienced member. In this process of initiation, Fleck wrote, *"an intellect is prepared for a given field; it is received into a self-contained world and, as it were, initiated"* (p. 54). According to Fleck, this initiation usually takes place through dogmatic teaching of what he called "textbook knowledge," that is, knowledge and methods that are squarely situated within the thinking style of the collective. After his discussion of thought collectives, Fleck developed his definition of thinking style further:

> It is characterized by common features in the problems of interest to a thought collective, by the judgment which the thought collective considers evident, and by the methods which it applies as a means of cognition. The thinking style may also be accompanied by a technical and literary style characteristic of the given system of knowledge. Because it belongs to a community, the thinking style of the collective undergoes social reinforcement. (p. 99)

The Power of Thinking Styles

In a cohesive thought collective, the thinking style may dominate to such an extent that individual members are confined to thinking through problems within the bounds of the style. This means that *what* a member sees, and *how* that member thinks and acts, depend on the thinking style of the collective. And this means, according to Fleck, that something (the "what" above) that is of the utmost significance to a member of one thought collective may be of no import to a member of another thought collective. Moreover, because thinking styles include methodological approaches (the "how" above), a method that members of one thought collective regard as bringing forward strong evidence may well be taken as anecdotal and unscientific by a member of another thought collective. Further, according to Fleck, the thinking style of a thought collective may determine not just the ways in which its members want to think and are able to think, but also the ways of thinking that they come to repudiate or even eventually feel aversion to.

Recall the seventeenth-century controversies about the geocentric versus heliocentric worldviews. The proponents of the two views *saw* different things when they observed the skies (the "what"), and neither was prepared to accept the other thought collective's *methods* of observation as providing valid evidence (the "how"). They certainly expressed aversion to the opposing worldview.

In the next section we illustrate how the ideas of thinking styles and thought collectives can enable critical reflections on psychological theory and research.

Active Assumptions and Passive Elements of Thinking Styles

Recall that Ludwik Fleck defined a thinking style as "*a definite constraint on thought, and even more; it is the entirety of intellectual preparedness or readiness for one particular way of seeing and acting and no other*" (Fleck, 1935/1979, p. 64). He was also careful to point out that the "thinking" in a thinking style is something more than a particular way of defining and using a set of theoretical concepts. To grasp the breadth of the term, the German philosopher Claus Zittel's explication is helpful:

> ... [Fleck's] detailed descriptions of "thinking-styles" make it clear that they are neither methods nor thinking forms; nor do they describe epochs or worldviews, nor characterize social groups. Rather, thinking-styles are understood as processes, circulations of ideas, and social practices, and the style-appropriate conditioning[6] of perception, thinking and action of researchers, which results from these ideas and practices. (2012, p. 65)

In line with his emphasis on social practices and style-appropriate conditioning, Fleck distinguished between the foundational *active assumptions* of a thinking style and its ensuing *passive elements*. He argued that the active assumptions on which a thinking style is built will render certain decisions, such as choosing a research method, almost self-evident or automatic, or in

---

[6] The term "conditioning" in this context should be read as "being shaped by," or "influenced by," and not in the technical sense of "conditioned reflex."

his terms, *passive*. That is, such choices follow directly and automatically, in Fleck's words, *passively*, as consequences of the active assumptions of the style. To illustrate, we can imagine a psychological thinking style that is based on the active assumption that psychological properties have quantitative characteristics. Note that this is an assumption, and not a proven fact, about psychological properties (see Michell, 1999). In Chapter 10, *Disagreements and Debates in Psychology's History*, we describe the emergence in early academic psychology of the (in Fleck's terms, "active") assumption that psychological properties have quantitative attributes and should be studied by quantitative methods. For a psychologist who has assumed quantitative properties, the choice of using quantitative measuring instruments will be automatic and self-evident. This makes the choice of such a method a passive consequence, in Fleck's terms.

But Fleck also argued the converse: When a researcher uses a particular research method, the researcher will inevitably also be applying the active assumptions of the style from which the method has followed. This will be true whether or not the researcher is aware of those active assumptions of the style. Fleck went so far as to assert that using a particular research method and its measuring instruments forces the researcher – knowingly or not – to accept the active assumptions from which they have passively followed.

The active assumptions of a thinking style, making up its core, tend to become established early in the life of the style. These assumptions then successively shape the further development of the thinking style, such as its canon of methods. Later researchers may not *actively* or consciously have chosen to accept those original active assumptions. They may instead have taken them over via the research methods they were taught (the passive elements), without being aware that they were also thereby accepting certain assumptions. Therefore, a psychologist who, for instance, relies on a quantitative method will – knowingly or not – be led to accept the active assumption of quantitative properties that is part of the thinking style of which that method is a part.

It is not difficult to find contemporary examples of how the active assumptions of a thinking style infuse researchers' methodological practices as well as the conclusions they draw when using those methods. We briefly mention two. The first example of such discussions is found in the current discussions and critiques of the framework, methods, and interpretations in research on "theory of mind," and suggestions for alternative frameworks (or thinking styles). See especially the close scrutiny of such research by Taylor et al. (2023).

Another example is the German developmental psychologist Markus Paulus's (2022) critical scrutiny of the well-known method of "Violation of Expectations" in psychological research on infant cognition. Paulus argues that this framework (which we might call a thinking style) contains several speculative ideas about infants' cognitive abilities (the active assumptions). These assumptions, he argues, have encouraged the use of overly "cognitive" methods (the passive elements) and interpretations of experimental results, for which other interpretations were equally likely or even more likely. Following Fleck, we would say that the VoE framework's active assumptions about infant cognition led to the presumption that the findings of the VoE method were proof of certain cognitive abilities. This pre-loading of expectations, at the same time, dissuaded the researchers from using other methods or from seeking other kinds of explanations for their own findings (of which there are several).

Remembering the connection between active assumptions and passive (or automatic) elements is crucial when applying the thinking styles framework to research in practice. We explore this framework further in the next section.

Further Thoughts about Active Assumptions and Automatic Consequences

It is essential to distinguish between the active and the passive (or automatic) elements of thinking styles. As we saw earlier in this chapter, Fleck argued that the *active* assumptions and the *passive* or *automatic* elements play very different roles in the research process. They should not be confused. Confusing them will cause one to misunderstand the whole research process in one's study. A researcher who confuses the active and automatic elements will, for instance, be unable to identify which elements need to be changed if things do not work out as expected (Binney, 2016a, 2016b). Steven Goldman, a US philosopher and historian of science, described the roles in this way: "... *the active associations being our choice of definitions, assumptions, and rules of reasoning, and the passive being the logical consequences of those choices*" (2021, p. 241). This is an accessible working definition, as long as we are aware that the "choice" of active associations that Goldman mentions is far from always made consciously by the individual researcher. It is probably more often taken over from seniors during one's education.

In fact, as we noted earlier, many active assumptions are introduced in the very early phases of a research tradition and then become implicit. This implicitness may make them difficult to discern today because they have, over time, become built into the very fabric of one's field. Fleck's awareness of such historical processes made him emphasize the importance of knowing the history of one's own discipline (1935/1979, p. 54). He also pointed out that the active assumptions of a thinking style often have a tinge of subjectivity and historical specificity – they are not the direct results of empirical observations and are therefore not what one usually means by "facts." On the contrary, active assumptions are the results of an agreement or decision made at one time in a thought collective on sometimes rather loose grounds (think of the geocentric view of the universe or the assumption of quantitative properties that we have mentioned previously). As is often the case today, it will be an agreement that the contemporary collective has taken over from an earlier phase or from an earlier collective. This quote from Roger Smith, a British historian of psychology, elaborates the idea nicely and takes it one step further:

> ...it is always possible, in any reasoning or body of thought, to find presumptions which that reasoning or body of thought cannot itself justify. There are always unfounded presumptions – in the claim which I am now making as in any other – and we can, "reflexively," make these assumptions the focus of inquiry. (2005, p. 56)

In this book, we are picking up on Roger Smith's conclusion that such assumptions can be investigated; they can be made the focus of inquiry. And we have chosen Ludwik Fleck's frame of reference to do this because it has its origin with a practicing researcher who was also knowledgeable about epistemology and the philosophy of science. This combination makes his tools for thinking, such as "thinking style" and "thought collective," easy to apply to the practices of psychologists – researchers as well as practitioners. While certainly not being the only possible framework for scrutinizing psychological theories and practices, Fleck's ideas contribute a language and a set of concepts that enables understandings of problems and shortcomings in the fields, topics, and questions that we investigate in this book.

CHAPTER 3

Culture, Communities, and Persons

Debates about the meaning of the word "culture" have a long history. In 1952, the anthropologists A. L. Kroeber and Clyde Kluckhohn (1952) counted 164 definitions of culture in the academic literature. They also offered their own definition. Culture, in their words, *"consists of the derivatives of experience, more or less organized, learned or created by the individuals of a population, including those images or encodements and their interpretations."* As Richard Shweder and Les Beldo (2015, p. 1) comment, definitions of culture have been *"frequently debated, doubted, distrusted, and scorned and associated with a variety of sins"* by many cohorts of English-speaking cultural anthropologists.

The question of what constitutes "culture" remains unsettled, and it has continued to be discussed and debated. Regardless of these debates about the proper definition of "culture," however, there seems to be little disagreement that human beings are inextricably part of culture. Culture remains a key concept not just in anthropology but also in social sciences such as psychology and sociology, as well as in people's everyday ways of talking about the world they live in.

Within the field of psychology, several kinds of questions have been posed regarding persons and culture. Some psychologists, often called cross-cultural psychologists, have been interested in comparing the behavior of people in various societies in a search for psychological phenomena or mental processes that are universal across cultures. For example, some psychologists have proposed typologies of human personality traits that they believe are universal. For other psychologists, referred to as cultural psychologists, the questions of interest concern the relation between cultural frames of meaning and individuals' behavior. For example, how do cultural meanings, culture-specific practices, or culture-specific institutions shape people's ways of thinking and behaving? Yet other psychologists take issue with the view of people as "cultural dopes" who blindly adhere to social rules and reproduce conventional ways of thinking and

26

acting. Instead, they envision human beings as persons with the capacity to resist dominant meanings, to negotiate new meanings, and to engage in actions that produce social change and ultimately cultural change. Using Ludwik Fleck's ideas about thinking styles (see Chapter 2), one could argue that collectives of psychologists who have adopted such divergent approaches to the questions about psychology and culture are basing their theories on incompatible thinking styles. Further (again according to Fleck), working within mutually incompatible thinking styles tends to make members of different thought collectives disinclined to listen to each other's arguments and findings. Such disinclination is not unusual when questions of culture and psychology are broached.

Even as debates about the best meaning of the term "culture" continue, the idea of culture remains a key concept in the social sciences. For instance, Richard Shweder and Les Beldo (2015), who are cultural anthropologists in the USA, offer the view of culture as an *interpretive community*. Such a community is comprised of individuals who share a set of communal assumptions. These shared assumptions include, for example, common beliefs, norms, values, language, and symbols. Such shared assumptions, and the shared meanings and practices that follow from them, enable members of the community to live and work together.

The definitions of culture in the preceding paragraphs bear little resemblance to the usages of the word "culture" in everyday talk. In everyday talk, the word "culture" is often used as if it were synonymous with geographic place. An expression such as "Asian culture" is an example. Note that Asia encompasses 48 countries, nearly five billion people, and well over 2,000 languages. The claim that there is a common set of norms, values, and customs across Asia seems improbable, to say the least. Descriptions of cultural differences between "the East" and "the West" are similarly improbable. Consider the common claim that "Eastern cultures" are collectivist, while "Western cultures" are individualist. Such totalizing claims conceal the considerable diversity among the many locales and social groups within the "East" as well as within the "West."

Let us also consider the everyday notion of culture as a repository for long-standing customs and ways of thinking. In everyday talk, people often use the word "tradition" to refer to such customs, rituals, and practices. For example, it is said that British people traditionally eat mince pies at Christmas time. The word "tradition" implies that such ways of doing things are common to every member of a social group and that those ways of doing things have been handed down from generation to generation. Not every British person eats mince pies, of course. Nor does every British person celebrate Christmas. More generally, what might be spoken of as timeless norms and practices likely are not timeless at all, but subject to many alterations over time. Often, members of a social group renegotiate practices that have come to seem old-fashioned, insensitive, or even offensive. For example, from the latter part of the twentieth century onward, many women in Western countries stepped away from the custom of changing their surname from their natal name to their spouse's name when they married.

In sum, cultural groups can be thought of as *interpretive communities*. That is, their members share certain beliefs, norms, and ways of being and behaving. These are neither static frameworks, nor are cultural groups totalizing or unchanging. Rather, members are often active in modifying and renegotiating aspects of their common understandings and practices. If one accepts this view of culture and of persons, what implications, if any, are there for psychologists interested in culture and cultural differences?

Psychological Studies of Culture

How might a view of culture as the product of communities of persons who continually negotiate and renegotiate local norms and meanings shape the knowledge interests and research conventions of psychology? This is a question worth considering, because for much of its history, psychologists, taking their cue from the natural sciences, sought to identify universal principles of human behavior. There was little attention in those days to cultural differences. Indeed, behaviorists, following the lead of B. F. Skinner, went even further and sought to discover general principles of behavior that applied to all organisms, not just humans. If we then fast forward a few decades, we find, as Henrich, Norenzayan, and Heine (2010) pointed out, that the (often universal) claims of psychology and some other social sciences rested largely on studies of highly unrepresentative groups of participants. Specifically, 90 percent of the participants were drawn from perhaps 12 percent of the world population. As we noted in Chapter 1, to characterize these unrepresentative participants, Henrich and his colleagues coined the acronym WEIRD – Western, Educated, Industrialized, Rich, and Democratic.

More recently, other critics (e.g., Sanches de Oliveira & Baggs, 2023) have pointed out that other core elements of conventional psychological research have often been "WEIRD" as well. These elements include the theoretical assumptions on which the research is based; aspects of the research methods, such as psychometric tests and other data-gathering procedures; and the publication outlets, organizational structures, and other resources, all based in WEIRD parts of the world. Addressing these criticisms requires deeper changes in the disciplinary practices of psychologists than merely studying more diverse groups of research participants.

The remainder of this chapter presents a few areas of human behavior that have been prominent topics of study by Western psychologists. We bring forward some of the cultural and historical variations in these behaviors and in the scientific theories and moral judgments that have been advanced about them. Our intentions are twofold: One goal is to underscore the importance of considering how such practices are embedded in the cultural and social surroundings in which they occur. The other is to draw attention to the situatedness of social and psychological knowledge, that is, of the psychologists themselves. If you are a student of psychology, you also might consider whether textbooks and research articles that you have read discuss such sociocultural particularities, rather than portraying WEIRD ways of thinking and practices as if they were universal and timeless. In Chapter 13, *Being a Discerning Reader of Psychology*, we take up some of these questions again, now in the context of reading psychological literature.

Early Mother–Infant Emotional Bonds: Theories, Concepts, Measurements

The development of mother–infant emotional bonds became a topic of considerable interest among both psychologists and psychiatrists during the latter decades of the twentieth century. This interest was spurred by the dominance of Freudian theories of child development, human personality, and psychopathology in the discipline of psychology in the US and many countries in Europe.

Attachment Theory, as the study of mother–infant attachment came to be known, originated in the work of John Bowlby, a British psychiatrist and psychoanalyst (Bowlby, 1951). Many of Bowlby's ideas about mothers and their babies were drawn from Sigmund Freud's assumptions about the pivotal role of early childhood in later patterns of psychological development, personality, and psychopathology. Bowlby postulated that human infants are biologically predisposed to develop a primary emotional bond with their mothers (or, in the absence of the mother, the primary caregiver). Bowlby (1988) held that the critical period during which the mother–infant bond develops is the first two and a half years of the child's life. The crucial element was the mother's intensive interactions with her baby. These interactions led the infant to develop an internal working model that would become the prototype for future social relationships throughout the rest of the person's life (Bowlby, 1951). Although Bowlby did not ignore fathers' roles in their children's lives, it was the mother–infant bond that was the central focus of attention for Bowlby and other attachment theorists.

Research on mother–infant interactions and the development of an emotional bond centered on a laboratory-based observational method called the Strange Situation Procedure. This method was developed by Mary Ainsworth, a Canadian developmental psychologist, and her colleagues (Ainsworth et al., 1978). The Strange Situation Procedure provided a standardized protocol for observing and then categorizing infants' behavior in a controlled setting in which the infants experienced two brief separations and reunions with their mother (or caregiver) as well as contact with a stranger. The Strange Situation Procedure was deemed to yield standardized and quantified indices of early childhood attachment. For several years, it held sway over research on mother–infant attachment by developmental psychologists in North America and Europe. There was also a strong interest in longitudinal investigations aimed at determining whether difficulties in mother–child attachment (such as avoidant behavior on the part of the child, or so-called insecure attachment) were associated with later difficulties in cognitive, affective, and behavioral domains. More recently, some neuroscientists have investigated whether different patterns of early childhood attachment were associated with later differences in brain activity. Others sought out molecular-genetic correlates of children's attachment bonds to their mothers. As of this writing, such studies have not yielded conclusive findings.

Mother–infant attachment has continued to be a key interest of developmental psychologists in European and North American countries. However, controversies have surfaced over the years. In the US, for example, when large numbers of women sought entry into the paid labor force in the late 1960s and 1970s, some proponents of Attachment Theory mounted strenuous objections to placing young children in the care of adults other than their mothers or close relatives. Various claims were advanced about possible negative effects on children. Some, like the child psychoanalyst Selma Fraiberg (1978), held that fulltime mothering at home was superior to any other care arrangement and imperative for the child's optimal development. However, in other Western high-income countries and in other regions of the world, childcare arrangements were far more diverse, often involving multiple caregivers. In the US, opposition to daycare faded as it became evident that many families required the income that women's paid work provided. The focus of attention turned to ensuring that the quality of the care provided to children was adequate.

A broader set of concerns about Attachment Theory was registered by anthropologists and cultural psychologists who studied families in settings outside Western high-income countries. Their observations of family relations and childcare practices led them to register strenuous objections to many of the claims made by Attachment Theory. In their edited volume *Attachment Reconsidered*, Naomi Quinn and Jeannette Marie Mageo, two US anthropologists, noted succinctly that *"the claims and constructs of attachment theory suffer from profound ethnocentrism"* (2013, p. 3). For anthropologists and cultural psychologists, this assertion did not come as a surprise. Indeed, many of them had long been skeptical of several key premises of Attachment Theory. For example, some doubted that intensive mothering and mother–infant bonding experiences were necessarily critical to a child's psychological development. They pointed to the wide variety of ways of caregiving, patterns of childrearing, and family structures across the world (Morelli & Henry, 2013). Others objected to the notion that there was a particular style of mother–child relationship that was necessary for a child's psychological health; some went a step further to question whether there was and ever could be a universal standard of children's "psychological health."

Other psychologists have brought forward methodological critiques asking, for example, whether the Strange Situation Procedure has the same import and meaning for all infants, regardless of their family's social and cultural background. At the same time, some feminists raised another set of objections to conventional Attachment Theory (e.g., Birns, 1999). In their view, several dubious assumptions are embedded in Attachment Theory about adult women's proper role and about the supposedly "natural" allocation of the care work for children to their mothers.

Sexes, Genders, and Sexualities across Time and Space

The second arena we consider concerns practices and ideas regarding gender identities, sex categories, and sexual desires. This arena involves a broad array of issues, especially from a global perspective, many of which are currently receiving considerable public attention. Here, we take up only a few. Many longstanding ways of understanding sex categories, gender identity, and sexual desires are in flux. Ongoing changes are often controversial, leading to acrimonious debate and disagreement in some quarters, as well as political mobilization and legal changes.

In many countries, legal and social prohibitions on same-sex sexual desires and liaisons have been relaxed, and social acceptance has increased. Homosexual relationships are no longer against the law, and statutes supporting marriage equality afford two people of the same sex the same legal right to marriage as two people of different sexes. Also, psychiatric diagnoses pathologizing gay men and lesbian women have been expunged from the official diagnostic codes. However, legal prohibitions and criminal punishment of homosexual acts persist in some countries, notably in Africa and the Middle East.

In many countries, social movements have emerged that challenge the idea of gender as a binary set of categories (i.e., male and female, as defined by a person's genital anatomy at birth). These movements press instead for societal, medical, and legal recognition of a larger number of gender categories (encompassing, e.g., alternatives such as nonbinary, genderfluid, genderqueer, transgender, and agender). As many readers will know, even though many people embrace the recognition of such categories, there are others who believe that this is damaging both to the individuals who embrace such categories and to the social order. Depending on local norms and beliefs, individuals who openly embrace alternative gender categories may be subjected to exclusion, harassment, discriminatory treatment, and legal constraints.

Although gender categories other than male and female have only recently received public attention in Western societies, many other societies have long acknowledged more than two genders. Perhaps the best-known example is in India, where *hijras*, who are people whose gender expression is nonbinary, have been recognized for over 2,000 years. Most *hijras* were born anatomically male; some of them elect to undergo a ceremonial castration as adults. Other *hijras* are intersex. That is, they were born with genitalia, chromosomes, or reproductive organs that do not fit neatly into a male/female binary. *Hijras* adopt feminine clothing, make-up, hair styles, and mannerisms. At least some *hijras* obtain hormonal and surgical treatments that produce female sex characteristics such as breasts. Groups of *hijras* usually live together in communal settings and support themselves by performing rituals to bestow blessings at weddings and births, as well as entertaining guests at these occasions by dancing and singing. Because their appearance as cross-dressing men often prevents them from gaining employment in mainstream occupations, some resort to sex work (Reddy, 2006). Spokespersons in the *hijra* community object to being called "third gender" because, as they argue, that term conceals the unique historical and cultural niche they have long occupied in India.

Another example is found in Thailand, where the *kathoey* is a group that also does not fit into a male–female binary. *Kathoey*, who are sometimes referred to as ladyboys, are male-to-female transgender individuals. Yet another example of gender-variant individuals – *fa'afafines* – is found in Samoa, a small country in the South Pacific Ocean. The term *fa'afafine* designates a cisgendered male who espouses feminine characteristics and behaviors from early childhood onward. In Samoa, people regard *fa'afafines* as distinct from typical boys and men; nonetheless, *fa'afafines* are well accepted in most parts of Samoan society. As adults, *fa'afafines* often choose to work as caregivers or housekeepers.

This brief discussion has focused only on a few examples of gender-variant individuals in present-day societies, but there are many historical examples as well. Even the few contemporary examples presented here indicate that gender-variant individuals are part of many societies. The social roles that they occupy, the occupations that are open to them, the degree of acceptance accorded to them by the public, as well as their legal rights and protections vary greatly across different societies and across time. Scholars who seek to understand the life experiences, aspirations, and sources of distress and wellbeing of gender-variant individuals must pay close attention to the cultural, political, and relational contexts in which their lives are embedded. It is important to note that attitudes, practices, laws, and medical edicts concerning gender-variant individuals are far from settled. As such individuals attain visibility and social prominence, this can lead to greater social acceptance; at the same time, it can also mobilize opposition and a political backlash.

Conceptions of Psychological Suffering

Popular ideas about what constitutes mental disorder vary widely across history and culture. Moreover, the moral, social, and legal judgments about such "disordered" behavior also vary widely across time and place. Perhaps it is more surprising that scientific knowledge has varied widely as well, as have the treatments thought to help sufferers. Chapter 8 takes up some questions about this in detail. Here, we briefly point to some examples of historical and cultural specificity.

The disorder that is now termed Schizophrenia Spectrum Disorder has been aptly termed "our most troubling madness" (Lurhmann & Marrow, 2016), and it occurs in all parts of the world, though the symptoms vary. Symptoms of schizophrenia can include hallucinations (such as hearing voices or visual disturbances), delusions (strongly held beliefs that are clearly false), and disorganized speech. Difficulties in forming and maintaining relationships are also common. These difficulties may become apparent in mid-adolescence or early adulthood, and they may recur (often with periods of remission) for the duration of an individual's life. Historically, people in Western countries who exhibited symptoms of schizophrenia were subjected to physical restraints such as strait jackets and chains, as well as ice baths, electroshock therapy, and sedation. In the 1930s, physical interventions such as insulin coma therapy and electroconvulsive shock therapy were used; and later, even lobotomy. Today, neuroleptic medications, discovered in the 1950s, offer varying degrees of relief, though they fall short of a cure.

Schizophrenia is expressed, experienced, and treated differently across cultural settings. For example, the content of hallucinatory voices in sufferers in India tends to differ from that typical in Western countries. Moreover, people diagnosed with schizophrenia in India seem to experience fewer episodes of the disorder, and the episodes tend to be shorter in duration.

The diagnosis of nymphomania emerged in Western biomedicine in the nineteenth century. Nymphomania was the name given to a female disorder that involved what was deemed to be excessive and uncontrollable sexual desire. This diagnostic category served to pathologize women whose sexual desires were regarded as unseemly for women. No such judgments were made about "excessive" sexual desire in men. Gynecologists prescribed a variety of supposed remedies for women, such as abstaining from meat, taking cold enemas and baths to "cool" the passions, and applying leeches to the genitals. From the mid nineteenth century to the mid twentieth century, in rare cases, some US physicians treated women and girls for masturbation by removing the clitoris (Rodriguez, 2014). Nymphomania is no longer recognized as either a medical condition or a psychiatric diagnosis. In most Western societies, ideas about female sexuality have changed dramatically.

A contemporary example of cultural specificity is the psychiatric diagnosis "Prolonged Grief Disorder" (or Persistent Complex Bereavement Disorder [PCBD]), a recent invention of US psychiatrists that was inserted into the *Diagnostic and Statistical Manual of Mental Disorders* in 2022. The diagnosis was said to codify a distinctive set of psychological symptoms that might occur subsequent to the death of a family member or an intimate other. The new diagnosis stirred considerable controversy among both clinical practitioners and researchers. Many objected to the attempt to set a universal standard for appropriate grieving, irrespective of cultural practices, local social expectations, and personal circumstances. How much grieving should be deemed "too much"? Which manifestations of grief ought to be regarded as psychopathological? What forms of grieving ought to be considered "excessive"?

On a more general note, the terms "culture-bound syndromes" and "cultural concepts of distress" are used to refer to conditions that are locally considered to be disorders. For example, an expression of distress common in Latin America is *Ataque de Nervios*, which involves episodes of uncontrollable crying or aggression, often triggered by stressful events. Another example is somatization – the manifestation of mental distress in the form of physical symptoms – which is quite common in many cultural groups across the world. Often, somatization can be seen as a physical means of registering anxiety or depression. Rather than experiencing feelings of anxiety or depression, people experience bodily manifestations such as feeling as if the soles of the feet are burning or feeling as if one's stomach is burning.

There are also examples of psychological syndromes that seem to be specific to a particular historical time. One example is Dissociative Fugue, a syndrome involving temporary amnesia regarding one's identity and other personal information and involving unexpected travel or wandering. As documented by Hacking (1998), such fugue states, which are now quite unusual, were more common in earlier times. A more familiar example of time-bound disorders is the emergence of eating disorders among adolescent girls and adult women in many Western countries in the final decades of the twentieth century, and the persistence of such disorders since then. The preoccupation with thinness was initially prompted by the popularity of "Twiggy," a young British fashion model who became a pop icon in the late 1960s. Twiggy's emaciated physique was imitated by fashion models and many female celebrities, as well as by many young White females. There was a sharp rise in clinical eating disorders, such as anorexia nervosa and bulimia nervosa, among girls and women.

Conceptions of the Life Course and "Stages" of Human Development

Different social groups, different social ecologies, and the differing demands of historical eras are connected with different norms and expectations regarding the tasks, obligations, and moral strictures placed on persons throughout the life course. Among contemporary middle-class social groups in many Western high-income countries, for example, autonomy and individual choice are typically accorded more importance than conformity to social rules. This is particularly true for males. Moreover, at least through childhood and adolescence, and perhaps early adulthood, children and young people may be subject to expectations for their behavior that are associated with a particular age period (e.g., the "terrible twos"). Some psychologists hold that these expectations reflect stages of biophysical maturation or possibly brain development (Steinberg, 2009). However, the striking variations in age-related expectations, both across societies and across historical eras, should caution us against presuming biological determinism.

As an example, let us consider adolescence, which is now widely regarded in Western societies as a pre-adult stage of life. The notion of adolescence as a specific period of human development was developed in the United States between 1890 and 1920. The psychologist G. Stanley Hall (1844–1924) put forward the idea of adolescence as a distinct phase of human development in his 1904 book *Adolescence*. Note that Hall did not believe that he had "discovered" a previously unrecognized universal aspect of human development. Rather, he regarded adolescence as the product of social changes that were taking place at the turn of the twentieth century. He used the phrase "storm and stress" to define adolescence as a time of turmoil, involving rebelliousness and conflicts with parents and authority figures, turbulent moods, and risk-taking behaviors. He argued further that, contrary to past practices, adolescents should not be expected to shoulder adult responsibilities.

The idea that adolescence is a stage of human development during which rebellion is natural and inevitable came to be widely shared by middle-class Americans and then gradually spread to several other Western countries. During their teenage years, young people growing up in Western societies are expected to assert their individuality and to achieve some distance from their natal family by adopting manners, tastes, ways of dressing and speaking, and so on that are different from, and often at odds with, those of their parents and other adults. Moreover, parents, teachers, and other adults anticipate that young people will engage in misbehavior, flout parental rules of conduct, and break laws (such as those involving alcohol consumption and illicit drug use).

Contemporary Western accounts of the psychological development of adolescents owe much to the work of Erik Erikson, a German psychoanalyst who spent most of his career in the US. Erikson, a revisionist of Freud's ideas, expanded on Freud's stages of child development, focusing especially on adolescence. For Erikson (1968), the central developmental task for adolescents is to resolve the crisis of identity. In Erikson's view, adolescence is a time when a young person seeks to establish a personal identity by trying out several self-presentations, roles, and ways of being. Ultimately, the young person can commit to a set of personal values, beliefs, and goals. As adolescence draws to a close, he or she emerges with a strong sense of a unique self, a sense of independence from their family of origin, and a feeling of control over their life. Erikson presented his ideas about the development of identity and self during adolescence as universal, in this way mirroring Freud's ideas about early child development.

However, if we consider ideas about the life course in different societies, Erikson's claim of universality seems doubtful. For example, in many cultural settings, there is no societal recognition of a developmental period called "adolescence." Rather, in many social groups around the world, the teenage years are not regarded as a period of rebellion against authority figures or a time when anti-social behavior is inevitable. This means that anti-social behavior or rule-breaking is not universally regarded as part of a natural stage of "becoming one's own person." Furthermore, in many cultural settings, establishing a sense of identity does not require "individuating" from one's family of origin. Rather, family solidarity is maintained throughout a person's life, with successive generations residing on adjacent land, and care for children and frail elders shared among family members. Interdependence among family members and "filial piety" are expected and valued throughout the life course.

In many cultural settings, crucial signifiers of the end of childhood and the beginning of adulthood are directly connected to bodily changes, such as menarche (a girl's first menstrual period). Menarche may be celebrated with public festivities and rituals that signify the girl's transformation into a woman. These rituals also signify that she is now marriageable. But although menarche signifies the entry into adulthood for a girl, it may not bring increased autonomy but instead lead to more restrictions. Boys, of course, also undergo various physical changes, such as the development of facial hair, the growth of testes, and voice changes. However, these changes are usually not celebrated or ritualized as the beginning of manhood, and they are not connected to restrictions in autonomy.

There is much more to be said about cultural variations in conceptions of the life course, the normative expectations of various life stages, social penalties for violating or refusing those expectations, and the challenges and satisfactions of various life stages. Our focus here has been largely on adolescence. However, as we saw previously, the idea of adolescence is a recent invention – less than 150 years old – and limited to parts of the world that are affluent.

Marriage

Marriage is a culturally recognized union between people. In many societies, this union is sanctioned by law, and it may also be subject to religious recognition. Marriages entail rights and obligations of spouses to each other, as well as to their children, and often to at least some extended family members. Marriage plays a significant role in regulating gender relations and in organizing social life and civil society, though this role varies widely across time and space. Some anthropologists argue that marriage is a cross-cultural universal, though some disagree. Moreover, the forms of marriage and the social practices associated with marriage vary substantially across social groups and across historical time.

Conventionally, marriage has involved two partners: a man and a woman. However, marriages between same-sex partners have sometimes been recognized, and they are now being legalized in an increasing number of societies. Moreover, polygyny – a form of marriage in which a man may have more than one wife – is practiced in several countries in Africa. In other countries (such as India, Sri Lanka, and Malaysia), polygyny is legal for citizens who are Muslims but not for others. Polyandry – a form of marriage in which a woman has more than one husband – is quite rare, and it is usually illegal. Typically, when polyandry is practiced, brothers in a family share one wife. This form of marriage often serves as a means to prevent a family's land from being divided into plots so small that they are no longer suitable for agriculture.

In many societies, heterosexual marriage is the default state of adulthood. Members of those societies expect that, as adults, they will marry and have children. They may also anticipate that marriage and family life will be an important source of personal fulfillment and life satisfaction (Abeyasekera, 2021). In some societies, marriages between kin (such as cross-cousins) are common and thought to be preferable. In many parts of the world, families arrange marital unions for their children. In many societies, marriage is not regarded solely as a partnership of two individuals; marriages also join families and familial lineages. Often marital arrangements include the payment of a dowry (goods, money, or property transferred by the bride's family to the groom's family) or a bride price (payment by the groom to the bride's family). Furthermore, in some social groups, families may demand proof of a bride's virginity in the form of a premarital gynecological examination.

Moreover, in most societies, many forms of inequality between husbands and wives (or cohabiting partners) can be observed. These may include formal legal statutes, formal and informal social and economic structures, mundane family life, and the allocation of responsibilities for childcare and family life.

Across the world, the grounds for formally dissolving a marital union vary widely. In some societies, marital partners are at liberty to make the decision that they no longer wish to be married. In other societies or in certain religious traditions, divorce may be proscribed except under the most extreme circumstances. In some religious traditions, men may divorce their wives far more easily than women may divorce their husbands. In short, while it may be true that all or most societies institutionalize some form of marriage, there is a wide variety of customary practices, state regulations, and religious and cultural conditions.

Emotions

Researchers have long debated whether emotions are internal, universal experiences or culture-specific practices shaped by the demands of the local social order. In these debates, anthropologists have shown that different cultural groups "hypercognize" different emotions. A "hypercognized" emotion is an emotion that is the object of frequent introspection and discussion among members of a social group. Among group members, there is an emphasis on or heightened awareness of the emotion. There may be an elaborate array of associations and distinctions made about the emotion, socialization practices, and perhaps rituals connected to a hypercognized emotion.

In what follows, we briefly take up envy, an emotion that is hypercognized in many parts of the world. Beliefs about the dangers of envy have long been part of the folk theories of many cultural groups living in the geographic region stretching from the Mediterranean Sea to the eastern boundary of South Asia. The traditional beliefs about the "evil eye" – which is the envying eye – hold that the malevolent forces unleashed by envy can cause bad things to happen to the person who is the object of another's envy. This belief leads to a strong concern to avoid arousing the envy of others. It is worth pointing out that, although people are afraid of the envy of others, the expected negative effects of being envied do not always involve fears of deliberate harmful actions by these others.

Beliefs in the force of envy may shape everyday practices and social relations. Consider Sri Lanka, where concerns about the dangers of being envied are often very strong. It is a common practice there to conceal one's good fortune from others. For example, people may be careful to keep positive events secret from relatives, colleagues, and neighbors. And if a family receives positive news regarding a child's exam outcome or admission to a prestigious university, they will take pains to conceal this from neighbors and relatives. Some families may take further steps to ward off the potential harm of the envy that they believe such good news would inevitably arouse. They may undertake ritual acts of cleansing such as burning incense or burying a charm or magic amulet on the premises of their household. A related example is that buildings under construction have a *pambaya* (a scarecrow) affixed to the topmost scaffolding; the *pambaya* serves to protect against envy by distracting attention from the evidence of the owner's good fortune. And mothers in rural villages may smudge the cheeks of their babies and toddlers with dirt to make the child look ugly and therefore less likely to arouse other parents' envy. We should note that envy is only one of the emotions that may be hypercognized. Another common hypercognized emotion is shame: In many societies, shame is regarded as a crucial aspect of social regulation.

Finally, while the emphasis on envy may seem exotic and foreign to contemporary Western readers, envy has sometimes in earlier times been hypercognized in Western societies. This observation should serve as a reminder of the decisive role of history in much cultural change.

Taking Culture into Account

The preceding examples point to the variability of cultural models of personhood and moral entailments. Even these few examples should alert readers to the importance of thinking carefully about, and even scrutinizing, psychologists' ways of studying persons. Are these ways, for instance, sensitive to the fact that certain behaviors and personal qualities may have a different moral valence for members of one social group than for another? To take just one example, the *items* on scales measuring psychological traits that have been standardized for Euro-American (often high-income) populations may well have a different meaning for other populations; indeed, some items may have no meaning at all. There is also the question of whether the *methods* used to measure psychological concepts are valid from culture to culture (Byrne & van de Vijver, 2010). In addition, there are deeper questions about whether the very traits, opinions, and concepts that are purportedly being measured by scales developed in Euro-American settings really make sense outside these settings. And, closer to home for Western psychologists, there is no reason to assume that "Euro-American" or "Western" settings are culturally homogeneous. Traits, scales, and research methods may well fail to be valid, or applicable, to all inhabitants of Western countries.

Moreover, indices developed for use at one point in time may not carry over to later periods in the same cultural setting. For example, the Attitudes Toward Women Scale (Spence, Helmreich, & Stapp, 1973) was used widely by researchers in the US and the UK during the 1970s and 1980s. But attitudes regarding women's proper roles were quickly changing in these countries, and items such as "Swearing is more repulsive in the speech of a woman than a man" were soon outmoded. It is likely that there have been similar shifts in indices of personal experiences such as marital satisfaction, happiness, or depression in response to changes in social values and popular culture.

Many researchers who aim to study humans as persons who are embedded in social relations and cultural contexts rely on some of the methodological and analytical practices that anthropologists and ethnographers have developed. We describe some of these practices in Chapter 14.

CHAPTER 4

Minds in Psychology

In English, the word "mind" is common in everyday talk. Other languages have other words that serve the same everyday purposes. The everyday meanings of these words usually cause little confusion. However, in scholarly contexts, the word "mind" and the corresponding words in languages other than English sometimes spark debate. In fact, debating about the mind is a very old activity that goes back at least to the very beginning of philosophy in all parts of the world from which there are written records. The debates still go on, especially in fields such as the philosophy of mind, consciousness studies, and cognitive neuroscience, and also among psychologists with a philosophical interest. Reading this chapter will make it evident that history, even some old history, is still with us when ideas about the mind are concerned.

The debates about the mind have concerned questions such as: Is there a specific location in the individual where thinking and other mental activities take place? If the location of thinking, etc., is the mind, how do the activities of the mind interact with, and influence, the other parts of the individual? How is the mind related to the person as a whole? And if the location of thinking, etc., is the mind, what kind of thing is the mind? Is it the soul, or is it something else? Is the mind a substance? If so, is it a material or an immaterial substance? Can there be immaterial substances? And where is this mind substance itself located – is it in some ethereal, nonmaterial space, or is it in the brain? Or is the mind perhaps identical with the brain? Finally, as it seems so difficult to locate the mind, could the word "mind" be just a shorthand for each individual's collection of capacities and abilities?

In this chapter, we offer glimpses of early and contemporary debates about the mind in order to sketch what we could call the conceptual landscape of ideas about the mind. Knowledge of this landscape is helpful in any evaluation of psychological theory and practice. We have found it particularly useful when working from the perspective of situated persons that we have adopted in this book. We restrict our discussion to Western philosophy and history of ideas, because those ideas form the basis of modern psychology. Scholars in other parts of the world have produced different ideas about the mind and about individuals and their minds, but those ideas have not influenced Western psychology substantially so far.

The chapter begins with a short history of Western dualist thinking about the mind, focusing on the influential writings by the French philosopher René Descartes in the seventeenth century and some of the knotty problems his ideas created. In the subsequent parts of the chapter, we present and discuss the various attempts to resolve these problems. We also discuss the thinking styles – in Ludwik Fleck's terms (see Chapter 2) – at the basis of the suggested solutions. These styles range from Descartes's dualist thinking style about the mind as the immaterial *res cogitans*, via the mind as an entity located in the brain, to the brain *as* the mind, and finally, to the mind as a set of capacities. We also look at the words that several different languages use for what is, in English, usually meant by "mind" and point to the risk of misunderstandings and the need for precision. There are many languages that do not have a word that corresponds completely to the English word "mind" and manage well without such a word.

The Western History of the Mind

When discussing the mind, some delving into the history of both philosophy and psychology is indicated, first because this will provide a sense of the considerable longevity of ideas about the mind. Second, this history also gives a sense of the persistence of these ideas and of what might make them change (Richards & Stenner, 2023). In European history, probably the most influential early thinkers about the mind are the Greek philosopher Plato (in the 300s BCE), the Roman church father Saint Augustine (in the 400s CE), and the French philosopher René Descartes (in the seventeenth century). They subscribed to *dualist* views, taking the mind and the body to be different kinds of substances. The equally well-known Greek thinker Aristotle (in the 300s BCE) subscribed to a different view, but this part of his thinking has not been as influential as his writings on other topics. Even so, his ideas about the mind have recently been taken up by philosophers who do not accept dualism. We describe some of their ideas in later parts of the chapter.

We focus here on the mathematician and philosopher René Descartes (1596–1650), because his version of dualist thinking about the mind and the body has been enormously influential – in at least two ways. First, his *ideas* about the mind were extremely influential and long-lasting, as we will see in the following sections of the chapter. Second, and maybe even more importantly, beyond his specific ideas about the mind, the *categories* and *words* he used when he wrote about the mind became central parts of the vocabularies of philosophers and scientists, psychologists included (Hacker, 2007). That is, later philosophers kept on using his categories when they wrote about mental processes, even if they were critical of his original ideas. And, inevitably, their use of Descartes's words and categories to express their thoughts came to set certain limits on what they were able to write about the mind, the body, and their interactions. This second legacy of Descartes's scheme is a good reason for including his writings in almost any book about psychology. Ludwik Fleck would probably have said that Descartes's words and categories became central parts of the active assumptions at the base of an influential thinking style: Cartesian dualism.

Res cogitans and Cartesian Dualism

Among Descartes's most long-lasting ideas was *res cogitans*. This is a Latin term, *res* meaning "substance," and *cogitans* meaning "thinking," as in the act of thinking. Descartes described *res cogitans* as a nonmaterial substance in which all higher, or conscious, mental activity occurs.[1] It has often been translated into English, first as "soul" and later as "mind." However, though there are similarities, Descartes's descriptions of *res cogitans* show that it was not identical to what is usually meant by the English word "mind."

A brief description of *res cogitans* would be something like this: It is an immaterial substance that is identical with the self and distinct from the body (which is *res extensa*, a material, i.e., extended, substance). It contains everything that is accessible to introspection: human understanding, will-ing, seeing, hearing, feeling, pain, and pleasure. *Res cogitans* is transparent to the individual and its contents are therefore also transparent to the individual. The individual knows the contents. Further, the contents are private, thus not accessible to others (Hacker, 2007; LaVine & Tissaw, 2015; Sprague, 1999; Tanney, 2022). It should also be noted that for

---

[1] The word *substance* usually denotes material phenomena; that is, phenomena that fit the definition of matter. Therefore, Descartes's notion that there might exist a substance that does not consist of matter and consequently is nonmaterial (or *immaterial*) while still being a substance has been problematic in the history of philosophy and has occasioned much debate.

Descartes all human sensations include a spiritual or experiential element that is distinct from the body's activities (Kenny, 1992).

For Descartes, the mind (or *res cogitans*) is both the container of private mental content and the subject, or agent, of psychological experiences and actions: It is the mind that has the experiences. Further, in Descartes's scheme, the mind, as an immaterial substance, and the body, as a material substance, are ontologically distinct from each other. The expression "ontologically distinct" means that the substances, mind and body, are able to exist by themselves, independently of each another (Dicker, 2013). But although Descartes took the mind to be ontologically distinct from the body, he argued that the mind is nonetheless in some way united with and interacts with the body, causing bodily changes such as movements of limbs and so on (Baier, 1985; Hoffman, 2009). This argument requires the "active" assumption (in Ludwik Fleck's terms) that a nonmaterial substance, such as the mind, *can* interact causally with matter. This assumption led to what has been termed *dualistic interactionism*. As we shall see later, dualistic interactionism created serious problems for Descartes's scheme.

As we mentioned before, Descartes's view of mind and body, often called "Cartesian dualism," and perhaps especially many of the terms he used to talk about mind and body, were adopted by many philosophers and psychologists after him. But his dualism was also, from its beginning, fiercely debated, and it still is (Lowe, 2009). The two most intensely debated issues are the mind–body problem and the problem of mental content and its location.

The Cartesian Mind–Body Problem

Cartesian dualism was part of more general habits of thought in his time, habits which took the world to consist of items that are unrelated to one another, existing independently, and having nothing in common (Chirimuuta, 2024). This makes these items, by definition, unable to interact because interaction requires some measure of connection or similarity. An obvious difficulty for Cartesian dualism was, therefore, how and where the mind, as an immaterial substance ontologically distinct from the body, could interact with the material substance of the body (Kenny, 1992). But for Cartesian dualism to make sense, mind and body had to interact somehow. Contemporary commentators repeatedly made Descartes aware of this requirement. Eventually, after unsuccessfully suggesting that the interaction took place in the pineal gland in the brain, he admitted to being unable to solve this problem. Even so, he insisted that interaction *did* take place (Dicker, 2013). Since Descartes's days, the mind–body problem in Cartesian dualism has repeatedly been brought up by many philosophers and some psychologists. It is still a contentious issue in modern philosophy and science.

The Cartesian Problem of Mental Content and Its Location
Descartes's image of the mind as the container of private mental content (knowledge, beliefs, judgments; perceptions, sensations, mental images) also met with difficulties. When one thinks of the mind as a container, one must ask what *kind* of *thing* the container is and *where* the container is located. The earliest choice of location was the immaterial *soul*, but this choice lost its appeal in the centuries following Descartes. We follow up on the issue of location later in the chapter, but first, we summarize the Cartesian scheme in thinking style terms.

The Cartesian Dualist Thinking Style about the Mind

In Ludwik Fleck's terminology from Chapter 2, we would say that, for several centuries to come, Descartes cemented *Cartesian dualism* as a particularly influential thinking style regarding the mind. First, his writings introduced what came to be a long-lived vocabulary for speaking about mental activities. Second, some of his ideas came to function as taken-for-granted "active assumptions" (Hacker, 2007). In this thinking style, the first assumption was that the mind (originally, *res cogitans*) is the seat of all higher mental activity. A further assumption was that the mind is a nonmaterial substance, followed by the assumption that the mind is nonetheless able to interact with the material body in *dualistic* interaction. In this way, the mind, despite being nonmaterial, is assumed both to influence the body and to be influenced by the body. This thinking style was based on the further assumptions that the mind is transparent to the individual and private to each individual. The Cartesian dualist thinking style was especially plagued by the two problems we mentioned just before: the mind–body problem and the problem of mental content. We discuss these problems in some detail in the next section.

From Descartes to Today

Large parts of Descartes's thinking about the mind have been discarded by modern Western thinkers, including psychologists. Some parts have lingered, though, and have caused continuing controversy in philosophical and psychological theorizing. We can identify the lingering parts in three characteristics of common word use about psychological matters. First, words are often used to portray psychological concepts as *possessions*. Second, words are often used as the names of assumed mental *entities*. Third, such assumed mental entities are often talked about as having a *location*, that location being the mind. (Sometimes these entities are, via a process of reification, also talked about as having *agency;* see Chapter 12.) All these characteristics of people's use of words to talk about the mind have their origins in Descartes's ideas about the mind (LaVine & Tissaw, 2015). We scrutinize the characteristics one at a time, though they are obviously connected.

Possessions

It is common to talk about psychological properties as something that people have, that is, as *possessions*. We can think about expressions such as "I have a feeling that . . . " "Have" is a very common word and easy to understand, but in the circumstances we are discussing here, it can be treacherous. Consider these sentences: "Lena has a comfortable chair." "Nicholas has very long arms." "Patricia has a bright mind." "Nils has excellent verbal abilities." In all these sentences, the word "have" expresses possession, but not the same kind of possession (Lavine & Tissaw, 2015; see also Smit, 2023). Having a chair seems different from having a mind. A chair is an object that one can acquire but also relinquish. It is an object that definitely is distinct from its owner. A mind, even if talked about as something that people have, is not something that one can acquire or divest oneself of. And people usually do not think about a person's mind as an object that is distinct from its owner. Having an arm seems different from having a chair or a mind. Arms are not like chairs because they are not separate from their owners and cannot be bought or sold, etc. But having arms is not like having a mind, either. Human beings can have both arms and minds, but they "have" them in rather different ways. An arm is a *part* of a human being, but it is a part that can be lost without turning someone into another person. That would not be true of someone's mind. The British philosopher Peter Hacker puts the trouble even more starkly by adding "is":

> . . . is the body one is identical with the body one has? How can one be identical with something one has? Or, since one can apparently doubt the

existence of one's body but not of one's mind, is one, as Descartes held, identical with one's mind? But a mind too is something one has, and if it is what he is, who has it? (2007, p. 234)[2]

A major source of the trouble with the word "have" in all these examples rests in the difference between the *superficial* (dictionary, or general) meaning and the *contextualized* (or deep grammatical) meanings of the word "have" in each of these specific places in the sentences (Lavine & Tissaw, 2015). Perhaps, then, when somebody uses the word "have" about their mind, we should think twice about which contextualized meaning of "have" they could be alluding to, and perhaps ask them to specify. The next section takes up some troubles with that which is being "had" when talking about the mind.

Mental Entities

In everyday conversations, the contextualized meanings of words such as "have" usually cause little trouble. However, sometimes the dictionary, or general, meaning of the word "have" (as in having a chair) "infects" a contextualized meaning. This happens, for instance, when one talks about somebody having a psychological property (such as an attitude, phobia, or prejudice) as being analogous to having a physical entity (such as a chair). The US philosopher Elmer Sprague, therefore, advises us to pay attention to how we use "psychological" nouns and to be wary of how the uses of such nouns in everyday language can trick us into thinking of psychological phenomena as mental *entities*:

> What is embedded in our language and obscures the facts is the view that where there is a noun, there must be an entity that it names. So [that makes us think that] thinking and thought, wishing and wish, hope and hoping, and so on, must be the names of something-or-others in the medium of the mind. (1999, p. 51)

The word "chair" is the name of a physical *entity* that can be owned and can be sat on. It exists independently, its existence is not dependent on any other entity. Would one also be entitled to take psychological states or properties (such as anger or extroversion) to be independent entities? No, because psychological states and properties are not *separable*. This means

---

[2] The reference in the quote to doubting one's body versus doubting one's mind comes from Descartes's reasoning up to his well-known conclusion *cogito, ergo sum* – because he is able to doubt (i.e., to think), he must have a mind, and therefore he must exist. Therefore, in this scheme, one can doubt that one has a body, but not that one has a mind.

that they are not entities or things that have independent existence. They cannot (unlike the chair) exist on their own, but require a *subject*, such as the human being, who is the one who, for instance, is in a state of anger or has the property of extroversion (Fuchs, 2018, 2021; Hacker, 2007; Kagan, 1998). The fact that a subject is required for psychological states and properties to exist means that words like "thinking and thought, wishing and wish, hope and hoping" in the quote above need to be seen as something other than the names of *entities* "in the medium of the mind." We discuss what this "something else" could be in the section about the fourth thinking style about the mind.

The Location and Nature of the Mind

Someone who thinks of psychological properties as mental entities that are somebody's possessions is likely to want to know where these entities are located. This has been a perennial question in philosophy for millennia, and it is still being asked and debated, especially in the fields of philosophy of mind and consciousness studies (Kind, 2020; Morris et al., 2018). The answer has often, or even usually, been the mind. Then there is the question of where the mind itself is located. While previously the soul was seen as its location, nowadays the mind is usually seen as located in the brain. Recently, some philosophers and researchers instead answer that the mind is not just located in the brain, but that the brain *is* the mind. Their answer provides one of the contemporary answers to the second question about the mind that has exercised philosophers, namely that of its nature. This is so because claiming that the brain is the mind necessarily means assuming that the nature of the mind is the same as the nature of the brain.

In what follows, we scrutinize these views and assumptions by juxtaposing the thinking styles that they inform. We begin with the thinking style that is based on the assumption that the mind is located in the brain.

The Mind as Located in the Brain: A Modern Dualist Thinking Style

The basic assumptions that inform this thinking style are familiar from the previous section. The mind is assumed to be something that it is possible to distinguish from all other things, and that interacts with some of these other things (such as the body). The mind is also assumed to have content; to be a *container* of mental entities. What is new is the assumption that the *location* of the mind is the brain, rather than the soul or some other nonmaterial thing or place (Fuchs, 2021; Glock, 2020). Does the assumption of the brain as the location of the mind help resolve Descartes's mind–body problem? Not really, its critics argue (Bennett & Hacker, 2022; Tanney, 2022). Locating the mind as a distinguishable kind of thing in the brain, in fact, presupposes dualism, though another kind than that of Descartes. The thinking it presupposes is dualist because when one thinks about the mind as "a something" that is *located* in the brain, this inevitably means thinking about the mind as something distinct from the brain (because a thing cannot be located in itself). And then one is faced with another version of the problem of mind–body dualism: how the located, distinct thing (the mind) and its properties could possibly interact with the bodily substance in which it is located (the brain). The philosopher Julia Tanney has phrased the problem succinctly:

> How can mental properties be affected by and have an effect upon physical and other mental ones? What used to be a mystery about interaction taking place in the pineal gland becomes a mystery . . about how to find mental "vehicles" and their "representational contents" in synapses and neural networks. (2022, pp. 100–101)

There are some seemingly self-evident "passive" consequences (see Chapter 2), to which this modern dualist thinking style leads: First, basing one's thinking on the *active assumption* that the mind is the only location of reasoning, thinking, knowing, and so on will invite psychologists to confine their research questions to psychological processes assumed to be mind-bound, that is, limited to what goes on inside an individual's mind. This mind-boundedness will inevitably place some limitations on what kinds of phenomena can be taken to be "psychological."[3] Perhaps it may be those limitations that have led many psychologists throughout the history of the discipline to confine their research to properties and activities assumed to be mind-bound, or *subpersonal*, that is, internal to each individual (Brinkmann, 2018; Sprague, 1999). The Australian philosopher Robert Wilson summarized these aspects of the thinking style by noting that ". . .*psychology is both mind laden (rather than mind free) and individual bound (rather than interpersonal)*" (Wilson, 2004, p. 29, emphasis in the original). Second, adopting such mind-ladenness has led many psychologists to pay little attention to the person as a whole, and even less to the person's social and cultural surroundings (Martin, Sugarman, & Hickinbottom, 2009).

---

[3] In Chapter 6, *Thinking Persons*, we take up the debates about the bodily and other boundaries of thinking and other psychological processes in some detail.

At this point, we should remember the self-evident character – or even sense of "naturalness" – of well-ingrained thinking styles. Thinking styles are, if we are to believe Ludwik Fleck, often not explicitly expressed or even conscious in a researcher's daily work, while still forming the taken-for-granted basis of much of the work. So, perhaps working within a modern dualist thinking style leads researchers to presuppose that the data that their research produces is, by definition, data about what goes on in the mind, and about nothing or nowhere else. That is how it would be if no other thinking styles, that is, no other interpretative frameworks, were available to a researcher.

Finally, we should consider Fleck's argument that one can draw conclusions from the methods used in psychological research, back to the active assumptions that make those methods natural or "self-evident" (see the section *Active Assumptions and Passive Elements of Thinking Styles* in Chapter 2 for details). As an example, the observation that methods (the passive elements) for studying subpersonal properties have long been common in certain parts of psychology should lead us to surmise that such psychological research has been conducted in accord with the active assumptions of a dualist thinking style.

Some contemporary thinkers and researchers avoid all discussion about the location and content of the mind and instead focus solely on what the mind does, hoping thereby to avoid the specter of dualism. Critics are often skeptical of their success, however. One critical argument holds that some version of dualism still lingers, not least the (unwanted) necessity of imagining an inner "homunculus" to be the interpreter of what the mind does (de-Wit et al., 2016; Hacking, 2004; Tanney, 2022).[4] Other researchers have taken the step of assuming identity between the mind and the brain. We discuss them in the next section.

The *Brain as the Mind* Thinking Style

Some contemporary philosophers and researchers, among them many cognitive neuroscientists and psychologists, subscribe to a view of the brain *as* the mind. Or, put another way: In this view, it is the brain that does all the work that in everyday talk is ascribed to the mind. According to this *monist* view, there is no need to postulate something, such as a mind, that is located somewhere, such as in the soul or in the brain. What people,

---

[4] *Homunculus* is Latin for "little person." The expression has been used in dualistic philosophy to designate an assumed agent in the mind that observes and reacts to activities in the mind.

in their everyday lives, take to be the contents and processes of their minds are, in this view, nothing but the physiological and chemical changes in their brains. Thoughts and all other kinds of mental content *are* brain activities; they are not the interpretations by some invisible agent (such as the mind) of brain activities. This monist thinking recognizes the existence of only one type of substance – matter – and it is, therefore, a strictly materialist view. If only material substance exists, there should be no Cartesian problem of interaction between different kinds of substances (Rey, 2010).

But, of course, there is also critique of this thinking style. One immediate critique is phenomenological and experiential in a general sense: saying that the brain *is* the mind does not explain how physiological changes in the brain can cause the psychological experiences and lived lives of human beings. This problem is sometimes called *the hard problem of consciousness* or *the explanatory gap*. If the universe is entirely physical, and should therefore be understood only in physical terms, how can there be one part of the universe – subjective experience – that seems so different? (Chalmers, 2021; Charles, 2021).

Further, some critics have pointed out that brain monism is, in fact, troubled by a version of the same Cartesian problems as the two earlier thinking styles. One major reason for this is that this thinking style, in spite of its monism, upholds the Cartesian "part" idea. To recapitulate: Descartes thought of the mind, or *res cogitans*, as the particular (in his case immaterial) part of the human being which was the location where mental events and processes occur. That part needed to interact with the material part of the human but, as critics pointed out, logically could not do so. A similar "part" aspect of the Cartesian view is assumed by the thinkers who adopt the second thinking style (the mind as located in the brain). While it seems unclear what these thinkers take the mind to be made of, they see the mind as the part where mental events occur. However, in contrast to Descartes, they see the mind's location as material: the brain. And the interaction problem remains.

Those who have adopted the third, the *brain as the mind*, thinking style will also be troubled by a type of Cartesian "part" view. The part in question now is the *brain* (Tanney, 2022). So there is still an interaction problem, now the problem of interaction between the brain (assumed to be the same thing as the mind) on the one hand, and on the other hand, the rest of the human being, including the body and the human being's psychological experiences and lived life. The Australian neuroscientist

Max Bennett, in collaboration with the British philosopher Peter Hacker, summarized this third style of thinking:

> Just as Cartesianism and classical British empiricism fostered the idea that human behaviour is to be rendered intelligible in terms of causal interaction between mind and body, the mind being the subject of volitional psychological attributes, so current neuroscience fosters the idea that human behaviour is to be rendered intelligible in terms of causal interaction between the brain and the body, the brain being the subject of volitional psychological attributes. (2022, p. 125)

The *brain as the mind* thinking style is also beset by an epistemological problem, that is, a problem to do with knowledge. For it to be possible to find out whether the thesis that the brain is the mind is true, one must be able to specify what kind of knowledge would count *as proof* of this thesis. And critics claim that it is far from obvious that it is possible to do this (Bennett & Hacker, 2022).

Summarizing the First Three Thinking Styles

In sum, these three thinking styles, though different, share two major *active assumptions*, that is, the foundational assumptions that, as Ludwik Fleck argued, tend to be taken for granted and seldom scrutinized. First, they share the active assumption that thinking and other mental processes take place *in some part of* the human being (either in *res cogitans*/the mind or in the brain). Second, they share the active assumption that this part interacts causally with other parts of the human being, thereby making those other parts change (Smit, 2021). This means that even the third, monist and materialist, thinking style contains a version of dualism; now between the brain on the one hand, and the rest of the human being on the other hand. This makes it look as if dualism is sneaking back from the "older" styles. And that defeats the purpose of materialist monism, which was to get rid of the old specter of dualism (Charles, 2021).[5] In the following quote, the Dutch philosopher Fred Keijzer therefore argues that conventional, that is, dualist, ideas of mind are still reigning in the contemporary cognitive sciences – and that they seem unlikely to be overturned very soon:

> The concept of mind is a powerful and influential conceptual structure that has a major influence on how the problem space of the cognitive sciences is

---

[5] We should note that the set of thinking styles that we have enumerated in this chapter does not exhaust the existing suggestions. See Charles (2021, pp. 1–3) for a more complete list.

conceived: an inner domain of reasons connected with inputs and outputs to an independently existing external world. This conceptualization is so deeply established and generally accepted that it is difficult to see it as a conceptualization that may be questioned. (Keijzer, 2022, lines 3044–3048)

The *Mind as Capacities* Thinking Style

An assumption that does away with the dualisms of the first three thinking styles takes thinking and other mental processes to be states or activities of human beings (rather than states or activities *in some part* of human beings). This means that mental processes and states are seen as states and processes undergone by *a whole* human being (rather than just by one of its *parts*, such as the mind) (Bennett & Hacker, 2022; Glock, 2020).

We have seen that several conceptual and logical problems inhere within the ways of conceiving of the mind that have their historical and philosophical origins with thinkers such as Descartes. These problems also surface in contemporary philosophy of mind, because many debates build on questions based in the second and third of the thinking styles we described previously (see, for instance, Bayne, Cleeremans, & Wilken, 2009; Chalmers, 2021; Tanney, 2022). Some philosophers have become disaffected with this dualist heritage and have looked for other tracks to follow in the history of ideas (Kenny, 1992). One such track reaches back to the Greek philosopher and scientist Aristotle, who lived in the fourth century BCE. Aristotle used the word *psuchē*[6] for what we would here approximately refer to as the mind. One of his major ideas was that psuchē should be thought about as the *powers of* living things. In this view, the psuchē is not something distinct from the body. It is not a thing, nor something located in a part of the body, and it is not a location. Rather, the term psuchē refers to the powers or potentialities that can be inferred from an individual's actions. In summary, then, the psuchē is not (like the brain) a part of the body, and not (like *res cogitans*) an immaterial substance separate from but connected with the body. The psuchē comprises the powers and abilities of the individual as a whole (Bennett & Hacker, 2022; Glock, 2020).

---

[6] It should be noted here that Aristotle's use of the word *psuchē* is not synonymous with the current use of the word "mind" or "psyche" but that it, at least for human beings, can be said to refer to the *capacities* that are usually referred to when the word "mind" is used (cf. Bennett & Hacker, 2022).

To give a sense of how some contemporary philosophers use Aristotelian ideas in their thinking about the mind, we quote four philosophers. First is Elmer Sprague, for whom:

> ...mind does not stand for another organ. It signifies a person's ability and proneness to do certain things, not some piece of apparatus without which a person could not do them. (1999, p. 7)

Then Peter Hacker, who has argued for a view of the mind as

> ...not a *thing* (an "entity") of any kind – just as horsepower and eyesight are not things of any sort. They are *powers*. The mind is an array of distinctive powers to engage in activities that characterize humanity. (2012, p. 71; italics in the original)

The German philosopher Hans-Johann Glock has argued that

> ... to have a mind is to have a range of cognitive, volitional, and affective capacities or abilities... whether a subject has mental properties depends on what she is capable of doing. (2020, p. 3)

Finally, the British philosopher Anthony Kenny has proposed:

> The mind itself can be defined as the capacity for behaviour of the complicated and symbolic kinds which constitute the linguistic, social, moral, economic, scientific, cultural, and other characteristic activities of human beings in society. (1992, p. 7)

If these uses of the word "mind" seem odd, think back to our observation at the beginning of the chapter: Descartes's terms and concepts became so ingrained in Western thinking that it is difficult to move outside them. The philosophers quoted above attempt to do just that – move outside of the Cartesian concepts and vocabulary. And their claims may seem odd at first. What, then, characterizes the assumptions about the abilities, powers, or capacities that constitute "mind" in the thinking style of these philosophers?

First, these philosophers assume that human capacities or powers are not things that could take up space. Therefore (in contrast to the first three thinking styles), they have no location. Second, capacities and powers are not assumed to be objects or entities of any kind. This is true of all varieties of abilities, powers, or capacities, both physical powers such as elasticity and mental powers such as cognition, perception, and imagination. Third, while abilities or capacities are not entities that take up space, they are assumed to be the *attributes* of entities or objects that do take up space. *Those* entities and objects have locations and are made of material substance – they are, for instance, entities such as human beings (Smit & Hacker, 2020).

We should observe that these assumptions, and the thinking style that they underpin, are not held by the majority of philosophers of mind or, indeed, by many neuroscientists or psychologists today. There have been debates about this fourth thinking style and its differences from, and contradictions of, the other styles described earlier in this chapter.[7] However, we argue that this thinking style brings a refreshing perspective both on the mind and on the brain, and on many psychological questions – enough to make it worth considering in the context of our perspective on persons as contextualized beings (Craffert, 2024; Glock, 2020; Smit, 2021, 2023).

What would be the consequences of adopting a thinking style that rejects the dualist idea of mind as a location or part (whether material or immaterial) of the individual, and instead focuses attention on the individual's capacities? One consequence could be to avoid the word "mind" and instead speak directly of the specific powers and capacities that are under consideration. As we will show in the following section about the array of different words for "mind," it is often easy to rephrase expressions that use "mind" into an active-verb format. For example, one can rephrase "keep this in mind!" as "remember this!" And so on. A second consequence may be weightier and perhaps more difficult for someone who is wedded to one of the first three thinking styles in this chapter to accept: One would have to refrain from thinking about the mind as the *subject* who has psychological attributes. If the mind is not a location or an entity, but a set of capacities or powers, it (the mind) could not be a subject that "has" anything. As we saw previously, capacities and powers are seen as *attributes* of entities (human beings, in our case) that can be the subjects of psychological attributes. To quote two of the foremost contemporary proponents of this thinking style:

> It is not the mind that is the subject of psychological attributes, any more than it is the brain. It is the living human being – the animal as a whole, not one of its parts or a subset of its powers. It is not my mind that makes up its mind or decides; it is not my mind that calls something to mind and recollects; and it is not my mind that turns its mind to something or other and thinks – it is I, this human being. (Bennett & Hacker, 2022, p. 74)

---

[7] For a retrospective on such debates, see Bennett & Hacker (2022, Appendices 1, 2, and 3); see also Fuchs (2021) and Smit (2021), for overviews and discussions.

How would proponents of this thinking style answer the questions that the three other thinking styles struggle with (the mind–body problem, the problem of location, and the problem of mental content)? The short answer is that they would not be asking those kinds of questions. If the mind is not a thing that forms a part (whether material or immaterial) of the human being, then there is no reason to discuss how "it" would interact with the body or the brain. And if the mind is not seen as a place that is the location of mental content, then there is no reason to look for such a location.

If one does not think of the mind and "the mental" as a kind of entity in the brain, but as a set of capacities, one will look at the activities and conditions of the *persons* who possess those capacities (Charles, 2021). It is, after all, persons who think, feel, act, talk, and so on. This necessarily makes persons the proper subjects to study. And persons, on this view, should be studied on their own terms, in accordance with their own ways of being. It is likely that many (perhaps most?) of these ways are activities that people do for a reason, and that these activities, therefore, cannot be causally explained by natural science laws or principles (Sprague, 1999). To study persons and their capacities (substituting now for the term "mind"), it is necessary to use concepts and methods that will help in understanding persons. In Chapter 12, we therefore look closer at the different kinds of explanations that are used about human behavior and experiences. And in Chapter 14, we present approaches to the psychological study of persons.

We should note that this thinking style does not lead to a lack of interest in research about the mind (i.e., psychological or other kinds of powers and/or capacities) or in research about neurophysiology and brain functions. Rather, thinking in terms of powers and capacities leads to a lively interest in scientific research aimed at finding out about the physical bases that enable humans to develop, possess, and wield these powers.

The Many Words for Mind And the Languages That Have No Such Word

We have written this book in English, and it therefore seems natural to use the word "mind" when we write. But we expect some of our readers to belong to other language communities (as does one of us), and so we here consider the words that a few other languages use to talk about mind-like phenomena. We also consider the many uses of the word "mind" in English. To begin, we should note that the word "mind" is unique to the English language. Some of its dictionary meanings are: the seat of awareness; the spiritual as opposed to the bodily part of a human being; consciousness; mental and psychic faculty; intellect; temperament; thoughts; ways of thinking (The Shorter Oxford English Dictionary). Other languages use several other words for mind-like phenomena (see below), and the meaning they ascribe to each of these words encompasses only one or a few of the several meanings of "mind" before. To illustrate, we present the words that some European languages use to (more or less) denote what English speakers mean by "mind."

The German word "Geist" (related to the word "ghost," and originally connected to the Greek word *pneuma*, for breath), means "spirits" as in good or evil spirits or ghosts, but it also means "spirit" as in morale, or in Zeitgeist, and finally also ability or intelligence. The Dutch word "geest" has the same etymology as the German word and is used to mean soul, consciousness, character, or presence of mind, and also spirit as in "team spirit," as well as spirit as in an evil spirit or ghost. The French word "esprit" usually denotes spirit (in the sense of "spirits" as above), soul, consciousness, and ability. The French word "âme" denotes soul in the meaning of sense or "heart," or spirit in the meaning of morale or atmosphere (and it was the word that Descartes used to denote the soul, when he wrote in French). The Danish language uses the word "sind" to denote the mental faculties that are responsible for thinking, imagination, memory, and so on, and also to denote the soul. The Norwegian language uses the word "sinn" to denote thinking, memory, emotions, will, and imagination, as well as the stream of consciousness and rational reasoning processes, and the word "sans" to denote the senses. As can be seen, none of these words corresponds completely to the English word "mind."

We look a little closer at words in Swedish because one of us is a speaker of Swedish and the other is a speaker of American English. When writing this book, we have become very aware that our respective languages use different kinds of expressions for many psychological phenomena. And we have seen how such mismatches sometimes make understanding more difficult. "Mind" is one example. Like many other languages, the Swedish language has no word that directly translates into "mind." Instead, several Swedish words and expressions are used to denote different aspects of mental life. In some settings the word "psyke" (derived from the Greek word *psuchē*, "soul" or "life") is used, often to denote mental life in general. But apart from this, psyke is not used like the word "mind" in expressions such as "to change one's mind." Swedish speakers do not say "to change one's psyke"; rather, they say in Swedish, "att ändra åsikt" (which translates literally as "to change one's opinion"). That is, no words like "mind" enter into such expressions in Swedish. In some settings, the Swedish word "medvetande" is used for mind. So, for instance, the English expression "philosophy of mind" has been translated into Swedish as "medvetandefilosofi." But even so, the Swedish word "medvetande" is not fully synonymous with "mind" – it can also be translated into English as "awareness" or "consciousness," which in English are not synonyms for "mind." Another Swedish word that is sometimes used for "mind" is "sinne," similar to the Danish and Norwegian words. In Swedish, though, "sinne" is most often used to denote the different senses. Now and then, the word "minne" (which means "memory") is used in expressions where English uses "mind." One can find this in Swedish expressions such as "hålla något i minnet" (which translates literally as "to keep something in one's memory") for the English expression "keep something in mind." But because the Swedish word "minne" really only means "memory," it cannot be used as a general translation of "mind," even though it fits in the previous sentence. Actually, in many, if not most, cases where English uses the word "mind," Swedish tends to use expressions that do not refer to minds: "Make up your mind!" translates as "Bestäm dig!" ("Decide!"). "What did you have in mind?" translates as "Vad hade du tänkt dig?" ("What had you planned?"). "To know one's own mind" translates as "Att veta vad man vill" ("To know what one wants"). And so on.

The purpose of this exercise in language variations is not to teach readers some Swedish words. The purpose is to make both English speakers and speakers of other languages aware that when the word "mind" is used in an English text, or by an English speaker, it is not always evident how it should be translated into another language (or even what is meant in English). Is this important? It is evident that it is important for readers whose first language is not English. They may have to think carefully before settling on the best translation of the word "mind" in a sentence. But might this exercise also be important for English speakers? We think so. English speakers need to be explicit about which aspect of the word "mind" they intend in specific settings, both for their own sake and for the sake of their listeners or readers. Expressions that use the word "mind" often refer to remembering, thinking, or wishing. These uses of the word are quite easy to paraphrase without using the word "mind" (look back at the examples from Swedish just mentioned before!). Such paraphrasing works because the *subject* of the psychological attributes in question is the person – not the mind. It is the person who remembers something, not the person's mind. It is the person's opinion that is changed, not the mind's opinion. And it is the person who knows what they want, not the person's mind.

English speakers and writers may be well advised to consider whether they can make their messages clearer by doing without the word "mind" when possible. Alternatively, they could be explicit about which of the many meanings of the word "mind" they are referring to (Glock, 2020). Or they could try to go even further and consider doing without thinking of mind as a container, a location, or a substance. As we saw, the "mind as capacities" thinking style that we discussed earlier is moving in that direction.

Other Dualisms to Worry About?

In a recent article, the Dutch philosopher Fred Keijzer (2025) has pointed out problems associated with a kind of dualism other than the ones we have discussed here. This is the commonly taken-for-granted *conceptual* dualism between the organism and the surrounding world (also a legacy of Descartes, like the earlier dualisms in this chapter). In Keijzer's view, psychological and neuroscientific theorizing would benefit from rejecting the assumed conceptual division between what is internal or subjective to the individual, and what is external or objective in the natural world. He argued, on the basis of comparisons of animals along the evolutionary scale, that there is good reason to see the individual's subjective point of view as just as much a part of nature as the external and objective world. Put slightly differently: if humans are part of nature, their activities, including their subjective points of view and experiences will by definition also be part of nature. In Keijzer's view, therefore, humans' subjective points of view should not be taken as conceptually separate from nature.

Keijzer's perhaps provocative ideas are still being developed, but it seems clear that a thinking style informed by his lines of thought would lead to yet other kinds of questions about "mind" than the ones we have presented here. In Chapter 6, about thinking, part of the discussion deals with ideas about cognition that are related to ideas like Keijzer's.

CHAPTER 5

Human Brains and Psychology

Today, psychologists often talk about human psychology and human brains in the same breath – much more so than just a couple of decades ago. There are now few psychological specialties in which the prefixes "brain-" or "neuro-" are never used. This is hardly surprising, considering recent developments in neuroscience, especially cognitive neuroscience. A reasonable question to ask, in a book like this, is what might be the implications of the increased brain focus in psychology for a psychology that is committed to the study of human beings as socially and culturally situated persons. Our answer to that question is: it depends! There are, of course, several ways to theorize about and talk about human brains. In this chapter, we discuss some ways that are more, and some less, able to take people's social and cultural situatedness into account.

Before we start, we want to emphasize that this chapter is *not* a critique of neuroscientific research. However, it does contain critiques of certain ways of *drawing conclusions* about brains and persons from such research.

The chapter begins with a description of human brains and some of their specific characteristics. A discussion then follows on the impact of cultural conventions on how people interpret biological phenomena, especially brains. We then look at the various metaphors that have been used through history for talking about the brain, and the impact that some metaphors still have on how people, including scientists, think about brains. In the next section, we look at how researchers and popular writers today describe the activities that go on in brains when people think, feel, and act. This is followed by a discussion of reductionist explanations of psychological functions and brain activity. We then present the different thinking styles that inform various understandings of brains and psychology. In the final section, we summarize some problems in contemporary psychological thinking about brains and in the language used for talking about brains. We end with suggestions for less problematic ways for psychologists to think about brains, brain research, and psychology.

Human Brains

Human brains are estimated to contain between 78 and 94 billion nerve cells and similar numbers of support cells (glia). Adult human brains weigh on average about 1.3 kg (2.87 lb), with a range of about 1.03–1.62 kg (2.27–3.57 lb). These differences in weight are not associated with differences in functions such as cognitive capacities. That is, having a heavy brain does not guarantee a high level of cognitive functioning, nor does having a light brain preclude it.

Human brains are usually described as divided into the cerebrum (Latin for "the large brain"), the cerebellum (Latin for "the little brain"), and the brainstem. The cerebrum is divided into two nearly identical hemispheres, each consisting of the cerebral cortex (Latin for "bark") and several subcortical structures. Some of these are the thalamus, the hypothalamus, the hippocampus, and the amygdala. Each hemisphere is divided into four lobes: the frontal (at the front of the skull), the parietal (just behind the frontal lobe), the temporal (on each side of the skull), and the occipital lobe (at the very back of the skull). The two hemispheres are connected by a large bundle of fibers, the corpus callosum (Latin for "tough body"). The cerebellum sits at the very back, beneath the occipital lobe. The brainstem is at the base of the brain, connecting the other parts of the brain to the peripheral nervous system via the spinal cord.

Structures and Functions in Human Brains

The processing and control of many functions are localized in specific brain structures. Two examples are processing of vision in the visual cortex of the occipital lobe and control of voluntary movement in the motor cortex of the frontal lobe. Most of the control of nonconscious functions such as heart rate and digestion is located in subcortical structures, many of which are in the brainstem. However, while the control of many functions is localized, this is not true of all functions. And also, many functions for which localization of control has been identified are, in fact, also influenced by activity in other brain structures that are distant from that localization (De Bari & Dixon, 2022). As just one of many examples, neural responses to visual stimuli occur not just in the visual cortex but also in motor regions of the brain that were traditionally not seen as having to do with vision.

This means that much neural activity is distributed across the brain in ways that differ from "classical" maps of brain functions. Thus, brain activation underlying psychological functions and processes, such as working memory, response inhibition, and semantic judgments (to mention just a few), is more distributed across the brain and overlaps more between functions than was earlier assumed. In a comment on what to learn from these findings, Paul Cisek, a Canadian neuroscientist, concluded: "*In short, the categories of concepts we inherit from psychology simply do not fit the brain*" (2022, lines 1040–1041). Put slightly differently, many of the psychological activities that psychological research and theory have identified (such as those mentioned just previously) are not accompanied by activity in specific brain regions. Does this mean that psychologists should adjust their categories and concepts to fit neuroscientific findings? Or would such an adjustment lead to putatively "psychological" categories that are unintelligible to people in general, or perhaps also to psychologists in general? Arguments in favor of switching to using neuroscientific categories are found in Pessoa, Medina, and Desfilis (2021), and more discussion about the question can be found in Cisek and Hayden (2021). The question is worth keeping in mind when considering reductive explanations of psychological phenomena in terms of brain processes. We take up such questions in a later section in this chapter, and also in Chapter 12, about explanations in psychology.

Plasticity in Human Brains

There is also *plasticity* in the brain: A particular region of the brain may be recruited for several tasks. This is seen, for instance, when an adult human becomes blind. Then, the brain area that was dedicated to vision becomes repurposed for other abilities (e.g., hearing). That is, human brains are adaptable and context-sensitive: when needed, brains are restructured, and the use of their parts is changed. Brain plasticity also means that the stable functioning of the brain as a whole is not completely dependent on perpetual stability of all brain structures. When a brain structure is damaged, other brain structures may take over its function, or the damaged structure may change so that its function is restored (De Bari & Dixon, 2022).

At birth, human brains are far from finished products; babies and young children need to interact with the surrounding world for their brain functions to develop properly. While brain plasticity is greatest in the early years of childhood, it does not cease after that. The structure as well as the functions of adult human brains reflect the life-long environment and experiences of each specific human being. Because both brain function and brain structure are experience-dependent, adult human brains can be seen as cultural products. In fact, even temporary blindfolding of sighted people initiates neural reorganization (Eagleman, 2020). Learning specific skills such as playing the piano or downhill skiing will initiate changes to a person's brain. So will the development of knowledge, for instance knowledge of mathematics or foreign languages. And so will familiarization with, and mastery of, changes in the technological and cultural environment. Such changes to people's brains are called *learning-driven plasticity* (Menary, 2014).

Brain Flexibility, Brain Research, and Everyday Life

Human brains do not only display long-term plasticity; they are also flexible and adjustable over much shorter time spans. This flexibility has an interesting, and for some, perhaps disconcerting, consequence for the interpretation of neuroscientific research. Such research usually uses simple stimuli that require simple responses from the participants. It typically screens the research participants from as much "extraneous" stimulation as possible, and the participants' movements are often restricted. However, because of the flexibility of human brains, it is difficult to say what research under such restrictive conditions can tell us about brain activity in real life, when conditions are not restricted. As Mazviita Chirimuuta, a British neuroscientist and philosopher, has noted:

> . . .the fact that use of simple artificial stimuli, like spots and bars of light, leads to simpler (i.e., more linear) neuronal responses is due to the inherent plasticity of the cortex. Neuronal responses tend to adapt themselves to the statistics of the prevailing stimulus regime and will show a more complex response profile when the stimuli themselves are more complicated, as with images encountered in the environment outside the lab. (2024, pp. 124–125)

That is, brain activity, being flexible, adjusts to the existing stimulus conditions – which, in experiments, are often simplified or even impoverished. This means that when the stimuli are simple, the neural responses will be simple. And that, in turn, means that finding a specific neuronal response pattern in an experimental study does not necessarily mean that the same response pattern will, or even can, occur in everyday life. In other words, simple stimuli and simple response requirements studied in an experimentally restricted condition will probably not provide much knowledge about how the brain functions in the complexities of real life. The ecological validity of such research may therefore be questionable, leaving it uncertain how much a researcher can reasonably generalize from findings in neuroscientific research to brain activity in everyday life (Nastase, Goldstein, & Hasson, 2021).

There are now efforts to study brains and behavior in more everyday situations (Maselli et al., 2023). However, just because of the brain's flexibility we just mentioned, researchers cannot expect that the theories, methods, conclusions, and categories that have hitherto been used in laboratory research will be appropriate for studying brain activity in more complex situations. As noted by the neuroscientists Paul Cisek and Andrea Green,

> Beyond new empirical methods and data, however, there is also a need for new theories and concepts to interpret that data. Such theories need to address the particular challenges of natural behavior, which often differ significantly from the scenarios studied in traditional laboratory settings. (2024, p. 1)

The knowledge about brain plasticity and flexibility, and of the distribution of brain functions, is of fairly recent origin. It contrasts with many earlier ideas about brain stability, and also with earlier notions of genetic determinism. Remnants of such earlier ideas can be found in accounts that neglect both the plasticity and flexibility of brains, and of people's – and their brains' – social and cultural embeddedness. An example of such neglect is the occasional popularity of pronouncements about *"the* human brain" or sometimes even *"the* female brain" and *"the* male brain" (for critique of this practice, see e.g., Joel, Hänggi, & Pool, 2016). Today, there is agreement among researchers that adult human brains are the products of experience. And experiences obviously vary between individuals, to a large extent due to variations in cultural contexts (Fuchs, 2018).

Interpreting Human Biology in Cultural Contexts

We know that cultural habits and traditions direct people's (including researchers') attention and, therefore, influence their ways of understanding that to which they attend. This is true also for how they understand biological phenomena: when people encounter a biological phenomenon, the phenomenon is already *interpreted*. In the words of Roger Smith, a British historian of the human sciences,

> If there are biological capacities in common among people, and it is an almost empty truism to accept this, it is not possible to describe these capacities independently of their expression in particular forms of cultural life. (2007, p. 35)

As an example, think about human infants and their need for a long period of care in order to survive to adulthood. This is a biological fact. However, this biological fact has been given different interpretations through history. For instance, in Western countries in the first half of the twentieth century, it was common to see infants as, by nature, unsocial and untamed. The caregiver's task was to discipline the infant into regular habits and obedience. In the same countries nowadays, infants are instead seen as, by nature, socially oriented but also fragile. The caregiver's task now is to establish the right kind of attachment between the infant and the caregiver. The biological fact of the infant's need for care remains the same. It is the interpretations that vary. Another example concerns how human reproduction has been described and understood through history, especially how descriptions of the functions of eggs and sperm have been modeled on the prevailing views of women's and men's supposedly "natural" roles in society (Martin, 1991, 2004).

Obviously, *un*interpreted biological processes occur all the time. But people, including psychologists, make sense of them through the culturally dominant images and ideas about biology of their place and time (Keller, 2010). Psychologists are therefore well advised to scrutinize their own culturally derived ideas of what is "natural" or "biological" and what is "cultural" or "learned" (Baggs, Raja, & Anderson, 2019; Heyes, 2018). Such scrutiny provides one way to become knowledgeable about the traps that cultural conventions and figures of speech may set for people's understandings. At the same time the scrutiny also helps in identifying misleading or otherwise unhelpful conventions. Conventions usually have historical pedigrees that may have tenacious holds on the members of a culture. We therefore take a look at the history of brain conventions by scrutinizing the most popular metaphors for "the brain."

Brain Metaphors: From Hearts to Electricity to Computers

Because brains are not available for direct observation, metaphors for "the brain" have played important roles throughout history. They still do, as we will see, when exploring the contemporary use of metaphors. A metaphor is, in principle, innocuous when it, for instance, offers a convenient shorthand for talking about complicated things. But metaphors have their dangers, too, as philosophers and neuroscientists have pointed out. When a particular metaphor becomes dominant in a field, there is a great risk that the images built into that metaphor will "freeze" how researchers use and understand words and concepts (Chirimuuta, 2024). When that happens, the metaphor will stand in the way of critical discussions and reevaluations (Cobb, 2021). Here we can note the similarity of this reasoning to Ludwik Fleck's discussion of the *active assumptions* that inform a thinking style.

If we go back far enough in history, we find that it was often not the brain, but the heart, that was taken to be the organ responsible for thinking and feeling. This is not surprising. After all, it is the palpitating heart that accompanies nervousness and fear, while there are no noticeable palpitations in the brain. This old idea of the heart as the emotional center is still with us in everyday expressions in many languages, such as "Her heart just wasn't in it"; "He took it to heart"; "I heartily agree"; "She lost her heart to him"; and "She broke his heart."

In the early modern era, dissections made it obvious that what the heart does is pump blood through the body. The brain seemed a more likely candidate for the functions of thinking, feeling, and body regulation. Early ideas of how the brain does this, such as those of the philosopher René Descartes, were borrowed from observations of blood circulation and envisioned the nervous system as a *hydraulic* system of liquid currents, flows, and pressures (Cobb, 2021). However, because cutting nerves did not cause any flow of liquid from the open nerve endings, the blood flow analogy was soon discredited. It was followed by various *mechanical* metaphors for what went on in the brain and the nervous system. The legacy of these metaphors remains in the use of words such as "impression," a term that suggests mechanical pressure or force of some kind when talking about the workings of the nervous system.

In the second half of the eighteenth century, *electricity* became a popular metaphor for the nervous system. This was so partly because it had, by then, become possible to conduct experiments directly on frogs' legs by sending electrical currents through the nerves, causing the legs to contract. The terms mostly used for electricity were those related to the behavior of liquids (e.g., "current" and "flow"). The popularity of the electricity metaphor, therefore, reintroduced these hydraulic terms into the thinking about brains and the nervous system.

The next metaphorical step came when the *telegraph* was invented in the first half of the nineteenth century. The telegraph became a powerful brain metaphor that remained in use for most of the century. The telegraph – like nerves – allowed almost instantaneous communication, and both could also enable action. Another parallel with the telegraph was the idea that nerves, like telegraph lines, all carried the same kind of signal, and that distinctions between messages were made by the receiver – in the case of the nervous system, by the brain.

By the end of the nineteenth century, it had become possible to study nerves and brains in more detail, and the findings of this research led some researchers to argue that the telegraph metaphor was insufficient. The nervous system, as these researchers showed, can change through experience, in contrast with the rigidity of a telegraph network. They argued that the *telephone exchange* (which was invented in the late nineteenth century) provided a more adequate metaphor for the brain. In a telephone exchange, the messages can be switched around in many directions, as they can in the brain. However, a telephone exchange actually has very limited flexibility – an obvious drawback of this metaphor. For instance, a telephone exchange has no feedback loops, while there are multiple such loops in the brain and the rest of the nervous system.

Lessons from the practicalities of installing telephone systems, and eventually electrical lighting, into buildings then led to the metaphor of a *wiring diagram* for the brain. An image of a wiring diagram of the electric system in a building was not difficult to transpose into an idea of the nervous system as also a kind of wiring that could be diagrammed in some analogous way. In the 1940s, during the earliest phase of the development of electronic computers, the idea of a strong similarity between the wiring diagrams of computers and the "wiring" in the brain took root. This is the origin of the *computer metaphor* for the brain – the idea that the brain is like a computer and, therefore, analogously to a computer, carries out computations that can model its surroundings in the present and predict the future consequences of its actions. We look a little closer at this image.

Modern Metaphors: Are Brains Like Computers?

Since the early days of computer development, the computer has been the most frequently used metaphor for the brain. The general idea of the computer metaphor is that what the brain does (in analogy with computers) is *process inputs* in order to deliver the right kind of *output*, and that the brain does so by the aid of computations. To do this, the brain is assumed to *encode* the inputs, use a chosen *algorithm* to manipulate the inputs, then store the information extracted from the manipulation and perhaps recombine it, and finally deliver the accurate output in the form of a *command* of some kind (Raja, 2022). There are a few different versions of the computer metaphor. However, the basic idea of brains as performing computations is common, together with terminology taken from computer engineering (Brette, 2022). So, *are* brains like computers? In the next paragraph, we present some facts about brains and computers.

To begin, the brain is an organ of the body and consists of living cells; the computer is a machine made of inorganic matter. While most computers have a hierarchical structure, the brain does not. In a computer, it is easy to identify and isolate the processes that carry out a particular computation; in a brain, it is not. This is so because the physical structure of a brain is much more complex than that of a computer, and because cognitive processes go on within, and are influenced by, the flow of countless other processes – within and outside of the brain. Because computers can be meaningfully described either at the level of hardware (the physical machine) or software (the program the machine is running), it is tempting to apply the same type of descriptions to brains. But such descriptions inevitably oversimplify or misconstrue the neurophysiological activity that is involved. The different functions of a computer have been designed by humans and are therefore easy to identify. Living systems such as brains have not been designed; they have evolved, and many of the tasks that they can perform are not unequivocally localizable to specific functional modules (Cisek & Hayden, 2021). Computer hardware is designed such that it does not change in a material way when it is used; in contrast, the biological cells that make up a brain change continually when the brain is active.

On the basis of these comparisons, it is perhaps not surprising that the computer metaphor, no matter how theoretically sophisticated, has led to simplified and often misleading pictures of how brains function (Cobb, 2021; Kelty-Stephen, Cisek, De Bari et al., 2022). In recent years, there has been a growing concern that the computer metaphor may be holding back theory development in both neuroscience and cognitive psychology (Brette, 2019; Chirimuuta, 2024; Fuchs, 2021; Keijzer, 2025; Miller, 2010). This worry has led to lively discussions among researchers from several disciplines about the fruitfulness (or not) of keeping the computer metaphor alive (see Matassi & Martinez, 2023). Fred Keijzer, a Dutch philosopher of neuroscience, argues against using the metaphor and points to several built-in conceptual problems. He also argues that these conceptual problems are deeply ingrained in current thought and therefore shape much of the ongoing scientific research:

> . . .the current cognitive and neurosciences rely on a conceptual dichotomy between a pregiven external environment and a representing internal mind or cognitive system. While many aspects of this dichotomy have been

challenged over the years, it still remains a default interpretation setting the dualistic problem space that drives much of the current scientific efforts in the cognitive and neurosciences. (Keijzer, 2025, p. 6)[1]

In the same vein, Paul Cisek noted: "*If brains do not fit the mechanistic hypothesis underwriting the computer metaphor, then the cognitive sciences may need to seek alternative metaphors based on the assumption that minds and brains are some other kind of natural systems*" (Cisek, 2022, lines 1317–1320). The worries about the computer metaphor can also be seen in attempts by several groups of researchers to find alternatives (Chirimuuta, 2024; Kelty-Stephen et al., 2022; Keijzer, 2025). Others worry less and argue that the solution will be new kinds of machines that can function as appropriate metaphors or analogies for the human brain (Bongard & Levin, 2021).

As we are writing this, there is much discussion but little unanimity about what the best alternative metaphor would be. Here are some suggestions that have been offered: One could get out of the dualism inherent in the computer metaphor by conceiving of cognition as fundamentally a biologically based phenomenon (Keijzer, 2025). One could think about cognition as something that goes on in a much wider set of organisms than humans and other primates, and learning from the strategies of these other organisms (Lyon et al., 2021). One could assume that the organism's environment is rich enough to enable "radical embodied computation" (Hasselman, 2022; see also Chapter 6, where we discuss extended and embodied cognition). One could think of brains not as primarily input-output devices, but instead as control systems that produce useful motor outputs (Bechtel, 2016; Cisek, 2022). One could try to develop complexity science, the interdisciplinary study of complex systems, in such a way that it can become a tool for studying brains (Favela, 2022). And so on. Note that, while these suggestions have moved on from the computer metaphor, some of them make use of computations (analogously to computers), while others do not.

Computation in the Brain?

A central feature of early computer metaphors for the brain was the idea of computation in the brain; that is, sequences of input – computation – output, and so on, akin to the sequences at the core of how a computer

---

[1] The arguments about dualism in the computer metaphor idea are parallel to those in Chapter 4, about minds.

functions. This feature proved to be such a powerful idea that, when many scientists in recent decades abandoned the early versions of the metaphor, they kept the idea that there is computation in the brain. Using Ludwik Fleck's terminology, we would say that the idea of computation was passed down from earlier thinkers as one of the *active assumptions* that inform large parts of neuroscience and cognitive science. An indication of the power of such assumptions can be seen in some terminology choices in neuroscience. The neuroscientific literature uses many concepts from engineering, especially computer engineering: neurons are described as mechanisms; these mechanisms are described as communicating via codes and using algorithms to perform computations, like computers do. This terminology could, in Fleck's terms, be seen as a *passive*, even self-evident, consequence of the active assumption of computation. And again following Fleck, one could argue that using a terminology that is based on an active assumption is likely to lead to a circle of research results that strengthen the force of that assumption. It may even be inevitable that they do. In the section *Methodological Circles* in Chapter 11, we describe this phenomenon in more detail.

Further, several critics have pointed out that when engineering terminology is used in reference to brains, it is often unclear with what meanings the engineering terms are used. Also problematic is that the meanings tend to differ between different computational approaches (Brette, in press). Among those who have challenged the computational ideas is the French neuroscientist Romain Brette. He concludes, after reviewing the debates, that "...*it is not at all obvious in what sense the brain 'computes,' if it does, and the metaphorical use of the word tends to bury the important questions*" (2022, p. 4). Brette therefore warns that the idea of computation in the brain may stand in the way of other questions that researchers ought to ask, such as questions taking into account that humans are biological creatures. Biological creatures are evolved, and evolution is not a kind of engineering; it has no predetermined goals or plans. According to Brette, this fact is often forgotten in cognitive and neuroscientific theory and research:

> Perception, cognition, agency, free will, consciousness are all biological phenomena. Even though we might try to replicate those phenomena in artifacts, the primary empirical source remains biology. Yet, strikingly, the study of cognition appears to be a branch of computer science rather than of biology... In neuroscience, the standard terminology of brain theory largely refers to a non-biological world, the world of machines made by humans – computation, implementation, algorithms, codes, optimization. (Brette, in press, p. 11)

Some neuroscientists and philosophers have warned that holding on to the idea of commonalities between brains and computers will hinder understanding of the ways in which the brain's biological activities and properties form the basis of human cognition (cf. Chirimuuta, 2024; Keijzer, 2025). Others have added that it is just as important to take into account that humans are *persons*, living socially and culturally situated lives. These arguments will feature in Chapter 6, about thinking. There we also present the debates about computational versus situated models of cognition.

What Do Their *Brains* Do When *Persons* Think, Feel, or Act?

We now examine how researchers, including psychologists, describe what goes on in a person's brain when that person thinks, feels, or acts. Researchers who study human brains for psychological purposes must bring together theories, explanations, and research methods from at least three domains of knowledge: knowledge about behavior, about psychological processes, and about the nervous system, including the brain. Combining them can be complicated because the concepts that are used in these three domains have different histories and different intellectual surroundings. A concept or explanation that works in one domain may be ill-suited or meaningless in the other domains. This is so because the concepts that are used in the three different domains are categorically dissimilar; that is, concepts in one domain do not "talk" about the same kinds of things as concepts in the other domains (Nachev & Hacker, 2014).

Disagreements about how to combine knowledge from the three domains can be seen in debates about how to understand what a person's *brain* does when *the person* thinks, decides, feels, wishes, and so on (Fuchs, 2018; Smit & Hacker, 2014). These debates often turn on whether words (usually agentic verbs) used to denote what people do can logically also be used to denote what their brains concomitantly do. While these debates may seem to be only about words and word use, they have both theoretical and practical consequences that psychologists who want to integrate knowledge about brains with their psychological knowledge should consider seriously. We give a few examples of how the combination of knowledge about brains, psychological processes, and behaviors is described in different types of media today:[2]

---

[2] We give no references to the selected publications, because our point here is to indicate the prevalence of a few ways of conceiving of brains, psychological processes, and behaviors, not to chastise or criticize specific writers.

(1)   Articles in neuroscientific journals usually describe how changes in people's brains *correlate with* changes in people's behavior: "Individuals who underwent training in creative thinking exhibited improved performance in math problem solving, as well as brain activation changes in several regions" (2023). "The main goal was to identify brain regions associated with memory consolidation" (2022). "[We wanted to] identify brain activity that corresponded to trial-by-trial changes" (2022). "Many brain regions show domain-specific correlations with the values of specific types of rewards" (2023). Many articles also suggest brain regions whose activity might be *necessary* for, or "underlie," certain cognitive processes: "fMRI has been used extensively to identify brain regions and networks that underlie a wide range of cognitive processes, including those that support cognitive control" (2023). "Structural integrity across these [brain] regions is critical for high-level math competence and efficient cognitive functions" (2023).

(2)   Other neuroscientific articles use active verbs that are otherwise only used about people to describe brain activity. These publications thereby ascribe the same kind of *agency* to brains as to persons: " . . . it is important to understand what and how the deaf brain sees" (2019). "How does your brain decide what you will do next?" (2021). "How does the brain decide what to do in novel strategic situations in the absence of direct experience?" (2022). " . . . the brain can take in only a fraction of that information at once. So how does the brain decide what to pay attention to and what to ignore?" (2020). "How does the brain decide which pieces of information should be integrated and which kept separate?" (2018). "We propose a neural generative mechanism by which the brain makes novel strategic choices" (2022). "[we study] the human brain's judgments of beauty [. . .] we assume that beauty decisions are the result of brain cognition and perception" (2023).

(3)   In popular books, it also seems quite common to use active verbs that ascribe *agency* to the brain, as in these examples: "Our brain is fantastic. It can take in enormous amounts of knowledge and think up goals, plans, and creative solutions. At the same time it can easily begin to work against us" (advertisement for a Swedish book). "Your brain . . . falls in love, and it can interpret complicated patterns, read between the lines and understand irony. But the brain also tricks you into making bad choices, and it rewards addiction" (advertisement for a Swedish book).

(4)   Some presentations of neuroscientific research on university websites also ascribe to brains the kind of independent agency that is usually reserved for persons: "Our brains like to predict as much as possible, then use our senses to course-correct when the predictions go wrong." "Her research indicates how the brain is constantly making decisions that then have to be converted into practical actions." "The brain tells us a story about the motion of objects. But that's not the only story it tells. It also tells us stories about more complicated aspects of our visual world, like color." "Your brain draws a lot of unconscious inferences, and it doesn't tell you that they are inferences."

In these collections of extracts, we find two different ideas about how to conceive of brain activity. The descriptions in paragraph (1), taken from scientific publications, use expressions such as "correlations with," "changes in brain activation," and "necessary activity." These descriptions do not use verbs that ascribe agency to brains. The descriptions in the other three paragraphs do. They all seem to be based on the assumption that, when someone observes *a person* thinking, deciding, feeling, and so on, it is, in fact, that person's *brain*, or a part of the brain, that thinks, decides, feels, wishes, and so on. This can be concluded from the use of agentic verbs that are mostly used about people to designate brain activity (verbs and verbal phrases like decide, see, construct goals, perceive, make plans and solutions, fall in love, understand irony, judge beauty).

Observations Are Not Scientific Facts!

Before we go on to the criticisms of agentic conceptualizations of what brains do, we must take a moment to consider, in a general way, what the findings of an empirical research study *can* show. To begin: A finding in a study (for instance, brain activity in a particular region) is *not a scientific fact*. A research finding is a set of observations acquired under certain (e.g., experimental and theoretical) conditions. Findings *become* scientific facts only by being interpreted by the researcher through the lens of the researcher's chosen theory (and therefore implicitly in the researcher's thinking style, as per Ludwik Fleck's arguments in Chapter 2). As an illustration, we can examine one of the quotes in the second paragraph (2), where the researcher writes that "the brain makes novel strategic choices." This researcher most likely has collected a number of *observations* of activity in certain brain regions when the *persons* who were being studied were making novel choices. The researcher has then, on the basis of a theory, interpreted the brain activity as proof that *the brain* was making choices. It is *this interpretation* that is claimed to be a scientific fact.

There is nothing unusual or strange about this procedure. It is what researchers do: A scientific fact is the outcome of how a researcher, within a particular thinking style and a particular theoretical frame, interprets a collection of observations. We would expect that researchers who work within different thinking styles and theoretical frames would draw different conclusions about what the *scientific facts* are if presented with the same empirical *observations*.

Critique of the "Agentic" Brain Idea

Thomas Fuchs, a German philosopher and psychiatrist, is among those who object to the conceptualizations of what brains do that appear in paragraphs (2), (3), and (4). Fuchs, therefore, has also objected to the accompanying "agentic" view of brains. In his words, *"The brain has neither mental states nor consciousness, because the brain does not live – it is only the organ of a living being, or a living person"* (2021, p. 121, emphasis in the original). He warns about the possible losses in analytical and theoretical power – that is, the losses of knowledge – that would ensue if conscious activities were no longer seen as the functions of a whole organism, but as activities performed by that organism's brain. In agreement with Fuchs, Max Bennett and Peter Hacker also criticize the agentic brain-centered view:

> We can observe whether a human being, a person, sees something or other – we look at his behaviour and ask him questions. . . . But what would it be to observe whether a brain sees something – as opposed to observing the brain of a human being when he sees something? (Bennett & Hacker, 2022, pp. 81–82)

Our comments on the four groups of extracts from research articles and popular presentations, together with the quotes in this subsection, point to some of the central debates about brains and psychology (see also Fuchs, 2018, 2021). Several themes in these debates will feature in the ensuing sections of this chapter. We first take up the question of reductionism.[3]

---

[3] One related debate in these fields that there is not enough space to take up here concerns what kinds of conclusions, if any, one is entitled to draw about the *content* of a person's thinking or feeling from measures produced, for instance, by neuroimaging techniques. See, e.g., Poldrack et al. (2017).

Reductive Explanations and the Brain

The most common type of reductive explanation is one that explains a phenomenon in terms of the properties of its constituents.[4] Such explanations are common in the natural sciences (Think about explanations of the properties of atoms based on the properties of elementary particles.) In disciplines such as psychology and cognitive neuroscience there is debate about such explanations. See, for instance, Abi-Rached and Rose (2013) for a thorough discussion of reductionism in neuroscience, which also has applications for psychology. Some researchers and philosophers argue that it is at least potentially possible to fully explain all human behavior and psychological attributes in terms of mechanisms such as brain activity and neural processes; that is, to "reduce" behavior to brain activity. Others argue that this will never be possible, because the logical connections between the domain of psychological attributes and the domain of neural processes are unknown, and perhaps unknowable (Robinson, 1995, 2010; Sharp & Miller, 2019). To exemplify, we quote one expression of the skeptical standpoint:

> ...the logical connections (of implication, exclusion, compatibility) between the different domains are exceedingly difficult to get into clear view. The relationships are not at all like those between, say, ionic and molecular descriptions of chemical phenomena. The different domains are not reducible one to another, and what explanations are appropriate to one domain may be inappropriate to another. How the description of phenomena in one domain bears on the description of phenomena in another is highly problematic. (Nachev & Hacker, 2014, p. 194)

In what follows, we present some recurring discussions focusing on the *conceptual* and *logical* problems of neuro-reductive explanations. Note that conceptual and logical problems such as these cannot be resolved by empirical research. They must be analyzed and resolved conceptually, and this must be done before attempting to study the topics involved empirically. (In Chapter 13, we discuss conceptual issues in psychology further and describe conceptual analysis.)

To begin, for a neurologically reductive explanation of a psychological phenomenon to be possible, the conceptual gap between the psychological and neurological levels needs to be closed. This is the same as specifying the logical connections between these levels that we mentioned just before the

---

[4] In Chapter 12, about explanations in psychology, we describe and discuss reductive explanations in psychology more generally.

quote. This would be possible if one could describe and define the psychological phenomenon of interest by using neurological terminology. Now, words and expressions such as angry, loving, caring, hostile, or undergoing a life-changing experience, for example, are words used on the conceptual level of *psychology*. On the *neurological* level, there are words such as neuron, synapse, brain structures, evoked potential, voxels, cortical networks (and so on, depending on which level of brain activity is in focus). These words can be used to describe *neurological correlates* of the psychological phenomena. But they cannot be used to describe these phenomena *as psychological* phenomena. That is, *psychological* meaning cannot be expressed with *neurological* words (Nachev & Hacker, 2014).

Explanations in terms of, for instance, reasons and wishes are *categorially* different from explanations in terms of brain mechanisms: the two types of explanations deal with different aspects of the world (Bennett & Hacker, 2022; Heyes, 2018; Robinson, 2016). The words on the psychological level are usually easy to relate directly to a person, a cultural setting, and a social context: persons undergo such experiences, and they always undergo them in specific cultural and social contexts. Neurological terms, on the other hand, describe mechanisms that do not refer to the person or the person's cultural and social context. The fact that many – or perhaps most – psychological phenomena involve a person's interactions with other people adds yet another layer of difficulties, because such interactive psychological phenomena cannot be meaningfully described in neurological terms.

We also need to consider the fact that the subject who is undergoing an experience or having a belief is a human being, whereas the "subject" that is in a brain state or is undergoing a brain process is that human being's brain. And, the critics point out, human beings are not identical with their brains – human beings *have* brains (Fuchs, 2018).

These discussions leave us with the question of how many psychological phenomena can be explained by using only terms that exclude person, culture, and social context. Maybe not that many. There may instead be areas of psychological experience where knowledge about brain mechanisms, though important for other purposes, does not add anything of *psychological* value (Kagan, 1998; Slife & Williams, 1995).

Another type of conceptual critique of reductive explanations is based on the logical *consequences* of a person's psychological attributes versus the logical consequences of that person's brain activity. For example, if a person believes something, that *person's* belief has the logical consequence of being right or wrong. If one took the person's belief to be identical with a brain state, then that brain state would have to have the same logical consequence as the person's belief: The consequence of being right or wrong. But while brain states or processes certainly have consequences, they cannot have *that kind* of logical consequence. It makes no sense to ascribe rightness or wrongness to a particular brain state or process (Sharp & Miller, 2019).

To summarize: Obviously, brains are involved in all psychological phenomena, but this need not mean that all *psychological* phenomena are ultimately best explained in the language of neurophysiology, thereby being reduced to neurophysiology. The many types of objections to reductive psychological explanations suggest that it would not be possible to derive laws for phenomena on a psychological level from laws derived at the neural level. (There are more objections than the ones we have mentioned; see Kostic & Halffman, 2023.)

A Thinking Style with Categorial Problems: *Encephalocentrism*

In this section and the next, we sketch and discuss two thinking styles that inform different ways of conceiving of brain activity. Think back to the extracts in the section "What do their *brains* do when *persons* think, feel, or act?" The extracts drawn from popular presentations (nos. 3 and 4) asserted that brains like to predict, brains fall in love, brains tell us stories, brains don't tell us that they make inferences, and brains can work against us. And in the second paragraph (no. 2) with extracts from scientific articles we read that brains see, brains decide, brains behave, brains think, and so on. These are assertions that it is brains – a part of human beings – that think, see, decide, behave, and so on.[5] Critics see such assertions as indications of encephalocentrism, or, in Ludwik Fleck's terminology, of an encephalo-centrist thinking style (from *enképhalos*, the Greek word for brain). Encephalocentrism is based on the (misguided, according to the critics) assumption that cognition is "*primarily or even exclusively a computational process occurring inside the brain*" (Glock, 2020, p. 1). In the encephalo-centric view, therefore, "*the real subjects of the fundamental cognitive states and processes are parts of individual organisms, and the ultimate location of cognition is within our skulls*" (Glock, 2020, p. 2; emphasis in the original).[6]

---

[5] An assumption that is related to this thinking style and often taken as integral to it is the idea of mental, or neural, representations in the brain. We discuss the questions and debates about such representations in Chapter 6, about thinking.

[6] In Chapter 6, about thinking, we take up the parallel debates in cognitive psychology about cognitive internalism versus contextualism.

To evaluate this critique, we have to ask if it makes sense to ascribe activities such as thinking and deciding, and so on, to brains, rather than ascribing them only to whole human beings. The expression "make sense" indicates that we are talking about *conceptual* questions, that is, questions that call for analysis of potential logical confusions in concept use.[7] Philosophers and neuroscientists such as Thomas Fuchs (2021), Hans-Johann Glock (2006, 2020), and Max Bennett and Peter Hacker (2022) argue that the encephalocentrist assertions in the extracts (nos. 2, 3, and 4) commit a particular type of conceptual error: *a category mistake*. Others disagree (cf. Searle, 2007).

A category mistake is the mistake of ascribing attributes to things in one category that can logically only be ascribed to things in another category. Ascribing an attribute to a thing that could not be a candidate for having that particular attribute is illogical, because it *makes no sense* to make that ascription. Therefore, such an ascription *has no meaning* (Glock, 2020). To elucidate the argument about category mistakes, we look at two sentences:

First, take the sentence, "*This horse is pink.*" This sentence is factually wrong, because there are no pink horses; therefore this horse is not pink. The person who says this must have misperceived the horse's color. But though it is *factually* wrong to ascribe the color pink to a particular horse, to do so is not logically wrong, because horses belong to a category whose members have color. Therefore it is not a *category mistake* to ascribe a color to a horse (though it is factually wrong, perhaps caused by misperception, to ascribe the color pink to it). This is so because it makes sense to ascribe colors to horses.

Now take the sentence, "*This argument is pink.*" This sentence is problematic in a very different way. To begin with, odd though this may sound, the sentence is not wrong. For this sentence to be wrong (or right, for that matter), there must be a way to decide if an argument is pink or not. And obviously, there is no such way. Arguments (in contrast to horses) do not belong to a category whose members have color. It, therefore, makes no sense to ascribe colors to an argument. Therefore, the sentence "this argument is pink" makes no sense. It commits the *category mistake* of trying to ascribe color to something (an argument) that belongs to a category to whose members it is not logical to ascribe color.

The critics of encephalocentrism argue that, just as it would be a category mistake to ascribe color to arguments, so too it is a category mistake to ascribe thinking, deciding, and so on, to brains:

---

[7] For more about concepts and concept use in psychology, see Chapter 13, *Being a Discerning Reader of Psychology*.

> Ascribing cognition to the brain is not just unwarranted or false, it is bereft of sense. It applies mental predicates or concepts to things that are not even potential candidates for satisfying these concepts. (Glock, 2020, p. 5)

According to the critics we have referred to in this section, brains do not belong to a category of things to which it makes sense to ascribe mental, that is, psychological, predicates. Consequently, the arguments and reasonings of the encephalocentrist thinking style commit a category mistake and are therefore logically invalid. In the next section, we describe how the critics of encephalocentrism understand what brains do.

Keeping the Categories Straight: The *Person in Context* Thinking Style

The critics we referred to above argue that activities such as thinking, deciding, and so on can only be ascribed to members of the category "human beings," and not to some part of human beings. From this perspective, a thinking style based on assumptions about the *person in context* makes sense, whereas the encephalocentrist style we sketched earlier does not. To consider whether this claim about the two styles makes sense, we have to begin by looking at what it means for members of the category "human beings" to do things like thinking and deciding, and so on.

Because people are human beings, they are usually fairly certain about what it means for a human being to behave, to think, to see, and so on (and often what it means for a human being to fall in love, to tell stories, to make inferences, or to work against other human beings – to take up a few of the earlier statements about brain agency). People can often directly judge whether another human being is doing one of these things. And if they cannot be sure, they can ask and be told by that other – truthfully or not, of course. Indeed, people often trust the other's account and usually have good reason to do so. Vision, behavior, decision-making, emotions, thinking and thoughts, and so on are concepts that people use in everyday language to refer to and observe activities by human beings (and in some cases also by other animals). Throughout evolutionary history, people have honed the use of these concepts and words into language tools that enable them to describe what persons (including themselves) are doing, thinking, and experiencing.

It does seem to be different with members of the category "brains." We cannot see if brains are behaving, seeing, thinking, or falling in love – hidden inside people's skulls as they are. Also, and in contrast to human beings, brains could not tell us if they were doing these things: brains cannot speak or write. So there is no possibility for direct evidence of thinking, deciding, and so on to be had from brains, such as there is from human beings. Instead, when researchers or popular psychology writers assert that brains decide, see, behave, fall in love, and so on, they tend to refer to laboratory measurements of some kind, such as fMRI data or evoked potentials. Arguing from the encephalocentrist thinking style, they take these measurements as evidence that it is the brain that performs behaviors, makes decisions, thinks, and so on. And many would accept that conclusion.

But many others do not accept these measurements as such evidence. Those who begin from the *persons in context* thinking style instead argue that what is measured by the laboratory instruments are activities in certain brain structures that correlate with, and are often necessary for, certain of the human being's behaviors, decisions, and so on (Lilienfield et al., 2017). But, these thinkers argue, such correlating brain activities are not signs that the brain is deciding, thinking, and so on; rather, they are signs that *the human being* whose brain it is, is deciding, thinking, and so on. These thinkers also point out that those who claim that brains think, and so on, have not been able to provide any empirical observations that show brains actually thinking, deciding, and so on. Some critics go further and argue that it is unknown what *would* show that brains do these things (Bennett & Hacker, 2022; Fuchs, 2018, 2021; Glock, 2020; Smit, 2021).

This last point forces us to consider what it *could mean* – if it could mean anything at all – to say that a brain thinks, decides, behaves, and so on. As we noted previously, these are words and concepts that humans have developed over millennia as descriptions of the activities that members of the category "human beings" engage in. The brain, of course, is not a member of the category "human beings." So perhaps one should be wary of applying these human-level concepts to parts of humans, such as brains.

The Problems of Parts and Wholes

There is something special about the differences between the two categories: brains and human beings. Brains and human beings do not just belong to *different* categories, but brains belong to the category *parts* of the human being. And this part-whole relationship creates some logical problems. To illustrate, let us consider two examples of parts versus wholes: First, the liver belongs to a different category than the human being does. Nobody would commit the category mistake of ascribing to the liver the attributes of thinking, deciding, and so on that we ascribe to the human being. Livers do not have the organs one needs to be able to think, decide, and so on. But there is more, because the liver is not just part of a different category than the human being, it is also a member of the category *parts* of the human being. This means that to ascribe thinking, deciding, and so on to livers would commit the further mistake of ascribing to a part (the liver) attributes that can only be ascribed to the whole (the human being). Such mistaken ascriptions of abilities to parts are examples of what has been called *the mereological fallacy*, mereology being the logic of wholes and their parts (Bennett & Hacker, 2022).

As a second example of parts versus wholes, we can think of airplanes and their engines. To begin, engines and airplanes belong to different categories: airplanes belong to a category of things that can fly; engines do not. Obviously, the actions of the engine are necessary for the flying, but the engine's action is not the flying. It is the whole airplane that flies. Further, engines belong to the category *parts* of airplanes. Therefore, to say that the engine is doing the flying is to commit a category mistake of the mereological kind; that is, it mistakenly ascribes to a part (the engine) an activity that can only be ascribed to the whole (the airplane).

Of course, far from all ascriptions of the same predicates to wholes and to their parts are mereological category mistakes. A classic example is suntan: a human being's arm can be suntanned, and so can the whole human being (Hacker, 2007). And so it is with pain: a human being's arm can hurt, and so can the whole human being (Glock, 2020). Those examples involve no contradictions and no logical category mistakes.

Against this background of non-brain examples of category mistakes to do with parts and wholes, we now turn to parallel arguments about brains and human beings. Those who do not accept that measurements of brain activity are signs that the brain (a part of the human) is thinking, deciding, and so on argue that such an assertion makes no sense; that it is nonsensical. This is how they argue for their position: For it to make sense to ascribe a *psychological* predicate (such as a psychological activity or state) to an object (such as the brain) that is a part of the human being, the object must be shown to be able to possess or evince that psychological predicate (such as to make decisions or be happy) that the whole human can evince. But the only criteria that exist for judging whether an object possesses or evinces such a psychological activity or state are human, or human-like, behaviors. It is therefore only meaningful to ascribe a psychological predicate to an object if that object can behave in human(-like) ways. And, because the brain (or its parts) cannot behave in human(-like) ways, it does not make sense to ascribe a psychological predicate to the brain or any of its parts (Bennett & Hacker, 2022; Glock, 2020).[8]

Philosophers such as Bennett, Hacker, and Glock emphasize that psychological predicates (such as deciding, thinking, feeling, and so on) apply only to human beings, not to brains or parts of brains. It is human beings who can behave in human ways, and therefore it is only of human beings that we can establish whether they evince some particular psychological predicate. To ascribe psychological predicates to brains is, therefore, to commit a category mistake, specifically of the mereological (part-whole) kind. To take an example, it makes perfect sense to say about human beings that they are blind or sighted. It makes sense because there are ways to ascertain whether a human being is blind or not. By the same logic, it does not make sense to say about a brain that it is blind or that it is sighted: there are no facts to be had that could ascertain whether a brain is blind or sighted. This means that only of a subject that *could* possibly see does it make sense to ask whether they are blind or sighted. Therefore, the question of sight or blindness is not applicable or relevant to brains (Glock, 2020).

If the critical philosophers, neuroscientists, and psychologists that we have referred to here are right, and it makes no sense to ascribe psychological properties to brains, why do so many people do this? One suggestion for an answer comes from the recent history of science: The neuroscientists of the first half of the twentieth century (such as Sherrington, Eccles, and Penfield) were wedded to a two-substance dualism (think back to the sections about dualism in Chapter 4). These researchers ascribed psychological predicates primarily to what they saw as the immaterial mind (one of the substances involved in the dualism) and only secondarily to the material human being and the brain (the other substance).

Practically all neuroscientists of more recent generations rejected this two-substance dualism. In its stead, most accepted some version of materialist monism. When they made this shift, they took the psychological predicates that their predecessors had ascribed to the immaterial mind

---

[8] We have borrowed, and paraphrased, this argumentation from Glock (2020, p. 5). In his original version, the logical premises and conclusions are set out in classical philosophical terminology. Further, on pages 5–7 in his article, Glock discusses and defends the premises he used in his argumentation. We found this defense convincing enough to use Glock's argument as the base for the rest of the argumentation in this section. Interested readers may want to double-check this in his article.

and ascribed them to the brain instead (see Bennett & Hacker, 2022, Part I, for details of this historical background). In these neuroscientists' view, then, the brain "became" the mind (in line with the third thinking style in Chapter 4). This seemed like the logical and straightforward move after having rejected two-substance dualism. From then on, many of the younger generation of neuroscientists conceived of the *human being's* psychological capacities as being the *brain's* psychological capacities. They were thereby committing a category mistake of the mereological kind that we described earlier.

The reactions of those who have been accused of mistakenly ascribing psychological attributes to brains have been varied. Many have refrained from engaging with the critique at all, perhaps taking the critical points to be no more than philosophical nitpicking and, therefore, irrelevant to empirical research and theorizing. Others argued that when they use psychological words to describe brain activity, they use these words meta-phorically and with only a weaker, "sort-of," meaning, not with the standard, "real" meaning of the words (Searle, 2007; and see Glock, 2020, for a critique of this argument). On this argument, a scientist who writes, for instance, that the brain decides is actually using that word with a special, metaphorical, and weaker meaning (as if it had inverted commas around it). This metaphorical meaning is taken to be different from the meaning of the same word when it is used about whole human beings. The critics retorted that it is quite unclear, and in fact is never spelled out, what exactly this brain-specific, weaker, and metaphorical meaning of psycho-logical words is supposed to be. The critics have further pointed out that even when scientists use psychological words about brains with the weaker "sort-of" meanings in the empirical parts of their studies, later, when they draw inferences from those studies, they typically use the same words with their standard meanings (Hacker, 2016). And this, the critics claim, means that they end up committing the mereological category mistake.

Other dimensions of the critique of committing the mereological cat-egory mistake have gone into which words can logically be applied to the body a person *is*, versus the body a person *has*, including the brain (see Smit & Hacker, 2014, for detailed discussions). We therefore take a look at the words in use for talking about brains and persons.

Words, Brains, and Persons

From the discussions in the previous sections, we would be prepared to conclude that those who are critical of ascribing whole-person psychological predicates to brains have a point. After all, as we noted earlier, psychological concepts and words are language tools with a long history of enabling human beings to describe, explain, and understand what human beings are doing, feeling, thinking, and so on. The meanings of these words are determined by their long-standing and ordinary, con-textualized, use by humans about humans. Further, a number of professional psychological terms have been invented in the recent century specifically to describe and explain what human beings are doing, feeling, thinking, and so on. These words all explicitly refer to the whole human being, and usually work well when they are used to do so. Thus, there is a correct usage of these words when they are used to refer to human beings; that is, there are established *rules* for their use and for the explanations of their meanings.

There seems to be little reason to expect that such whole-human-being psychological words would automatically also be the logically correct words to use for describing and explaining what is happening in some *part* of a human being. To quote Svend Brinkmann, a Danish psychologist, the way language works, "*...mental concepts can be applied only to living creatures with a certain range of behaviours – and the brain is not a creature in the required sense*" (2018, p. 38; see also Fuchs, 2018). As a parallel, we can think back to the airplane: when we describe what an airplane does, we use one kind of vocabulary (it flies, at a certain altitude and a certain speed). But to describe what some part of the airplane, such as the engine, is doing, there is no point in using the vocabulary of flying. That would make no sense. Instead, one will have to use words that describe what engines do, such as consuming fuel and compressing air.

From Words and Brains to Psychological Practices

At this point we must step back and ask what, if anything, these discussions are in aid of. Is the argument about category mistakes and parts and wholes just a case of hair-splitting among philosophers? Or is it something that psychologists should take seriously? That is, are there any drawbacks or risks associated with committing the category mistakes we have pointed out? Might there be some substantial negative consequences if psychologists were to attribute characteristics to brains that should only be applied to human beings? For instance, could such attributions lead practicing psychologists, such as clinicians, to pay more attention to a person's brain activity than to the person's experiences and living conditions? The risk of such a narrowing of focus and interest would certainly worry a cultural psychologist. We think it ought to worry all psychologists. To quote Hans-Johann Glock,

> Mental and biological phenomena reveal themselves only when we go beyond the brain and consider not just the whole organism, but the organism in the context of its environment, in the context of its form of life. (2006, p. 159)

Is there a risk that encephalocentrism, in the form of a narrow brain or "neuro" focus, will take over in the psychological disciplines, thereby reducing or even eradicating attention to the whole person, or, as we prefer to say, the person in context? Thomas Fuchs (2018, 2021) worries that there is such a risk. He worries that a change toward what he calls a narrow encephalocentrism may be underway in many parts of the human sciences. He is critical of the tendency today that, in his words, "*[s]ubjective experience and indeed human consciousness itself must now be naturalized and reduced to physical processes*" (2018, p. xvii). According to Fuchs, in many professional settings where psychologists are active it is no longer enough to provide *psychological* knowledge about a person. He claims that for psychological knowledge about a person to be taken seriously today, it often has to be expressed as, or complemented with, "neuro-knowledge" about the person.

The naturalizing and reductionist tendencies that Fuchs worries about are based on the philosophical position that is usually called materialist monism or physicalism. This is the view that the psychological is nothing over and above the neurological. This position is heavily debated today and is not generally accepted as a valid ground for knowledge about humans and human life (Keijzer, 2025; Tanney, 2022).

Fuchs especially warns, as an answer to our questions above, that a shift in a naturalizing physicalist and reductionist direction in the discipline of psychology brings with it a risk that psychologists – researchers and practitioners alike – will lose interest in human beings as persons in context. Fuchs also worries that psychologists in the process will also lose the *ability* to approach a human being as a whole person. A similar worry has been expressed by Andrew Scull, a US historian of psychiatry, after describing modern American psychiatry's move toward an increasingly "biologizing" brain focus squarely based in the encephalocentric thinking style that we sketched earlier. Scull warns that "*[t]o think of the brain as an asocial or presocial organ is …profoundly mistaken. So, too, is the crude parallel notion that mental illness – the breakdown of our cognitive and emotional life – is just brain disease*" (2022, p. 383).

We take all this to indicate that encephalocentrism and its problems and consequences are important for psychologists to discuss and investigate further. See especially Fuchs (2018, 2021) and Rose, Birk, & Manning (2021). In Chapter 8, about psychological suffering, we also discuss some of these issues.

Studying Human Brains

Upon reading this chapter's criticism of the encephalocentric thinking style, some readers might suspect that we who have written this book are against brain research. This would be a misreading: we are not. Of course researchers should study brains! Researchers who adopt something like the person-in-context thinking style study brains *as* brains, that is, as parts of human beings, which is what brains are. Such researchers thereby refrain from attributing characteristics to brains that can properly be ascribed only to human beings. These researchers, for instance, study particular brain activities that might be *necessary* for certain psychological predicates or that might *accompany* such predicates. And these researchers do this without aiming to eliminate "the psychological" as a meaningful explanatory level. Such research, in combination with the insight that each individual human brain is a product of each individual person's experiences and cultural surroundings, makes for research that is compatible with the persons-in-context approach that we favor in this book (Bennett & Hacker, 2022; Fuchs, 2021).

As in all research on humans, it behooves neuroscientists to take into account that the humans whose brains they study in their experiments are *persons*, with all that means of social and cultural situatedness. If two persons are differently culturally situated, then their brains will certainly also be differently culturally situated – for, as we noted at the beginning of this chapter, there is no such thing as *the universal* human brain. All brains are different, and a major proportion of what differs between them is due to each person's experiences throughout life.

Therefore, the differences between the persons who take part in a neuroscientific study (or, in fact, in any psychological study) will make them, including their brains, differentially affected by the laboratory setting.

Persons are likely to have different attitudes to being tested in the experiment, and they will be affected by those differences. Different persons are likely to understand the instructions that are given in different ways and, therefore, be differentially affected by them. Persons are likely to have different ideas about the aims of the experiment, and these differences are likely to affect the results. Different persons are likely to feel different levels of trust in the experimenter, and that will certainly affect the results (Frisch, 2022). All these differences, combined with the fact that experimental tasks often have very low ecological validity, will inevitably make it risky to draw far-reaching conclusions about the participants' real life from brain data gathered in much experimental brain research. Stefan Frisch, a German neuropsychologist, therefore suggests that instead of focusing heavily and mostly on brains, researchers ought systematically to "*...see mental states not as connected to brain states, but to brain-organism-environment-states. One and the same brain area activation would thus be related to different mental states, depending on the modulating context of the rest of the brain, the rest of the organism and the environment to which the organism is related*" (2022, p. 917, note 3).

We conclude with a thoughtful reflection by Roger Smith:

> Whatever the empirical advances in neuroscience actually are, it is still possible to argue that the understanding we seek about human subjects fundamentally, and irreducibly, concerns meaning, values, social rules, and the expressive world made possible by language. As a matter of principle, no material, causal theory can replace the search for knowledge of meanings, values, rules, and language without a total change in our forms of life and in the significance that life has for us. It is, perhaps, possible to imagine a form of life in which nothing has meaning, there are no rules or conscious judgments of significance and there is no language. But it is not the present human world. (2007, p. 110. Copyright © 2007 Roger Smith)

CHAPTER 6

Thinking Persons

It is not in any way controversial today to say that thinking takes place in social and cultural settings and is influenced by these settings. What is controversial, though, is whether this observation tells us anything about the actual activity of thinking itself. That is, is the *activity* of thinking, even when it is influenced by objects in the surroundings, something that takes place exclusively inside the thinking person's brain? Or do thinking activities sometimes involve, or even integrate, objects and activities in the thinker's surroundings? These are some of the questions we discuss in this chapter.

The chapter begins with a brief review of how thinking has been conceptualized by philosophers and others through history. We follow this with two sections on modern conceptualizations of thinking in cognitive psychology. First, we describe computational approaches, and then what are called the 4E-approaches (extended, embodied, embedded, enactive cognition, and cognitive integration). We then compare the assumptions and thinking styles on which the various approaches are based. We end the chapter with a discussion of whether and how the different approaches are compatible with a view of persons as embedded in sociocultural contexts.

A Very Brief History of Thinking Persons

Long before there was an academic discipline of psychology, philosophers and other thinkers speculated about thinking and sometimes also investigated thinking. We can recall the different views of ancient philosophers such as the Sophists, Socrates, Plato, and Aristotle, as well as later philosophers such as René Descartes, John Locke, David Hume, and Immanuel Kant. Do thoughts emanate from somewhere, like "the world of ideas," which infuses them into a person's soul, as Socrates and Plato argued? Or does a person create thoughts in the daily, often competitive, interaction with compatriots or adversaries, as a Sophist would have it? Or should thinking, as in Aristotle's view, be seen as the activities and abilities of the whole person, including the body, rather than only of the soul or the mind? Or, as Descartes argued, is thinking an activity exclusive to the person's soul or mind – an activity that very specifically does not involve the person's body?

In more recent times, with the emergence of different philosophies of mind and the field of cognitive psychology, several kinds of offspring of these early philosophical ideas have emerged. Inspired by the first developments in computer science and in the tradition of Descartes's ideas about thinking as exclusively processes in the mind, there was the "classical" computationalist cognitive science view of thinking as information processing in the form of mental or, more recently, neural computations (see Chapter 5 about the computer metaphor for the brain). More recently, other kinds of theories about thinking have been developed, partly inspired by the Aristotelian view of thinking as involving not just the mind but also the person's body and surroundings.

Terminology

In this chapter, we have chosen the verb "to think" as our general point of departure, because its many everyday uses cover most of what is of interest to us here. To think can be to reason from premises to a conclusion. It can be to reflect, that is, to deliberate about something. It can be to muse, as in daydreaming. It can be to imagine, as in to think something to be possible. It can be to remember, as in to think about the past. It can be the act of referring to somebody or something. To think can also be to take a stand, such as when inferring or concluding something. It can be believing or assuming that something is true. It can be attending to the task at hand. It can be engaging intelligently and cleverly in a task or in speaking. It can be coming up with the best counterargument against an opponent's argument in an ongoing discussion. It can also be working out a way to get out of an uncomfortable social position that arose because of a *faux pas* that one had just committed. And much more.

There are many verbs that are closely related to the activity of thinking, such as "to know," "to understand," "to believe," "to imagine," "to reason," "to reflect on," "to ponder," and so on. Often, the noun "cognition" is taken as the umbrella term that subsumes all these words. In this way, cognition has become a concept with a heterogeneous set of referents (Susswein & Racine, 2008). And indeed, in reading the research literature, one finds that the uses and meanings of the term cognition have varied substantially across time and vary across writers and theoretical traditions today.

The noun "cognition" is derived from the Latin verb *cogitare*, which means "to think." It should follow, then, that the noun "cognition" would be used to denote the activity of thinking. But, as we hinted just before, it turns out not to be quite so straightforward. The research community is not in agreement about what expressions such as "cognition" or "a cognitive process" should be taken to mean. Is cognition a manipulation of symbols with specific syntactic properties, as classical cognitive psychologists and computational theorists would have it? Or is it the spread of activation across a network of brain cells, as a connectionist might argue? Or should it be reserved for the psychological activity of thinking? Or is it something else entirely? We recommend readers that consider the many, sometimes contradictory, uses of the term "cognition" in psychology and other disciplines. These uses are by now so varied and, some critics claim, so inconsistent that perhaps it would be best to abandon the term altogether (cf. Costall, 2023). We do not take a stand on this issue, but we find it easy to sympathize with those who think this inconsistency is a problem.

Leaving the details of terminology aside, we agree with the approach to terms for thinking that the Australian philosopher of cognitive science Richard Menary has taken. For Menary, "*...it is quite natural to be pluralistic about cognitive processes and vehicles; as such, there is no single genuine 'cognitive kind'*" (2010b, p. 230). This stance makes sense in light of all the different activities that the expression "to think" can refer to. We also agree with Menary's further assertion that people (including researchers) have a fairly good sense of what a cognitive *task* is. Cognitive tasks are, for instance, to perceive things in the world, to remember them, and to use memories to solve problems and draw conclusions. On this basis, we can think of cognitive *processes* as processes that play a central role in enabling a person to complete a cognitive task (Rowlands, 2003).

In this chapter, we describe two general approaches to thinking. The first approach has its home in modern cognitive psychology. The second approach is connected primarily to a broad group of theories sometimes called "distributed cognition" or "situated cognition." The two approaches are based on different views of where and how people's thinking takes place. A recent overview article summarized the disagreements between them as "*the dispute between those who think of the mind as a computational and representing system on the one side and those who think of the mind as interactive and dynamical on the other*" (Casper & Artese, 2022, p. 3). As can be gleaned from this characterization, the disagreements are based on different thinking styles about the mind (see Chapter 4). And it may even be that the disagreements are, at bottom, due to different basic assumptions about what kind of activity "thinking" (or cognition) actually is. For instance, should thinking be *defined as* something that could only take place inside a person's mind or brain (depending on the exact theory)? Or should thinking be *defined as* something that may, and often does, include tools and other items outside the person's mind (or brain) in the actual process of thinking?

Does Thinking Take Place in a Computational and Representing System?

Cognitive psychology is usually described as the scientific study of how people and animals process information, or of how the mind represents and uses information about the outside world (Gilhooly et al., 2022). Cognitive psychology is a fairly young branch of the discipline of psychology. To a large extent, it is the product of the "cognitive revolution" of the late 1950s and early 1960s. The early steps of this revolution were inspired by contemporary (1940s–1950s) ideas of how the nervous system works, some of which we described in Chapter 5 (and see De Bari & Dixon, 2022). Toward the end of the 1950s, the early successes of computers, and of the concepts and terms used in computer science, inspired the development of modern cognitive psychology (Glenberg, Witt, & Metcalfe, 2013; Wilson, 2004). As a consequence, several central ideas in cognitive psychology came to build on a view of the mind as fundamentally a computational entity, and cognition as computational processes inside that entity (Johnson & Erneling, 1997; Núñez et al., 2019). The expressions "information processing approach," "computationalism," or "cognitivism" are often used more or less synonymously for this view (Marraffa & Paternoster, 2012). In recent years, computational approaches have become increasingly sophisticated and are sometimes combined with connectionist ideas (Eysenck & Brysbaert, 2018; Spivey, 2023).

In the computational approaches, cognition is seen as a form of computation. This means that cognition consists of using rules to manipulate formal symbols. When such computation is implemented in brains, the symbols are represented by neuronal states, and these states can be changed by brain processes according to computational rules or algorithms[1] (Brette,

---

[1] An algorithm is a sequence of instructions that has to be followed in exact detail in order to solve a specific problem, typically in mathematics or computer science. An everyday example would be the rule for performing long division on paper.

in press). The results of the internal computational processes in the brain are usually called *mental representations*. Some of the early inspiration for the idea that there are *representations* in the mind came from the ways that computer scientists conceptualized and described the steps that were necessary for computer processing, and especially the end results of those steps (Tanney, 2013). Contemporary representational approaches to cognition conceive of mental representations as the information-bearing structures of the cognitive system. These structures are defined, for instance, as *"inner representations such as an image or a verbal concept of some external reality"* (Gilhooly et al., 2022, p. 4). A cognitive process, then, is the transformation of mental representations, and a cognitive state is the storage of such representations (Dołęga, Roelofs, & Schlicht, 2018; Pagel, 2019; Zahnoun, 2018). In this view, *"the mind is in the business of manufacturing representations of the world, building the world inside the brain and . . . transformations of these representations comprise cognition"* (De Bari & Dixon, 2022, lines 1375–1377). The study of how such representations are formed, stored, and used *"is the essential business of cognitive psychology"* (Gilhooly et al., 2022, p. 4).

However, there is disagreement among theorists about what mental representations actually *are*, and even whether anything like representations really exists. Many cognitive psychologists and philosophers take it for granted that there are representations of images or verbal concepts in the mind (or, for cognitive neuroscientists, in the brain); that these can represent the outer world; and that the representations can be read and used by the mind. Others, however, question the basic idea of mental or neural representations and argue that cognitive psychologists misunderstand the word "representation" when they apply it to describe what goes on in the mind or the brain. These disagreements touch upon central assumptions in much of cognitive psychology, and we therefore say a little more about them in the section *"Debates about Mental Representations"* later.

"Classical" cognitive psychologists conceive of cognition as in principle a matter of input–output conversion of information through cognitive processes (i.e., computations). These processes are assumed to rely entirely on the formal features of the information symbols in combination with the rules for manipulating such symbols. Note that the view of cognition as an input–output process preserves the structure of the earlier behaviorist stimulus–response paradigm. Whereas in early behaviorism, all attention was on outer "behavior," such as the overt response to a stimulus, computational cognitive psychology created what has come to be called "the sandwich model" of cognition, entering "cognition" between the stimulus and the response (Brette, in press). Further, much cognitive theory has conceived of the cognitive architecture as innate and therefore universal across all humans (Glock, 2020; Wilson & Clark, 2009).

It has traditionally been the task of cognitive psychologists to identify and study cognitive processes, and the task of cognitive neuroscientists to study how the brain, via mental or neural representations, enables these processes. In recent years, however, these tasks and interests have increasingly blended. That is, large parts of contemporary cognitive psychology are concerned with the brain to a greater extent than was common earlier. It is, indeed, not unusual for present-day cognitive psychologists to argue the physicalist position that cognitive processes *are identical with* brain processes, and that cognitive states *are identical with* brain states (for more discussion of this issue, see Jungert, 2017; Slife, Burchfield, & Hedges, 2010; Williams & Gantt, 2022; Zahnoun, 2020). Note that this claim is quite different from the uncontroversial observation that cognitive processes *depend* on brain processes and that cognitive states *depend* on brain states. Also in line with the physicalist position, some contemporary cognitive psychologists conceive of mental representations as physical objects in the brain that have semantic properties (i.e., they argue, carry meaning) (Smortchkova, Dołęga, & Schlicht, 2021). As a consequence, it is not unusual today to talk about "*neural* representations."

In both the original cognitive view and the contemporary physicalist views, it makes sense to conceive of cognitive processes as necessarily occurring only inside the brain of the person who is thinking. This *internalist* view presupposes a strict and impenetrable boundary between, on the one hand, the brain-internal, really cognitive processes and mental (or neural) representations, and, on the other hand, all brain-external aids or scaffolds (Menary, 2015; Wilson, 2004). We can consider a pocket calculator from this perspective. A pocket calculator helps one to calculate a sum more quickly and more efficiently, and perhaps more correctly, than does in-the-head counting. In the internalist view of cognitive psychology, the calculator and the use of the calculator provide external scaffolding that can facilitate cognitive processes. However, seen from this perspective, the scaffolding must not be confused with cognition: An external scaffold is, therefore, by definition, not taken as a component of the individual's cognitive system in this view (Adams & Aizawa, 2010b; Rupert, 2010).

The idea of *the mark of the cognitive* is central here. It defines "the cognitive" as consisting of "*. . .processes that (a) are recognizably cognitive, (b) take place in the brain, (c) do not take place outside of the brain, and (d) do* not cross from the brain into the external world" (Adams & Aizawa, 2010a, p. 69). A common expression is that this definition sets *"the bounds of cognition"* (Adams & Aizawa, 2010a, p. 69). On this definition, nothing that happens, or exists, outside a person's brain could ever qualify as cognitive.

To sum up: Two assumptions in much contemporary cognitive psychology are, first, that nervous systems, including brains, are computational, and, second, that information processing is necessary for cognition to occur (Miłkowski, 2018b; Miłkowski et al., 2018; see also Rodríguez-Flores et al., 2023). On this basis, cognitive science and cognitive psychology have the tasks of identifying the mental or neural representations involved in this processing, finding out what their content is, and learning how the representations are used to control behavior (Bechtel, 2016). A third assumption is that cognitive processes can, by definition, only take place internally, inside the cognizing agent's mind or brain (Rupert, 2004). By this third assumption, thinking (or cognition) becomes *defined* as activity in a person's brain. Note that defining thinking in this way is based on a conceptual choice, not on empirical observations of where thinking takes place.

Critique of Computational Models

Computational ways of conceiving of cognition have been challenged in recent years. For instance, connectionist ideas have become increasingly popular, reducing some of the formalisms of computationalism (Spivey, 2023). However, critics argue that connectionism is beset by some of the same problems as the classical theories, especially problems surrounding the idea of mental representations (Brinkmann, 2018). See also Jaeger et al. (2024, p. 3), who argue that *". . .natural agency, cognition, and consciousness are, at their very core, not computational phenomena, and if we restrict ourselves to study them by purely computational means, we are likely to miss the point entirely."* This comment resonates with critiques coming from philosophers and neuroscientists who question the general soundness of modern cognitive psychology's conceptual basis. These thinkers have also pointed out that it is quite odd that the discipline of cognitive psychology should seem closer to computer science than to human biology (Brette, 2024). Human thinking, after all, takes place in humans, not in computers. Philosophers of cognitive science, such as Fred Keijzer, concur, and argue that a viable cognitive psychology needs to take into account that the creatures who engage in human cognition are human beings, who are, at bottom, biological and social creatures (Keijzer, 2025).

There has also been increasing criticism of the typical experimental settings in cognitive psychology and cognitive neuroscience which allow a very limited range of behaviors (such as button pressing). See also Chapter 5, about brains, where we referred to Mazviita Chirimuuta's (2024) observations on the consequences of using very simple tasks in highly restrictive experimental circumstances. According to the critics, the ecological validity of such research is doubtful; it may not tell us much about cognition in real life. This critique has led to a movement that encourages computational cognitive research that studies rich behavior (Maselli et al., 2023).

Critics also challenge the three basic assumptions that we described in the previous subsection (for more on this, see the later section on thinking in an interactive and dynamic system). Finally, cognitive psychologists have also been seen as committing the mereological fallacy (which we discussed in Chapter 5) by attributing agency to subpersonal cognitive properties. In the words of the US historian Ruth Leys, the critics call into question *"the validity of cognitive science's attempt to eliminate the role of the person – by treating his or her actions as the product of direct causal links between perception and behavior"* (Leys, 2024, p. 45). As can be expected, the internalist and computational view has also been defended against such critiques (cf. Adams & Aizawa, 2010b; Miłkowski, 2018a; Miłkowski et al., 2018; Rupert, 2004, 2009).

Debates about Mental Representations

The expression "mental representation" has now appeared several times in the text. The meaning of that expression, as well as the logic of using it to denote what goes on in people's minds or brains, is an object of debate. Here, we briefly introduce these debates and give a glimpse of some issues about mental representations that have been, and still are, especially contentious (Favela & Machery, 2025; Oliveira, 2021; Smortchkova, Dołęga, & Schlicht; 2021; Spackman & Yanchar, 2013).

The critique of representationalism has generally focused on what is meant by the expression that something *represents* something else, and on what should be taken as the requirements for a representational relationship to exist. Reading those who are critical of representationalism is, therefore, also a way of clarifying to oneself what one would (or could?) mean by statements that contain the expression "mental representation." We can think about statements that there are mental representations in people's minds; that a cognitive process is the transformation of mental representations; or that a cognitive state is the storage of such representations (these examples are quotes from earlier in this chapter).

Some critics have argued (in analogy to how people typically observe and use external representations) that, for a *mental* representation to be able to fulfill a representative function, one would have to postulate an inner agent that observes this representation and interprets it, that is, reads its meaning off it. What or who could be that agent? The critical argument here is that theorizing in terms of mental representations forces the theorist to assume the existence of one of those inner "homunculi" that have for so long plagued dualist theories about the mind and the brain (Glock, 2015; Susswein & Racine, 2008). This problem harks back to the discussions of dualism in Chapter 4, about the mind.

Others have put forward critiques based on the generally accepted meaning of the words "to represent" and "representation." In the accepted dictionary meanings of these terms, a minimal condition for something to qualify as a representation of some other thing is that the first thing (the representation) conveys some *information* about the second thing (Bennett & Hacker, 2022; Glock, 2006). We can think about a painting of an apple that resembles an apple (in technical terms, it is a representation in the form of an *icon* of an apple). Because the painting resembles the apple, it conveys information about the apple (such as its shape or color), and it is thereby able to stand for, and thus represent, a real apple. In other cases, a representation can be a *symbol* for that which it represents, such as a linguistic symbol like the word "cat" used to represent a real cat, or the picture of three golden royal crowns that represents the kingdom of Sweden. There is a convention, that is, a publicly acknowledged agreement, about what those three golden crowns stand for. Note that the picture of the three golden crowns is not an icon, because it does not resemble the country of Sweden. It is a symbol. Especially important to note here is that symbolic representations such as words, signs, and pictures of golden crowns, can only function as representations when there are *public conventions*, or norms about their meanings. That is, for something to be a symbolic representation of some other thing, there must be a publicly agreed-upon use of the first thing as a symbol for the second thing (Brinkmann, 2018). On this understanding, we can see that representations by definition have to be public.

It is doubtful whether the requirement that representations be public and subject to social convention can be fulfilled by what is usually meant in the literature by mental or neural representations (Bennett & Hacker, 2022; Chirimuuta, 2024; Glock, 2006, 2015; Tanney, 2013). There is, of course, neural activity going on concomitant to seeing or remembering either a picture of an apple (an icon) or a picture of the Swedish three crowns (a symbol). This is not in question. What is in question, though, is how that *neural* activity could be the subject of the kind of *public* agreement, convention, and norms that are necessary for representation in the usual sense of the word. Neural activity is, after all, by definition private and not open to public inspection, negotiation, or agreement. Further, ascription of *meaning* to the icons or symbols in question (such as meaning "an apple" or meaning "the kingdom of Sweden") is necessary if they are to function as what is normally meant by representations. And it is difficult to see how neural activity, on its own, could have what is usually meant by "meaning."

Some of those who argue in favor of using the concepts of mental or neural representations have reacted to the criticism by tweaking or bending the accepted meaning of "representation" that we described previously such that a thinner meaning of the term is implied. So, for instance, Chirimuuta (2024) argued that some concept of neural representation is needed, though it may have to be so "thinned" out as to be only distantly related to the dictionary meaning of the term.[2] Poldrack (2021, p. 1322) has also argued for the necessity of representation, in the form of "...*patterns of activity that bear a systematic relationship to the structure of the external world and play a causal role in behavior.*" Here, a critic would retort that the phrase "a systematic relationship to the structure of the external world" describes a *correlation*, not a representation. The critic would then point out that while a causal relationship is an important and worthwhile research finding, it is not proof of representation (cf. De-Wit et al., 2016). For more about these discussions, see Anderson & Champion (2022), who also touch on the issue of mental versus neural representations.

A recent example of cognitive research that engages critically with the representation question is an article by Di Rienzo, Myin, & van Dijk (2024). They studied the creation and maintenance of social norms in concrete settings. On the basis of their findings, they argued that normativity is best understood as *performed interactively* by people in social settings, and not as based on (assumed) mind-internal rules and representations. These researchers therefore claimed that, at least in the case of norms, one can do away with the need to posit mental representations in individuals.

[2] In Chapter 5, about brains, the section "*The Problems of Parts and Wholes,*" we described a somewhat parallel discussion about the legitimacy of using psychological words with "metaphorical" or "thin" meanings when describing the activities of brains.

We leave the representation debates with a quote from a recent article that reported a study of how neuroscientists and psychologists today use terms such as "representation" in their research (Favela & Machery, 2025). The main conclusions of the study were, first, that researchers have quite unclear concepts of representation; and second, that the meanings given to the term "representation" vary substantially between researchers. On this basis, the authors pose a number of questions about representations that need to be answered:

> What do neuroscientists mean when they apply the concept of representation to particular brain states? How do they decide whether a brain state is a representation? And what role does the assignment of representational status to brain states play in theories and descriptions of empirical results? Would anything be lost if these theories and descriptions were reformulated without the assignment of representations? (Favela & Machery, 2025, p. 216)

Does Thinking Take Place in an Interactive and Dynamic System?

We now move to the approaches on the *interactive and dynamic system* side of the dispute (see Casper and Artese, 2022, in the *Introduction* to this chapter). These approaches are sometimes described as signifying "the pragmatic turn" in cognitive science and have also been given labels such as "distributed cognition," or "wide cognition" (Baggs & Oliveira, 2024; Engel, Friston, & Kragic, 2016; Robbins & Aydede, 2009). In the words of the German philosopher Hans-Johann Glock, what unites these approaches is that they "*treat psychological concepts as means of making sense of others and ourselves, rather than as metaphysical lasers that 'carve nature at its joints,' in Plato's striking phrase*" (2020, p. 11). Cognition, in this view, does not originate from stimuli and is not primarily about ingesting and processing data from the surroundings. Rather, cognition is about actively creating networks of meanings in the individual's context. Perceiving, thinking, and moving are interconnected, and cognition is mainly for action – "action" here in the sense of exploratory and inferential actions (Menary, 2016; Pezzulo et al., 2015). In this view, therefore, cognitive processing – that is, thinking – has its origin in an action, usually integrated with an intention. These approaches are anti-Cartesian[3] in the sense of being opposed to seeing an individual's mental processes as always fully and solely determined by what is going on inside the mind. Therefore,

---

[3] See Chapter 4, on the concept of mind, for details about Descartes's ideas.

in the words of the Australian philosopher of cognitive science Robert Wilson, "*in order to understand central aspects of cognition we look not to what's in the brain but what the brain is in*" (2004, p. 212).

Partial precursors to these approaches can be found in pragmatist philosophy and in some early psychology. One example is Lev Vygotsky's (1978) developmental psychology in the 1930s. Another precursor is behavior settings theory in the 1940s and 1950s (Aunger et al., 2024; Baggs & Oliveira, 2024; Kalis, Pascoe, & Segundo Ortin, 2024). Yet another example is James and Eleanor Gibson's ecological psychology in the 1970s (Gibson, 1979; Gibson & Pick, 2023). In the view of the Gibsons, perception is always action-oriented, and people directly perceive, and act upon, the opportunities for action (called *affordances*) that the environment offers (Oliveira & Chemero, 2015). As a precursor outside psychology, we should remember Ludwik Fleck's thoughts on thinking as a social activity, which we described in Chapter 2. He argued that thinking can never be fully understood or explained without taking the thinker's context into account. In his view, an individual's thinking is always structured by that individual's location in a particular social environment.

Several approaches to situated or distributed cognition have appeared in recent decades, such as "extended cognition," "embodied cognition," "embedded cognition," "enactive cognition," and "cognitive integration." They are often summarized as *4E cognition* (Newen, De Bruin, & Gallagher, 2018). For detailed introductions to these approaches, including their historical backgrounds, see Wilson & Clark (2009) and Roth & Jornet (2013). See also, for example, Favela et al. (2021) and Hydén (2014, 2017) for examples of empirical studies in this tradition.

What unites these approaches is a *definition* of cognition as something that may involve more than just a person's brain. However, although the approaches are often talked about as one family, some basic assumptions differ among them. One important axis of variation involves ideas about the ways in which cognition, especially memory, can be extended through social interactions (Sutton et al., 2010; see also Menary, 2010a, 2010d, for further discussion of differences). However, beyond the differences, these approaches are united in that all take exception to the basic assumptions of the internalist approaches that we described in the previous sections. Because they all take people's context into account, they can all be characterized as *contextualist* approaches.

Cognitive Integration, Cognitive Tools, and Enculturation

We have chosen the *cognitive integration* approach as our example. It was suggested and developed by Richard Menary in the early 2000s (2007, 2010b). A cognitive integrationist thinks of cognitive processes as "*hybrid, straddling both brain and bodily manipulation of environmental vehicles*" (Menary, 2010b, p. 228). The word *vehicles* here denotes the bearers of mental content. A "mental content" cannot exist without something that "has" it. That something is its *vehicle*. In the cognitive integrationist view, the vehicles of mental content can be located either within the biological boundaries of the person or in the person's surroundings. Examples of *internal* vehicles are a person's mental states, such as beliefs and hopes, and a person's mental activities, such as believing and hoping. Some examples of *external* vehicles are tools that a person can manipulate for writing, such as pens, keyboards, and computers.

Cognitive integrationists see the internal aspects of cognition (via vehicles such as mental acts) and the external aspects of cognition (via bodily manipulation of external vehicles such as pens) as integrated into a whole – that whole being cognition (Menary, 2007). In the integrationist view, it is the learning of *practices for manipulating* the external vehicles and the information they contain that extends people's cognitive abilities, not the external vehicles themselves (Menary, 2012; Trybulec, 2015).

In line with these ideas, there is evidence that learning to use external tools influences visual perception. For instance, Jessica Witt, a US cognitive psychologist, has shown that when a reaching tool, such as a baton, is used, an observed object appears closer than when the tool is not used. In her words, "*Tools affect how the world looks. Tools change the action capabilities of a person, and with these changes come corresponding differences in visual perception*" (Witt, 2021, pp. 679–680).

In the integrationist view, internal and external processes and vehicles are coordinated with one another when a person performs a cognitive task. Menary (2007) uses writing to illustrate this. Bodily manipulating an external vehicle (when writing, a pen or a keyboard) enables a person to perform cognitive tasks that would have been difficult or perhaps impossible without access to that external vehicle. It is possible to act upon written text (the product of using an external vehicle such as a pen) in ways that it is not possible to act upon internal mental content (the product of an internal vehicle such as the mental act of remembering). As a result, a writer who has written down a sentence on paper or screen is able to perform cognitive tasks involving that sentence. Some of these tasks would be very difficult or even impossible to perform before the sentence was written down. The written sentence is therefore seen as an external component of the writer's total cognitive system, with which the internal components of the same total system interact.

According to the cognitive integrationist, having access to external vehicles and to the activity of manipulating them gives a person new cognitive abilities compared to only having access to internal vehicles. This is a main reason for the integrationist claim that bodily manipulating external vehicles (vehicles such as pens for writing) should be seen not just as enabling external storage of information but as actually a part of the thinking itself. This means seeing cognitive activities and abilities as not solely, and in some cases not even essentially, neural (Clark & Chalmers, 1998; Menary, 2007). In sum, then, a cognitive integrationist views cognition as based on the integration of internal neural processes with the bodily manipulation of external vehicles (Rowlands, 1999). For such cognitive integration, *cognitive tools* are essential.

Tools come in several forms, and cognitive tools are different from practical tools. There is archaeological evidence that *practical tools* have been in use by humans and their precursors, as well as by other animals, since time immemorial. (For an interesting general discussion about psychological aspects of human tool use, see Mangalam et al., 2022.)

Explicitly *cognitive* tools are of far more recent origin than practical tools. The available archaeological evidence points to an origin approximately 10,000 years ago (Donald, 1993, 2009). A cognitive tool is a tool made by humans to enable completion of a cognitive task. Such tools help a person to think through the steps of the cognitive task all the way to its completion (Gillett, 2022). Examples of cognitive tools are *symbolic tools* such as diagrams, writing systems, and computer languages; *sensory tools* such as telescopes or microscopes; and *tracking tools* such as rulers, maps, radar, and the Global Positioning System (Menary & Gillett, 2022). Further, *language* provides communicative links between people and thereby unequivocally extends what people, especially people collectively, are able to think, and therefore able to do with their cognitive tools (Christiansen & Chater, 2022).

Cognitive integrationists argue that using a cognitive tool does not merely improve a person's ability to complete a particular cognitive task. Using the cognitive tool also changes the *nature* of the task from what it was before the cognitive tool was introduced. And when the nature of the task has changed, that change will transform the person's cognition during the specific task. Over time, and as a result of many such changes, the totality of the person's cognitive capacities will be transformed (Menary, 2012). In these processes, culture, and especially processes of *enculturation*, play important roles.

The term *enculturation* refers to the processes of learning to use cognitive tools (Menary, 2013; Menary & Gillett, 2022; Vold & Schlimm, 2020). Through enculturation, a young person's biological faculties are transformed by the conjunction of their own ongoing cognitive development with their learning in their local cultural environment (often called their cognitive niche). Enculturation is, therefore, not a process of being "subjected" to enculturation, but rather a process of actively modifying and even constructing one's own cognitive niche (Allesøe Christensen, 2023; Kendal, Tehrani, & Odling-Smee, 2011; Menary, 2010d). The results of enculturation are, in the words of Menary and Gillett (2022, p. 364), *"integrated cognitive systems that incorporate tools and cultural practices as proper parts of those systems and not just as developmental or causal scaffolds."* For the integrationist, then, culture and cultural norms and rules are central to cognitive processes; in some cases, they should even be seen as parts of cognitive processes.

The cultural origin of cognitive tools and their use imbues cognitive tools with culturally based *cognitive norms* for the proper ways to use them (Menary, 2010c). We can think, for example, of the various culture-specific ways to perform the cognitive task of long division on paper. These different ways exemplify what Menary and Gillett (2017) call *culture-specific cognitive practices*. These are normative patterned practices that develop when a certain cognitive tool is becoming integrated into a particular setting. Culture-specific cognitive practices are defined as

> ... patterns of activity spread out across a population that are physically embodied, repeated, and stable habits that are shared by members of a cultural-cognitive niche and which are reliably involved in how human agents interact with each other and their various environmental resources. These stable patterns of activity arise from habitual interactions, which also shape that activity. (Gillett, 2022, p. 646)

Many culture-specific cognitive practices are (as in the case of long division) taught in schools in distinctly normative ways: the teacher corrects mistakes and shows the right way to perform the practices. Menary and Gillett (2022) argue that it is by learning such *normative cognitive practices –* that is, through the process of enculturation – that specific cognitive tools become integrated into a person's cognitive system. Note that learning normative cognitive practices (i.e., learning to think and act in certain culturally correct ways by using certain cognitive tools) always takes place in a specific social and cultural setting.

The research topics based on the ideas of cognitive integration and enculturation are varied. They include the development of autobiographical memory (Nelson & Fivush, 2020); joint attention, planning, and group coordination in naval navigation (Gillett, 2022; Hutchins, 1995); the evolution of cognition in social interaction (Heyes, 2019); mathematical cognition (Fabry & Pantsar, 2021); and reading and writing (Fabry, 2018).

Not all scholars in the 4E community agree with the cognitive integrationists, of course. For example, some are more restrictive about the role of context and culture in cognition, and some are more expansive (Cash, 2009, 2013; Wilson, 2004).

Comparing the Approaches to Thinking Persons

In this section, we compare the different approaches that we have presented, focusing on what we see as the significant elements – such as the active assumptions – of their respective thinking styles. Remember that Ludwik Fleck (see Chapter 2) characterized a *thinking style* as consisting of a thought collective's common preparedness to see, act, and think in one way, and often in no other, in relation to the collective's work and its objects of study.

Internalism: A Thinking Style of Individual-Based Cognition

Much of cognitive psychology was originally inspired by concepts and ideas in computer science. As a result, cognition has been seen as consisting of brain-internal processes of converting information input into behavioral or linguistic output. The conversion takes place through (usually) computational cognitive processes that result in the transformation of mental representations. Mental representations are the information-bearing structures of the cognitive system, nowadays increasingly seen as physical structures in the brain; and cognitive processes are increasingly seen as identical to brain processes. Cognitive scientists and cognitive psychologists use experiments to identify the mental representations relevant to a particular cognitive process, identify their content, and learn how they are used to control behavior.

The features mentioned just above presuppose some foundational *active* assumptions, such as: nervous systems, including brains, are in some sense computational; cognitive processes can take place only inside the cognizing agent's mind or brain; and after one has controlled for all "outside" influences on an individual's mental states, something *internal* of genuine psychological interest will remain to be studied (Adams & Aizawa, 2010a; Wilson, 2004). These assumptions erect an impenetrable boundary between the brain-internal cognitive processes and mental representations on the one hand, and any brain-external (secondary) phenomena on the other. Taken together, these assumptions point to an overarching characteristic: internalism or individualism, and we have therefore labeled this way of thinking about cognition the *internalist thinking style* (Menary, 2016; Wilson, 2010).[4]

Those who have adopted the internalist thinking style assert that, while it is true that individuals are impinged upon by factors in their surroundings which may cause changes in the contents of their minds, it is always factors inside the individual that actually determine their mental states. Consequently, in this view, it is in the nature of mental states to be, in some ways, independent of the character of the external world (Wilson, 1995, 2004).

Internalism and Universalism

Internalism in psychology often appears in company with a *universalist* thinking style. Universalism is the perspective that "*sees human action as a function of general laws relatively independent of time and space*" (Faulconer & Williams, 1985, p. 1179). In an argument related to Ludwik Fleck's ideas about thinking styles, the Canada-based historian of psychology Kurt Danziger (1997) has described how a combination of universalist and internalist assumptions has come to be written into the research methods of large parts of the psychology discipline. In a later publication, Danziger pointed to some consequences of this combination of assumptions that are of interest to us here:

> In traditional Western psychology, a particular version of universalism is linked to a particular form of individualism in a combination that is deeply engrained in the discipline's investigative practices. This combination takes the form of what has been called "Cartesian psychology" (Wilson, 1995), based on the belief that the scientific generalizations of psychology pertain to intra-individual processes and characteristics. Examples of these are variables of personality and intelligence as well as most of what has been

---

[4] We prefer the term "internalism" because the word "individualism" also carries a political meaning which we do not intend here.

investigated under "cognitive processes." The western cultural roots of Cartesian psychology are glaringly obvious, yet its preconceptions are so deeply enmeshed with the procedural norms of traditional scientific psychology that alternative approaches have long been subject to disciplinary marginalization. (Danziger, 2006, p. 272)

Note Danziger's emphasis on how the preconceptions of universalism and internalism in traditional Western psychology are *"engrained in . . . investigative practices"* and *"enmeshed with the procedural norms of traditional scientific psychology."* Danziger here echoed Ludwik Fleck's description of a thinking style as *"the entirety of intellectual preparedness or readiness for one particular way of seeing and acting, and no other"* (1935/1979, p. 64). Also, note Danziger's remark that it is this enmeshment of the preconceptions with the traditional research methods in psychology that makes it difficult to see any value in approaches to psychology that are based on thinking styles other than internalism and universalism. We have chosen to point to the combination of the internalist and universalist thinking styles here because we have judged this combination to be especially likely to be at odds with a view of people as culturally and socially situated persons.

But we also note that there are several other aspects of internalist cognitive psychology that are worth exploring critically: For example, the assumption that the studied phenomena have quantitative characteristics (see Chapter 10, the section about measurement in psychology); the assumption that there are inner, that is, mental representations of the outside world in the form of images or concepts (we gave a glimpse of the debates about this earlier in this chapter); and the assumption of causality and, thereby, of determinist explanations (see Chapter 12, about explanations). These aspects also have thoroughgoing methodological consequences for research, and they are all being debated today (for more on these debates, see Casper & Artese, 2022; Glock, 2020; Marraffa & Paternoster, 2012; Zahnoun, 2018).

Contextualism: A Thinking Style of Culturally Integrated Cognition

The "4E" approaches to cognition are united by a general thinking style that we have labeled *contextualism.*[5] A contextualist thinking style is not

---

[5] Some thinkers use the label "externalism," but we have decided against using this term, because it may lead associations away from what we see as the central idea, namely, the constant interaction and integration of "internal" *and* "external" aspects of people's everyday lives. Some researchers instead use the terms "situated," "interaction," and "interactionism"; however, these terms have many other uses in the psychology discipline and may therefore cause confusion.

unique to cognitive psychology; it is also found in disciplines such as biology, where research has shown that certain physiological processes (such as energy transfer, metabolism, and homeostasis) actively involve the organism's surroundings and, therefore, cannot be satisfactorily explained by organism-internal processes (Turner, 2000). Cognitive contextualists argue that external coupling is a core human cognitive resource that has an evolutionary basis: "*the biological brain has in fact evolved and matured in ways which factor in the reliable presence of a manipulable external environment*" (Clark & Chalmers, 2010, p. 31). They point to vision and language as prime examples (Menary, 2010c; see also Chapter 7, about language). Heyes et al. (2020) have developed the hypothesis of *cultural evolution* – contextually rather than genetically based evolution – of advanced cognitive abilities such as meta-cognition, that is, people's ability to monitor, talk about, and control their ongoing cognitive processes.

The central common feature of the cognitive contextualist thinking style is the assumption that cognition is the result of integrating and coordinating internal and external cognitive activities and resources. Cognitive *tasks* are assumed to be hybrid, in the sense of reaching across brains and bodies to the manipulation of external vehicles. As a consequence, bodily manipulation of external vehicles is seen as part of cognition. Further, having access to external vehicles, and manipulating these vehicles, will help a person develop new cognitive abilities (Wilson & Clark, 2009). And because cognitive tasks, and integration of external resources, always take place in specific contexts, cognitive contextualists take exception to the internalist thinking style's assumption of universalism. Instead, the assumption of *cultural specificity* is basic to the cognitive contextualist thinking style (Haslanger, 2019).

Many cognitive contextualists have worked to develop new methodological frameworks to use in empirical studies of people's thinking and problem-solving (Glock, 2020; Morgan, 2017). This has been felt to be necessary because many of the questions of interest to cognitive contextualists concern people's thinking and problem-solving in real life rather than in laboratory settings. The research methods used by cognitive contextualists are therefore varied and often cross disciplinary boundaries. They range from experiments using neuroimaging, such as fMRI (Fabry, 2018; Menary & Gillett, 2022), to case studies using ethnographic and other qualitative methods, such as narrative studies (Gillett, 2022; Hydén, 2014, 2017), and to varieties of computer modeling (De Jaegher et al., 2017).

Thinking Styles and the View of Persons as Culturally and Socially Situated

In this book, we have adopted a view of persons as living in social and cultural settings that organize the broad contours of their daily life. In this view, it is only within such organizing settings that the sophisticated cognitive and agential capacities of humans can be fully developed and persist. Further, because the details of how daily life is organized vary across time and place, and across class and ethnic groups, the details of what it means to *be a person* also vary. Against this background, it is not surprising that we should find the contextualist 4E approaches the most congenial. They take the situatedness of persons seriously, in a thorough manner that the internalist approaches have not done yet. While internalist cognitive psychological approaches have provided much interesting research and theory, they may, in fact, tell us rather little about how people think and solve problems in real life. One reason for this is that there are several aspects of what is commonly meant by "thinking" that have not typically been in focus when cognition has been studied in the internalist mode. Think of the many meanings of "to think" that we mentioned at the beginning of this chapter, for example those that are based in the fundamentally argumentative, inescapably social kinds of thinking that go on in debates and discussions (cf. Billig, 1996). To further elaborate the contextualist stance and critique, we quote Robert Wilson once more:

> It is not simply that particular models of problem solving, like the General Problem Solver (Newell, Shaw, & Simon, 1960), are mistaken in detail. It is that the entire approach to problem solving, where problems are well-defined and involve at their heart [a] search through a problem space in some effective manner, fails to connect with real-world problem-solving. Such approaches fail, basically, because the way in which they define the process of problem solving and the strategies they propose, are neither the ones that people use, nor do they reasonably approximate those strategies. (Wilson, 2013, p. 24)

Psychologists (researchers and clinicians) who favor a contextualist view of humans are especially interested in cognition as the "real-world problem solving" that Wilson points to in the quote. These psychologists do not begin their studies by looking for "inner" entities such as (cognitive) processes, knowledge, beliefs, attitudes, and so on. Rather, they begin with people's practices. They study people as they interact with one another, and they study how people solve problems in various everyday settings. Therefore, their research interests are not expressed in conventional "cognitive" terminology. These psychologists study people's thinking and other cognitive activities as parts of social behavior and not just on their own, nor as the "inner" causes of behavior (Potter, 2012).

Toward a Unified Person-Oriented Psychology of Thinking?

Though the two thinking styles that we have identified are poles apart, there may be movements toward integration. We therefore end this chapter by referring to a recent collaboration among twenty-eight cognitive scientists and psychologists from almost as many countries, and from across the different approaches that we have described in this chapter. These scientists advertise that they want to "*. . .highlight the opportunity for a figure-ground reversal that puts interaction at the heart of cognition. The interactive stance is a way of seeing that deserves to be a key part of the conceptual toolkit of cognitive scientists*" (Dingemanse et al., 2023). The twenty-eight researchers refer to several studies that feature varieties of interactive, or *contextualist*, stances (Dingemanse, 2020a; Dutilh Novaes, 2013, 2021; Enfield & Sidnell, 2022; see also Chater, Zeitoun, & Melkonyan, 2022; Rączaszek-Leonardi et al., 2023; Spivey, 2023). The concluding words in the collective's article stress the centrality of interaction in context, or in our words, of contextualism:

> We have argued for a recentering of the cognitive sciences around interacting minds. Are there any aspects of cognition that can fully be understood from the perspective of single minds? We do not know, but we submit that a reversal of the burden of evidence is in order. The watershed divide between the mental and the social has always been at best a convenient fiction [.]. As we come to terms with forms of cognition not centered on single brains, interaction looms large as the crucial connective tissue: ontologically prior, epistemologically fundamental, ecologically sound. As the cognitive sciences enter their next phase, interaction will be core to the enterprise of understanding how minds are made. (Dingemanse et al., 2023, p. 5)

CHAPTER 7

Language and Psychology

Language and human life as we know it are inseparable. Humans understand their world and themselves through language because humans live in a world that is mediated mainly by language (Richards & Stenner, 2023). It is by learning to use the language of their community that children become self-aware and fully participating members of that community – become what we mean by *persons*. This, of course, also means that language is an essential, or even a defining, part of life in human communities; language is one of the basic social institutions. It is not surprising, therefore, that psychologists and others who study people in their cultural communities are interested in language, especially language in everyday use (Clark, 1996; Hacker, 2013; LaVine & Tissaw, 2015). Recent decades have seen an increasing interest in studying language as *action*, indicating a shift away from mainly studying language as *thought*. This quote from the British psychologist Derek Edwards about what language is *for* summarizes this interest:

> We need to approach language as designed for discourse, for public performances, rather than having public actions as a kind of lucky consequence of people representing things mentally, in what happens to be a fortuitously shared meaning system. (1997, p. 259)[1]

Here Edwards is alluding to, and taking sides in, one of the major controversies among language researchers since the beginning of the 1960s: the evolution of human language. Did human language arise from early human beings' needs to cooperate and communicate publicly with one another, and did it thereby become shaped for such activities? Or is language a capacity that arose from mutations in the human brain that

---

[1] Edwards is here using the word "discourse" in its lexical meaning of a discussion of a topic, either in speech or in writing; or a connected series of utterances (OED). Other meanings of "discourse" are used, for instance, in some parts of modern *discursive psychology* (see, e.g., Edley, 2001; Wetherell & Edley, 1999).

created a universal grammar enabling humans to form mental representations of their world and their experiences? Researchers on both sides of this controversy have, over the years, produced much research and theory, combined with speculations and heated debates. It is nearly impossible to approach language and psychology without engaging, at least superficially, with these debates. We therefore begin the chapter with a section about the evolution of human language. We then describe and discuss different views of language use. This is followed by a section on practical aspects of talk in interaction, such as the functions of joint action and common ground in conversations. We then present two different views of how words get their meanings: the representational view and the anthropological view. Then, we suggest two different language-focused thinking styles that are common in research on language by psychologists. In the final section, we describe some psychological research approaches to people's talk.

Evolution and Human Language

There has been much speculation about the evolutionary origins of human language. Some theorists favor *usage-based* theories, based on everyday interaction among humans. These theorists argue that human language had its origin in hominids' and early humans' need to cooperate and communicate in order to survive. These theorists suggest that the origins of language are social and that language, therefore, is a basically intersubjective ability and consequently culturally local (Christiansen & Chater, 2018, 2022; Enfield & Sidnell, 2022; Levinson, 2023; Levinson & Evans, 2010). This makes language an extension and further development of early humans' nonlinguistic social and communicative behavior, such as body gestures. The psychological and linguistic research in this tradition focuses on the social dimensions of language use, such as people's need to manage their own accountability in the give-and-take of communicative interaction (Enfield, 2022). These researchers suggest that language *learning* and everyday language *use* are more closely connected processes than has hitherto been assumed. Some even suggest a unitary model of language comprehension and production (i.e., use). And some researchers further suggest that language learning should be seen as akin to skills learning in general. This would mean that knowledge of – that is, proficiency in – language is knowledge of the practical "knowing how" type, rather than knowledge of the cognitive "knowing that" type, as had long been claimed (Chater, McCauley, & Christiansen, 2016; Chater & Christiansen, 2018).

Other researchers, the *biolinguistic* theorists, seek natural-scientific explanations of language. Some of these theorists argue that human language has its origin in mutations in nonspeaking early humans that produced dedicated brain structures containing inborn general rules for language production (Berwick & Chomsky, 2016; Pléh, 2019). According to what has been termed the *nativist argument*, it is these inborn general rules that make it easy for young children to learn any existing language. The general rules also produce, in each learner, unconscious knowledge of the specific rules of that particular learner's mother tongue (Chomsky, 2006). In this view, language proficiency tends to be seen as a cognitive capacity of the "knowing that" type (Graffi, 2019). In their research, biolinguistic theorists tend to focus more on language production as an individual cognitive achievement (the term "generativity" is often used to characterize this focus) and less on social aspects, such as communication between individuals through language.

There is, of course, no way to test directly for the different evolutionary origins that the different theories propose. Lacking this possibility, researchers who are interested in language evolution tend to use the explanatory strategy that philosophers call *abduction*, or *inference to the best explanation*.[2] The typical situation is one in which a researcher has, or gathers, a collection of data and then develops a hypothesis which, *if it were true*, would explain the data. If the researcher can find no other hypothesis that equally well, or better, explains the data, the researcher may, at least temporarily, conclude that the chosen hypothesis is probably true (Grice, 2015; Michell, 2012). Obviously, because of its nature, inference to the best explanation cannot be conclusive, for it is, in principle, always possible for somebody else to develop a new, and perhaps better, hypothesis. This means that an inference to the best explanation of the origins of language can, at best, be indicative, but never conclusive.

For detailed overviews of the debates about language evolution, including input from linguists, psychologists, neuroscientists, and geneticists, see, for instance, de Boer et al. (2020); Christiansen & Chater (2018, 2022); Dabrowska (2015); Hagoort (2019); Levinson & Evans (2010); Pléh (2019); and Smith (2020). Of late, there have also been a few attempts to create consensus between the opposing views on the evolution of human language (Pleyer & Hartmann, 2019).

---

[2] In Chapter 12, about explanations in psychology, we describe the practice of inference to the best explanation, also called abduction, including its major drawbacks.

Following recent developments in evolutionary biology, genetics, and epigenetics, an increasing number of researchers are leaning toward the usage-based theories. We, therefore, highlight a few more features of these theories.

First, theorists favoring the usage-based view reject the idea of a dramatic mutation as the origin of language evolution in humans. Instead, they argue that early humans developed spoken languages gradually and that they did so in the ways that were enabled by the preconditions offered by their then existing bodily (i.e., brain) features, combined with the *then* existing patterns of social interaction (Christiansen & Chater, 2009, 2022). In other words, early humans could develop only the types of languages that their brains enabled them to produce and interpret. And – what is especially important – the languages that early humans developed had to be learnable by their children. After all, the absolute majority of language learners in the world have always been young children (Isbilen & Christiansen, 2020).

Second, as we mentioned earlier, in the usage-based view, "worded" language arose as an accompaniment to, and eventually a refinement of, the gestures, sounds, and other kinds of body language that were already in use in local communities of early humans. In this view, worded language, like gestures, is primarily a medium for accomplishing social actions (Chater & Christiansen, 2023; Christiansen & Chater, 2022; Edwards, 1991; Levinson & Evans, 2010).

Third, some linguists argue that it was human beings' particular ways of interacting that originally made language possible. These linguists also argue that the emergence of language enhanced this form of human intersubjectivity even more. Central to the development of such enhanced intersubjectivity, these theorists argue, was the phenomenon of *accountability*, that is, the development of shared *group norms* that regulate conversations and other interactions. In this view, enhanced intersubjectivity could not develop without accountability, and language is necessary for accountability (Enfield & Sidnell, 2022).

In the usage-based view, the evolution of language took place through *cultural* selection that operated on *socially* developed, and therefore *socially inherited*, language variants in the communities of early humans (Heyes, 2024). In plain words: each generation of humans learned from their previous generation and then, in turn, taught the next generation. This inter-generational process included any linguistic changes and improvements that had been made along the way. No genetic changes would be necessary for this kind of evolution. Here, it should be noted that culture, as an evolutionary force, enables infinitely faster evolution than "genes-alone" evolution could ever do. This insight has led researchers to focus increasingly on the cultural facets of human language evolution (Tamariz & Kirby, 2016; Tamariz & Vance, 2020).[3]

Not surprisingly, many researchers combine the usage-based view of language evolution in early humans with an interest in how people use language in their everyday lives today. This is the topic to which we turn in the next section.

Language in Use

People use language – spoken, signed, or written – to communicate with one another and often to influence one another. That is, people use words to *do* things, and those doings usually, in one way or another, involve other people. Words can be used to demand something from somebody else, or to ask forgiveness for being too demanding. Words can be used to inform somebody about something; to ask somebody about something; to warn somebody about an impending danger; to congratulate somebody on their birthday; to affirm something that a client says in therapy; or even to declare a couple to be married. In sum: people can do many things with words.

People's use of language has mainly been studied in two different research traditions. The first is the *product* tradition of language studies, based in the discipline of linguistics. It includes the detailed study of the speech sounds, words, and sentences that people produce. In this tradition, words and sentences are usually studied as linguistic phenomena, often separately from the social circumstances in which they were uttered (Pléh, 2019). The other tradition is the *action* tradition, with its origins in sociological, anthropological, and philosophical studies of people interacting. Researchers working in the action tradition are interested in people's situated social actions, and their intentions in those situations (Clark, 1996, 2006). Both traditions have achieved important results. However, we argue that for psychologists, research in the action tradition, with its emphasis on how people use language in everyday interactions with one another, is of especial interest.

---

[3] This increased focus on *cultural* evolution seems to be a more widespread trend among evolution researchers generally. A recent review of the research literature on the general "culture-versus-genes" question in human evolution concluded:

"The literature suggests that group-level cultural evolution is more adaptive and more rapid than genetic evolution in humans. This difference has caused an increasing fraction of human life to be mediated by culturally evolved group-level practices and technology, and a decreasing fraction by genetic traits. Available evidence suggests that this trend is ongoing and accelerating" (Waring & Wood, 2021, p. 7).

The Action Tradition in Language Studies

According to researchers in the action tradition, language use arises in, and is part of, people's joint activities. This means that, to account for the words that are used in an interaction, one must understand the *joint activity* that is going on in that interaction (Clark, 1996). This means that language use involves much more than the words. Just as important as the words are the numerous nonlinguistic features of the situations in which people use language. Some of the most important features are the speaker's and listener's gestures, facial expressions, tone of voice, and so on. Also important are the physical venue and the formal or informal pre-definitions of the interaction, including the relationship (e.g., hierarchical, friendly, adversarial) between the speakers. A large part of the meaning that gets created in an interactive speech situation is negotiated and determined through nonlinguistic interactions and by nonlinguistic cues (for more details, see Dingemanse, 2020b, 2024). Therefore, in many cases, it would not be possible to discern what went on in a situation from knowing only the words that were uttered. Herbert Clark, a US psychologist, has studied linguistic interactions – *communicative acts* – in detail. In his words:

> For each utterance, speakers and addressees must coordinate the speaker's vocalizations with the addressee's attention to those vocalizations, the speaker's wording with the addressee's identification of that wording, and what the speaker means with what the addressee understands the speaker to mean. (Clark, 2006, p. 129)

As Clark also observed, "*Some of the basic principles of language use are really general principles of joint action, and to understand language use, we must look to the broader principles*" (1996, p. 60). In Clark's view, because a communicative act such as a conversation is a type of joint activity between speaker and listener, one needs to learn about the general features of joint activities to really understand how conversations work. Clark, therefore, urged psychologists interested in psychological aspects of language and language use to study language in this broader sense. Important aspects to study are *joint activities*, *coordination*, and *common ground*.

Joint Activities, Coordination, Repair, and Common Ground

According to Clark, the totality of the *joint activity* in a communicative act where two or more speakers are present is made up of both linguistic and nonlinguistic elements or cues (Clark, 1996). In many types of joint activity, these elements will be well known to members of the same culture or subculture. When that is the case, people entering into a joint activity can already presuppose a great deal of what will happen and of what they themselves should say and do. Think about playing a game in which all players know the rules. Or think about the variants of formal rules of etiquette in many settings. According to Clark, joint activities can vary on at least five dimensions: scriptedness, formality, verbalness, cooperativeness, and governance or egalitarianism (Clark, 1996, p. 30). Given these dimensions, the participants in a joint activity can be expected to take on different *activity roles*, depending on their cultural backgrounds, expertise, and so on. And, of course, each participant also brings their own personal identity, including their beliefs and wishes, to the joint activity.

To get a sense of the composition of joint activities, including what the participants can presuppose, one could do what Clark has done, and note down all the interactive, linguistic, and contextual details in an interaction such as buying a few items in a shop. Someone who reads just the words that were uttered during such an interaction might not be able to find out what kind of interaction it was, much less what kinds of items were bought. A film of this interaction without the spoken words would make it possible to identify the joint action, though not those – probably important – aspects for which language is necessary. Language use and contextual details in a joint activity require each other; they are inseparable (Clark, 1996).

In a communicative act where the participants have common interests and goals, the actions of, and the outcomes for, each participant depend upon the actions of the other participants. Therefore, to reach their common goals, the participants must *coordinate* their individual actions during the communicative act. (As an example, think about two persons carrying a heavy and wide bed up a staircase.) This coordination is what makes an act a *joint* activity. In many well-known situations, coordination is not a problem; the participants will already have enough knowledge in common for all to know what to expect from each of the other participants. In other, less well-known situations, people may have to work hard at coordinating their behavior into a *joint* activity. For detailed studies of such coordination work in spoken interaction, see, for instance, Chater, Zeitoun, and Melkonyan (2022), and Dideriksen et al. (2023).

A central part of this coordinating work is people's ubiquitous habits of *interactive repair* of their own and each other's utterances when they talk to one another. Speakers tend to "repair" their own or each other's utterances when *accountability* is, or risks becoming, a problem for one of them, that is, when they are on the verge of transgressing some shared norm.[4] Such interactive repairs contribute greatly to, and may in fact be foundational to, the impressive resilience and flexibility of human language. The Dutch linguist Mark Dingemanse and the Australian linguistic anthropologist Nick Enfield have argued for the basic roles of joint action and interactive repair:

> ... through the use of interactive repair, dialogue is regulated by social norms, which provide "stable expectations for navigating our social world" (Hawkins, Goodman, & Goldstone, 2019, p. 158). Such expectations, often unspoken, can be defined by two qualities of normative behaviour: (i) the behaviour is not noticed or commented on when the norm is followed (subliminal), and (ii) it is noticed and commented on when the norm is transgressed. (2024, p. 34)

Performing a joint activity together several times makes the performance progressively easier; that is, joint activities are cumulative. They can accumulate to form the basis of the participants' *common ground*. Participants share a common ground when they know about each other's knowledge and ideas about the joint activity in question, and when this knowledge is openly acknowledged and shared between the participants (Enfield & Sidnell, 2022; Stalnaker, 2002). There are in principle two possible types of shared basis for common ground. The first type is evidence about each other's cultural communities. The more participants share a cultural community, the more *communal common ground* they will have. The second type is evidence that comes from the participants' direct experiences of one another. These experiences lead to their *personal common ground* (Clark, 1996).

Apart from these kinds of explicitly shared bases for common ground, people usually assume that the people they meet share most of the basic experiences of being human, such as having similar sense organs and so on, and will take these assumptions as bases for common ground. However, sometimes personal common ground is not necessary: For many types of frequently occurring communicative acts, communities have developed *conventions* about what to expect from participants in different activity roles (think about the coordination of the musicians in a symphony orchestra, or the coordination of the participants in a marriage ceremony). Most likely, whenever one finds such a convention, one can assume that it developed as the solution to a coordination problem (Clark, 1998; Hawkins, Goodman, & Goldstone, 2019).

---

[4] We return to questions about accountability in conversations later in the chapter.

In everyday life, people may classify themselves and one another by personality traits or other personal characteristics. Does this mean that personality traits and other individual characteristics are useful for establishing common ground? Herbert Clark says no. He argues that classification by traits is a very different thing from classification by community and cannot substitute for it:

> In using language, we classify people so that we can identify the conventions and other information we share with them. Traits are no good for this purpose. They are dispositions that people have more or less of, which don't lead to categories. There is also no evidence that we seek to establish mutual beliefs about our personality traits. We would have to if we were to use them as a basis for common ground. Personality traits have little to do with background expertise in actions that require coordination. For establishing common ground, we must classify by communities. (Clark, 1996, p. 106)

Of particular interest to a culturally oriented psychologist is the communal common ground that members of the same cultural community establish. After all, a cultural community is not just any collection of people. A cultural community is defined by the fact that its members share some substantial common ground, and usually that they have developed a *consensus* about the community's most central interests, beliefs, and values (see Chapter 3). Many thought collectives, as we discussed in Chapter 2, would qualify as cultural communities; their thinking styles then serve as major parts of their common ground and consensus.

In the next two sections, we discuss another aspect of the linguistic life of cultural communities: word use and the meanings of words.

How Words Get Their Meanings: The Classical View

In this section, we take up the classical or representational view of what it is that makes words mean what they mean. In early representational theories about language, the meaning of a word was taken to be the idea that it stood for. More recent representational theories see the meaning of a word as the mental representation for which it stands (Gilhooly et al., 2022; Smortchkova, Dołęga, & Schlicht, 2021; Sprague, 1999). These theories are based on a view of psychological predicates (i.e., words such as "believe," "think," and "intend") as being the *names* of an individual's subjective experiences or mental states. Thus, in this view, words such as these get their meaning through being associated with a particular private experience or state of a person. How would this work?

We can begin by considering how children learn the meaning of words for public phenomena such as colors: by watching another person point to a sample such as an object (perhaps a ball) of a particular color, and say, for instance, "That ball is blue." The colored ball serves as a public standard for judging something to be blue, that is, for the word "blue" to be the name of that color. The blue ball can be seen as a standard or rule for what can be termed "blue" in the same way that a meter ruler is a standard for length. To understand the meaning of color words is, therefore, the same as mastering the existing cultural rules for using those words (Smit, 2021).

Can the same principle be applied to learning the meanings of psychological words such as "believe," "think," and "intend"? That is, do people learn the meanings of psychological words by associating them with their own feelings and experiences? Do those feelings and experiences serve the same function as the colored ball did? For this to work, it would have to be possible, again in analogy with the color example, for an inner experience that only the individual has access to, to function as the cultural standard for the correct use (and thereby meaning) of a psychological word, just as the blue-colored ball functions as the standard for the color word.

This analogy encounters several difficulties. Here are some: what would, in the case of subjective experiences and feelings, be the parallel to another person's pointing to, and naming, the blue-colored ball that served as a sample in the example of learning colors? That is, what would (or could?) serve as a sample in analogy to the publicly observable colored ball? And how would one, again in analogy to the colored ball, compare an inner experience to some standard object or sample (which object? where?) to determine whether they match (Smit, 2021, esp. pp. 1209–1210)? These and similar critical questions about the possibility of private meanings of words have been intensely debated among philosophers.[5] Max Bennett and Peter Hacker have summarized their view of the debates and of the results of asking the questions above about psychological properties:

> . . .psychological terms are not names of psychological properties, acts and activities in the sense in which "red" can be said to be the name of a colour property, "to wave" can be said to be the name of an act, and "to dig the garden" can be said to be the name of an activity. (2022, p. 114)

---

[5] The debates were largely triggered by the Austrian philosopher Ludwig Wittgenstein. In his famous *private language argument*, he used the thought experiment of "the beetle in the box" to argue against the possibility of a language that is private to a person. Bennett & Hacker (2022, esp. pp. 111–114) provide a critical discussion of these arguments.

How Words Get Their Meanings: The Anthropological View

For those who are dissatisfied with the classical view of how words get their meanings, what has come to be called the "anthropological" view of language is an alternative. This view suggests that when one asks for the meaning of a word, what one wants to know is how the word *should be used* (Hacker, 2001). The presence of "should" in that sentence is important because it indicates that *norms* are essential for word use and, therefore, also important for word meanings. Norms are the often-unspoken rules and expectations for people's conduct (in this case, their word use) that are shared among people who belong to the same speech community (Hawkins, Goodman, & Goldstone, 2019). In this view, what a word means is determined by how the members of the speech community use it.[6] To explain the meaning of a word, one is required to describe the rules for its use, that is, give a standard of correctness for applying that particular word. And because these rules are norm-based, and norms are shared, the rules for word use are, by definition, public and based on a social agreement.

In the case of the blue-colored ball described earlier, one can point to it as a publicly agreed-upon standard, thereby teaching a child an existing public rule for the use of the word "blue."[7] When it comes to words for psychological experiences and actions, things seem different. As we saw above, the pointing-and-naming strategy that works for colors does not work for teaching the rules for using psychological words. Psychological words do not function as names of psychological properties in the same way that the word "blue" functions as the name of a color. For instance, psychological words cannot be taught by pointing to a sample. Further, because there are many kinds of psychological words, such words are taught in many different ways. But they are not taught in the same ways as color words and other words for publicly observable phenomena are taught.

---

[6] We should note here that the fact that word usage determines meaning does not imply that the meaning of a word is *identical* to its use. To draw that conclusion is to misunderstand the anthropological view of language. Indeed, there are words that have a use but no meaning. This is true, e.g., for proper names such as personal names. They can be used even though they do not mean anything relevant for their use. It is also true for the morphology, that is, the forms, of words: It is connected to word use but not to word meaning (Hacker, 2013).

[7] We should note that the public rules for applying the word "blue" vary between language communities. That is, the wavelength spectrum that is used for applying "blue" to an object is not the same in all language communities.

If we follow the anthropological view of language and see word meaning as determined by the rules for word use in a speech community, we would look at how various psychological words – words such as "feel," "remember," or "trauma" – are used and taught in particular speech communities. That is where we will find their meanings. The rules for using a psychological word – the rules that give us the meaning of that word – are part of the speech practices where that word occurs. Consequently, it is in people's (including professionals') talk and writings about psychological states and experiences that researchers should study how "psychological" words get their meanings (Wetherell, 2007). In the anthropological view of word meanings, the rules for word use, and thereby the meanings of words, are always products of particular speech communities in particular historical periods. In Herbert Clark's words:

> There is no such thing as a word simpliciter. Words belong. They belong to particular communities for whom they are conventional solutions to recurrent problems and there is community-wide expertise. And there is a plethora of communities that each of us belongs to. The result? We each have personal lexicons that are structured by the communal lexicons each lexical entry belongs to. The words we share are anything but haphazard, a fact we know and make use of. (1998, p. 86)

In a community or a historical period other than our own, a particular word may well have quite a different use and, therefore, a different meaning. A famous historical example in the English language is the word "silly." It originated before 1200 from the Old English and Germanic word *gesælig*, meaning "happy." Its use and meaning in English changed over the following centuries, first to "innocent," then to "weak," then to "unfortunate and pitiable," and eventually, in the sixteenth century, to "foolish." Meanwhile, its cognates in other Germanic languages (such as "salig" in Swedish and "selig" in German) have kept their original meaning. This example, though old history by now, should serve as a reminder to scholars, including psychologists, that word meanings may differ in important ways over time, and between subcultures in the same larger language community. Also, writing this book has repeatedly reminded us that we belong to two different Germanic language communities (English and Swedish). Like the word "silly," some words in the two languages that seemed identical to us had acquired diverging uses and, thereby, diverging meanings over time.

In psychology and its neighboring disciplines, there is also such "drift" in word meanings. One example can be found in the changes in the accepted rules for use, and thereby the meanings, of the word "trauma." The original medical meaning is taken from the ancient Greek word τραύμα (transliterated as "trauma"), which means an externally inflicted physical wound or damage. It later acquired the (still strictly medical) meaning of the internal medical state or condition that resulted from the externally inflicted wound or damage. Later still, the word gradually acquired the figurative meaning of a psychological shock that such a medical state might occasion. By the late twentieth century, this figurative meaning widened further to include psychological injuries caused by emotional shocks or the memories of such shocks, and not just by physical damage. In short, while the word "trauma" initially denoted an externally inflicted physical injury, it now, in popular usage, denotes an internal psychological state irrespective of the presence of physical injury.

In the anthropological view of language, to understand a word is seen as akin to an *ability* (thus, not a state).[8] Understanding a word is the ability to grasp the meaning of that word, including *being able to* follow the (often implicit) socially based rules for its use. As is true for other abilities, there are criteria for word understanding: first, to know the correct use of a word; second, to be able to give a correct explanation of the word's meaning in its specific context; and third, to respond in an appropriate way to somebody else's use of the word (Hacker, 2001). The words "correct" and "appropriate" in the previous sentences point to the *normativity* of language – the recognition that, in speaking a language, speakers follow certain constitutive *rules* that are shared among the members of their language community. These rules are seen as akin to the rules that one follows in a game: they are *guides* to people's language conduct. But they are not unbreakable laws. The rules are also *warrants* for one's chosen conduct, and they are *standards* for judging the correctness of one's conduct. Like the rules of a game, these rules are known to the speakers in a speech community, which is, of course, necessary if they are to function as standards (Hacker, 2013).

Words are often used to denote *concepts*, and in the anthropological view of language, what we have said earlier here about words and word use has parallels for concepts and concept use. Concepts are seen as human cultural creations that an individual learns while learning how to use the words that, in their language community, express particular concepts. This learning is what it means to master a concept. As an analogy, we can

---

[8] See also Chater, McCauley, & Christiansen (2016) and Christiansen & Chater (2022) for more about the view of language use as a skill in line with other human skills.

think about instruments or tools made by humans: Acquiring and mastering a concept can be seen as comparable to learning and mastering the use of an instrument or tool.[9]

To fully possess a concept requires that one is able to correctly use a word or phrase that expresses the concept and that one can respond correctly to somebody else's use of the concept. Furthermore, it requires one to be able to explain what one means when using the concept. These features – word usage, responses to others' word usage, and explanations of words – can be deployed in correct or incorrect ways; they therefore need to be learned. There are always cultural *norms* for correct concept use, norms that are developed and upheld in each language community (Bennett & Hacker, 2022). Moreover, because concepts are cultural creations, they can change.

Thinking Styles in Language Studies

In the section on debates about the origins of human language, we pointed to two distinctly different views of what language *is* and, therefore, also what it *does*: the biolinguistic tradition and the usage-based tradition. Beyond the shared insights that human language requires a human brain and that learning a language is easier for children than for adults, these views are based on very different ideas. These ideas form some of the *active assumptions* of two different thinking styles.

The biolinguistic thinking style is built on two assumptions. One is that language production is almost wholly dependent on brain structures and the inborn rules residing in these structures. The second is the assumption of *universalism*: that these structures and rules are nearly identical in all humans (Faulconer & Williams, 1985, p. 1179). Further, the biolinguistic thinking style carries an assumption of *internalism* about language functioning. The internalist assumption leads to seeing that which occurs within the physical boundaries of an individual as fundamentally determinative of the mental states (including the language production) of the individual. There is little need to refer to much, or anything, outside the individual. This view is akin to the cognitivist-internalist view of thinking that we described in Chapter 6. *Nativism* about language is another assumption at the basis of the biolinguistic style. From a nativist perspective, language acquisition is seen as maturational, that is, as a biological process driven by specialized inborn

---

[9] For more on discussions about concept use in psychology, see Chapter 11.

cognitive machinery (Wilson, 2004). Coupled to these assumptions about that which is being studied (language) is an ambition to restrict research to the methods and explanatory tools of natural science, and eventually to integrate language studies with the natural sciences (Chomsky, 2000).

The usage-based thinking style is built on the assumption that language evolution originated in, developed from, and served the general communicative needs of early human communities. A shared assumption in the usage-based tradition is, therefore, the *contextualism* of language, both as it evolved over evolutionary time and as it is learned by individuals today (Levinson, 2023; Levinson & Evans, 2010). This means that researchers in the usage-based tradition take exception to the assumption of universalism. Instead, in line with the assumption of contextualism, they highlight the immense variety of human languages and the differences between them. The view of language as having social and cultural origins implies an *anti-nativist* assumption (Enfield, 2022; Holler & Levinson, 2019). Several linguists (if not all) who work within a usage-based thinking style argue for an *ability assumption*: that knowledge of language should be seen as a kind of "knowing how," an ability akin to the many kinds of procedural *skills* that humans acquire and wield in their daily lives (Chater, McCauley, & Christiansen, 2016; Christiansen & Chater, 2018, 2022). This view signals what we may provisionally call a *generalist* assumption. It suggests, first, that language comprehension and language production are the same skill; and second, that both can be understood and studied in ways that have been found valid and useful for other human skills. A usage-based thinking style, therefore, assumes the centrality of the social settings in which language is acquired, and of the social and communicative needs that language use serves.

Psychological Approaches to People's Talk

It makes sense that psychologists should be interested in studying people's talk. After all, it is probably most often in their talk that people express their psychological concerns and their experiences. And, if one can believe the emerging theories about the evolution of language that we mentioned earlier, there is also reason to believe that people's talk and social actions have always been shaped by their interactions with others, thereby, by default, becoming intelligible to those others. In this view, because language and other cultural practices originally evolved in interactions between humans, it is inbuilt in the nature of talk and other cultural practices that they are intelligible and learnable by people in the same community (Edwards, 2012).

As we have already noted in this chapter, talk can be studied in several ways, from several perspectives, and with several different purposes. In psychological research, some ways have hitherto been more common than others. Because of the predominance of experimental and psychometric methods in psychology, the study of people's "free" and "unbounded" talk has hitherto not been very common in psychological research. However, psychologists who are interested in the study of culturally situated persons are also interested in studying people's unbounded talk in everyday settings. Over recent decades, this interest has led many psychologists, often in collaboration with researchers in other disciplines, to develop methods and theories that enable such study. These approaches are often summarized by umbrella terms such as interpretative research or qualitative methods (Magnusson & Marecek, 2015; Ritchie et al., 2014).

Here, we point to some ideas that can form a useful basis for the psychological study of talk. These ideas have their roots in fields such as linguistic anthropology, psycholinguistics, conversation analysis, and discursive psychology. They share basic assumptions with the usage-based thinking style that we sketched before. Thinking in usage-based terms invites a close study of communicative events and the contextualized cognitive processes that make up such events (Enfield, 2022). It also involves an interest in how people use talk to get things done or make things happen – that is, how talk typically is *action*.

Much inspiration for these studies comes from Herbert Clark, whose work we briefly described earlier in this chapter. Especially important parts are Clark's emphasis on language use as *joint activity* and on the social necessity for speakers to *coordinate* their actions in order to uphold or create *common ground*.

Inspiration also comes from the originators of conversation analysis, the US sociologists Emanuel Schegloff and Harvey Sacks, and the US sociolinguist Gail Jefferson. They formed a tradition of detailed study, for instance, of the micro-processes of *conversational turns*. Inspiration has also come from discursive psychologists in the UK, such as Derek Edwards, Margaret Wetherell, Nigel Edley, Jonathan Potter, and Michael Billig (see esp. Wetherell, Taylor, & Yates, 2001). They have contributed a focus on the *social accountability dimensions* of talk; that is, the fact that no neutral positions are available for speakers in conversations. These psychologists' ideas thereby also offer an entry point for studying the *wider socio-cultural dimensions* and normative bases of talk. Such contributions are, as we see it, particularly important for psychologists interested in socially and culturally situated persons.

Here are some glimpses of what psychological approaches to talk, based on the above inspirations, might focus on: What people say in a conversation is nearly always *oriented* toward achieving some specific action (such as informing, questioning, congratulating, and so on). And because situations vary greatly, a person's aim to achieve a particular talk-action may require different utterances and strategies in different conversational settings. People are typically quite adept at taking such situational differences into account and adjusting what they say to the particulars of each occasion. This ubiquitous adjustment of speech to situational specifics, expectations, and norms has been labeled the *indexicality of talk* (Clark, 1996; Edwards, 1991, 2006). Discursive psychologists argue that *"[t]here is therefore no point, for example, in picking quotations out of context and presenting them as what somebody thinks. Analysis of discourse has to respect the indexical, interaction-oriented, action-performing nature of its phenomena"* (Edwards, 2006, p. 47). People's actions – talk as well as all other kinds of action – have to be interpreted with reference to where and when they occur, and to the local situational context as well as the wider cultural context.

Discussions can exemplify the indexicality of talk. To understand the meaning of a speaker's words in a discussion, one needs to consider not just the position that the speaker is arguing for, but also and especially the positions that the speaker is arguing against. These positions form the *argumentative* context (Billig, 1996). If one disregards the argumentative context, some of the meanings of the words used – their argumentative meaning, or the argumentative work that they are meant to do – will be lost.

Sometimes a speaker's utterances in a discussion will implicitly take into account and argue against an unuttered argument that the speaker expects another speaker to propose. By doing this, the first speaker may be able to nullify the power of the unuttered argument and perhaps prevent it from ever being uttered. Michael Billig has labeled this forestalling ability *witcraft*: an ability that *"involves reasons being framed cunningly to answer, and thereby contradict, other reasons"* (Billig, 1996, p. 115). For a researcher to note down instances of "witcraft," for instance in an interview, is one possible way to identify controversial issues that may be worthy of closer study. The issues may be anything from large social questions about which there is controversy in society, to events in the immediate social context of the discussion that provoke a speaker to engage in witcraft. The appearance of such defensive rhetorical strategies in a speaker's talk may signal that the speaker worries that their own *social accountability* is in jeopardy. We therefore now turn to accountability.

To every conversation or discussion, people bring their notions of, and ambitions for, their own and others' social accountability within (and often beyond) the particular setting. This awareness has been labeled the *tyranny of accountability* in human affairs: " ... *an ever-present possibility of being noticed, praised, blamed, questioned, called out, and judged. We act knowing that our actions will be observed and, to a significant extent, knowing how they will be regarded*" (Enfield & Sidnell, 2017, p. 21). Thus, speakers entering a conversation are aware that they will be held accountable for the appropriateness of their contributions to the conversation. Being found out as providing an inappropriate contribution, and thereby breaking a norm or appearing ignorant, will place a speaker in a *troubled* conversational position. Most speakers are wary of the risk of finding themselves in such troubled positions and therefore engage in some kind of *accountability management* (Edley, 2001). Accountability management denotes speakers' handling of their part in a conversation such that they are able to maintain an untroubled position or manage to navigate out of a troubled position. This maneuvering may sometimes also involve an attempt to move somebody else – present or absent – into a troubled position. The details of accountability management in everyday conversations have been an important focus of study for discursive psychologists and linguists (Horton-Salway, 2001; Wetherell, 2012).

We stop here, hoping that this short exposition of a few of the many ideas for the psychological study of language use in context has given some sense of its possibilities.

CHAPTER 8

Social and Historical Perspectives on Psychological Suffering

In this chapter, we explore issues concerning mental distress and dysfunction and the care for those suffering from such difficulties. The chapter focuses on Western high-income countries, which are the areas of the world in which the "psy" professions have flourished and have had a strong sociocultural influence. We describe successive efforts to devise a satisfactory framework for categorizing disorders. The chapter also offers a very brief history of Western ideas about the causes of mental disorders and their treatment. We also call attention to the influence of the sociopolitical and sociocultural surround on the ways in which persons with mental disorders are supported and cared for. Much of the chapter draws on studies of the US, an area of the world in which the fields of psychiatry and psychology are widely viewed as offering help for a wide variety of problems in living.[1]

Many words that originated in the psychiatric lexicon have become part of the everyday vocabulary of emotional distress and psychological dysfunction used by English speakers. That is, terms such as "traumatized," "hysterical," "neurodivergent," "enmeshed," "co-dependent," "OCD," and "on the spectrum" have jumped from the technical vocabulary of mental health providers into everyday conversations. In the latter, they convey a jumble of meanings. We discuss some of the ramifications of such migrations in Chapter 10, about psychology's history. Moreover, advocacy groups have often coined pseudo-diagnoses that resemble *bona fide* psychiatric diagnoses to bolster their political agendas. Some examples are "post-abortion trauma syndrome," "ROGD" (rapid onset gender dysphoria),

---

[1] As we will note in more detail at the end of the chapter, different vocabularies for talking about psychological suffering direct thinking about such suffering into different channels. The dominant vocabulary today is based on biomedical thinking, and many critics have expressed serious reservations about this vocabulary and its biomedical basis. However, we found, when writing this chapter, that we had to use this vocabulary in order to write our condensed history of psychiatric diagnosis. There are at present no other vocabularies available in the institutional settings of modern psychiatry.

"male delusional dominating disorder," "narcissistic abuse trauma," "internet addiction," "media use disorder," and "climate anxiety." (As of this writing, none of these pseudo-diagnoses appear in the official nosology of mental disorders.) As the forms of suffering for which people seek psychological care multiply, cultural ideas about what constitutes suffering shift. Moreover, ideas about what constitutes the good life and the conditions required for wellbeing shift as well.

In tandem with the upsurge of descriptions of distress (and perhaps an upsurge of actual experiences of distress as well), the mental health industry has burgeoned in many parts of the developed world. In the US, for example, the traditional complement of helpers – psychiatrists, clinical psychologists, clinical social workers, and psychiatric nurse practitioners – has been increased by large numbers of life coaches, counselors, faith-based counselors, and therapists who claim expertise in various somatic therapies. While the training requirements, certification, and licensure of psychiatrists, clinical psychologists, and clinical social workers are closely regulated, other helpers may have little or no formal training regarding diagnosis and treatment. There is wide variation among such practitioners in their beliefs, theoretical orientations, and practices.

In many parts of the world, the venues where mental health care can be obtained have shifted dramatically in the past decade. The internet offers a prime example: Numerous websites now purport to assess a user's mental health via brief self-administered checklists of symptoms. The website may render a diagnosis and then prescribe and sell psychotropic medications online. There are also many websites that offer to connect users to a therapist of their choice at any time of the day or night.

Moreover, many clinical practitioners shifted to conducting therapy online or via telephone during the Covid19 pandemic and the ensuing lockdown. Modes of therapy included video appointments, voice calls, and conversations on messaging platforms. Though the pandemic lockdown is no longer in effect, telehealth, as it is often called, seems to be an enduring legacy of the Covid19 pandemic, at least in the US. Moreover, there is high interest today in the use of artificial intelligence technology for mental health care. Some mental health professionals make use of chatbots for the initial screening of potential patients and for generating case notes. Some use such apps to administer Cognitive Behavioral Therapy exercises, guided meditation, or relaxation procedures. All told, the venues for receiving mental health care have expanded dramatically, at least in Western high-income countries.

At the same time, psychiatric medications have also become widely available. In the US, these medications can be prescribed by general medical practitioners as well as psychiatrists; there are lobbying efforts to change legal statutes to grant doctoral-level psychologists prescribing authority as well. Moreover, in some countries, certain psychiatric medications can be purchased at pharmacies without any prescription at all. In the US, one person in four receives at least one prescription for psychiatric medication in any given year. This includes anti-depressant drugs and anti-anxiety drugs. In addition, significant numbers of children (primarily boys) receive medication that is intended to treat attention deficit hyperactivity disorder (ADHD). It should be noted that often these medications are prescribed without a formal assessment of the patient's psychiatric status by a qualified practitioner.

In what follows, we examine a piece of the history of mental health care. We first consider the history and status of modern diagnoses of psychological disorders. We focus on the successive revisions of the *Diagnostic and Statistical Manual of Mental Disorders* (hereinafter DSM), published by the American Psychiatric Association and used throughout the US and in many other Western high-income countries. Then we turn to a brief overview of efforts to alleviate psychological suffering – efforts that the social historian Andrew Scull (2022) has labeled "desperate remedies." In the final section, we briefly consider emerging social movements led primarily by persons who are the users of mental health services, in particular patients and their families. (We note that in the US, those who make use of mental health services may refer to themselves as "consumers" or "service users," terms chosen to avoid the stigmatizing connotations of "mental patient.")

Diagnosing Psychological Suffering

Here we consider scholarly and professional knowledge regarding psychological suffering. We first take up some issues regarding diagnoses, that is, the formal systems of categories for codifying psychological suffering. We focus on the *Diagnostic and Statistical Manual of Mental Disorders* (DSM), the first edition of which appeared in 1952. The successive editions of the DSM have provided the lexicon by which professionals convey information to one another about patient care. The DSM has also served to define which kinds of suffering are recognized as treatment-worthy. Its categories may also convey implicit moral values, as, for example, labeling "alcohol misuse disorder" as a mental disorder rather than a moral failing. As in biomedicine, the totality of diagnoses serves as a conceptual framework for synthesizing professional knowledge. Also, as in biomedicine, the different versions of the conceptual framework in recent history have been held together by powerful thought collectives, united by their central thinking style (Binney, 2016a).[2] In what follows, we briefly trace the successive revisions of the DSM since its first edition was published in 1952.

DSM-I

The DSM-I (1952) was designed as a compendium of common psychiatric disorders. Its content was heavily influenced by psychoanalytic theories, and much of it was couched in the language of psychoanalysis. This is not surprising. At the time the DSM-I was compiled, psychoanalysis was the dominant theoretical orientation of mental health professionals, especially psychiatrists, in the US and in much of Europe. The DSM-I offered only brief descriptions of the symptoms of psychiatric disorders. These descriptions were drawn from clinicians' experience, not from systematic empirical research. The authors of the DSM-I did not attempt to compile a glossary of standardized terms to assist readers. In total, the DSM-I contained about 60 diagnostic categories. It was just over 100 pages long – roughly one-fifth the length of the current edition of the DSM, the DSM-5.

Many of the diagnostic categories in the manual were not sufficiently detailed to enable practitioners to make consistent diagnoses of a patient over time, nor for different practitioners to make the same diagnosis of a particular patient. The technical term for such consistency is reliability. Reliability refers to the extent to which the diagnostic criteria are sufficient to enable diagnosticians who make use of those criteria to make the same diagnosis. To be useful, a category system must have high reliability. That is, two diagnosticians who apply the diagnostic criteria ought to arrive at the same diagnosis of a patient. Further, use of the diagnostic criteria should yield the same diagnosis for a patient at two points in time. As we will see, despite continual efforts to improve the reliability of the DSM categories, the goal of adequate reliability has remained elusive.

DSM-II

The second edition of the DSM (1968) was also criticized for its reliance on psychoanalytic concepts and psychoanalytic language. The lack of reliability

---

[2] The expression "thinking style" should not be confused with the use in psychiatry of the expression "thought style" to denote certain ways of thinking connected to a particular diagnosis (such as a "ruminating thought style" in people suffering from depression).

in diagnostic judgments also remained a serious problem. Like the DSM-I, DSM-II was relatively brief – slightly more than 130 pages long.

DSM-III

Published in 1980, the DSM-III was the culmination of six years of intensive effort by a work group of US psychiatrists. The intense revision process was sparked by a looming crisis for the psychiatric profession, as we will describe later. The DSM-III marked a sharp break from the two previous editions of the DSM. Indeed, the DSM-III transformed the knowledge base of US psychiatry. It put forward several novel foundational principles of mental health care in the US. It also set in motion broad changes in the social relations of clinical practitioners, notably the "dethroning" of psychoanalytically oriented practitioners.

The impetus for re-imagining mental disorders was specific to the US health care system. It was based in an acute crisis of legitimacy for psychiatrists in the US. With the rise of corporatized medicine and large healthcare systems, it became imperative for psychiatry to re-define itself as a branch of medicine (Wilson, 1993). Otherwise, psychiatrists would be cut out of insurance reimbursement systems. Among other changes, a top-to-bottom makeover of the DSM was required, a process that was spearheaded by the psychiatrist Robert Spitzer.

The changes initiated in the DSM-III drastically altered both the content of psychiatric diagnoses and the decision-making process involved in diagnosing a patient. The new manual (the DSM-III) was 494 pages long, nearly five times longer than the DSM-I, and it contained much more substantive information, including information drawn from empirical research. It also included more than 80 additional diagnostic categories. In most instances, these were not newly discovered disorders. Rather, the manual drew distinctions within previous categories and suggested different approaches to treatment. For each of the diagnostic categories, a set of symptom criteria was given. The use of these symptom criteria improved diagnostic reliability considerably, although diagnostic judgments remained considerably less reliable than those of biomedicine.

The editors of the DSM-III described the manual as "atheoretical." That is, the manual put aside theoretical explanations of mental disorders, such as those that drew on psychoanalytic theories. Instead, it focused on describing and classifying observable symptoms. These descriptions were modeled on those in use in mainstream Western biomedicine, and they also drew on the language of biomedicine. In that way, the DSM-III served the goal of inserting psychiatry into the overarching framework of biomedicine. In fact, the DSM-III is often said to have "re-medicalized" psychiatry – a feature that has been criticized as reductive and shortsighted by some practitioners and theorists. In any case, the description of the DSM-III as "atheoretical" is shortsighted. The DSM-III may indeed have focused on the description and classification of symptoms and eschewed explanation, but the choice of what was important to describe and classify was not "atheoretical."

The "medicalization" of psychiatry has remained in place from 1980 to the present. It has served to re-shape both clinical care and research priorities. Reliance on metaphors drawn from biomedicine to speak about psychological suffering has contributed to a decisive shift toward biologically oriented psychiatric research. The thought collectives of psychiatric professionals in many Western countries came to presume that biological factors (e.g., faulty genetic inheritance, neurophysiological malfunctions, or a brain disorder) are responsible for psychological disorders. Drawing on Ludwik Fleck's terminology, one would say that this presumption indicates the dominance of a *biomedical* thinking style in these collectives.

DSM-IV

The DSM-IV was published in 1994. This revision included some efforts by the American Psychiatric Association and the World Health Organization (WHO) to "harmonize" the DSM-IV and the forthcoming revision of the WHO's International Statistical Classification of Diseases and Related Health Problems (ICD-10). This goal of "harmonization" was an indication of the growing use of the DSM's categorization system outside the US, as well as the increasing impact of US-based theory and research beyond the US.

The DSM-IV introduced several revisions. These included a substantive addition to the process of clinical diagnosis. Rather than limiting the outcome of a clinical assessment to deciding on one (or several) clinical diagnoses, the DSM-IV instructed practitioners to complete what was called a "multi-axial" diagnosis. The intention was to prompt a fuller and more holistic view of the patient and thereby deepen the diagnostician's understanding of the person beyond a simple one-size-fits-all categorical judgment. Multi-axial diagnoses directed the clinician's attention to social, personal, cultural, and environmental factors that contributed to the person's difficulties. The multi-axial scheme included five "axes": Axis I: clinical disorders; Axis II: personality disorders and mental retardation; Axis III: general medical conditions; Axis IV: psychosocial and environmental problems; and Axis V: an assessment of overall functioning. In essence, the "multi-axial" assessment had the goal of broadening and deepening clinicians' attention beyond the assessment of psychiatric symptoms to the whole person and the relational, social, and cultural surround in which they were embedded.

Unfortunately, this effort to deepen and widen clinicians' attention to whole persons was a failure. It turned out that diagnosticians simply skipped the multi-axial assessment. Some claimed that they worked under too much time pressure to undertake it. Others said that they lacked the cultural competence required to complete it. Therefore, the multi-axial assessment was dropped from subsequent DSM revisions. In our view, this was a missed opportunity to improve clinical care. There is every reason to believe that focusing attention on situated persons rather than on symptoms would have led to improved care and better outcomes (Probst, 2014).

DSM-5

The DSM-5 was published in 2013. The revision process took some 14 years, and it engaged a much wider range of experts – including not only psychiatrists, but also psychologists and neurologists – than previous versions had. The DSM-5 introduced several substantial changes. For example, categories of disorder were reorganized into a new framework that drew on emerging theories about a shared etiology of some disorders. The DSM-5 also made use of the term "spectrum" to underscore that many mental disorders can be ordered along continua of varying degrees of severity and varying levels of impact on patients' lives. Autism, for example, was renamed autism spectrum disorder, and autistic people are now sometimes assessed as having one of three "levels" of disability. As another example, schizophrenia was renamed schizophrenia spectrum disorder.

Certain revisions in the DSM-5 generated strenuous objections within the professional community. Some of these disagreements also spilled into the popular press, especially in the US. One controversial revision involved changing the criteria for several diagnoses in ways that lowered the threshold for diagnosing a person as having that disorder. Such changes, of course, would greatly increase the number of people who would receive a diagnosis and be referred for treatment. Allen Frances, the US psychiatrist who had chaired the task force that produced the DSM-IV, criticized such revisions, which he termed a "hyperinflation" of diagnoses. In his book *Saving Normal* (2013), Frances expressed several concerns about this hyperinflation. One was that the hyperinflation of diagnoses led to what seemed to be "epidemics" of childhood disorders such as ADHD, autism, and childhood bipolar disorder. Moreover, he worried that the revisions ran the risk of diagnosing quirks and eccentricities as mental disorders. Moreover, hyperinflation of certain diagnoses would contribute to the over-prescribing of psychiatric medications. Frances's concerns seem to have some merit. For example, data gathered in 2022 revealed that some 15 percent of boys in the US had been diagnosed as having ADHD; many of them had been prescribed long-term psychiatric medication (Danielson et al., 2024).

The DSM-5 also introduced some controversial new psychiatric diagnoses. One example is Prolonged Grief Disorder, defined as profound grieving for more than 6 to 12 months following a death of a significant other. This contrasted with previous editions of DSM, which had included a "Bereavement Exclusion." The Bereavement Exclusion cautioned against diagnosing a person as clinically depressed if that person had recently experienced the death of a loved one. The developers of the DSM-5 proposed not only to eliminate the Bereavement Exclusion but also to add a new diagnosis, Prolonged Grief Disorder. Opponents of this new diagnostic category objected to imposing a uniform time frame that would distinguish "normal" grieving from mental disorder. They pointed out that a wide range of circumstances may surround a death and shape the experience of loss. Moreover, as cultural psychologists noted, expectations, forms of grieving, and ritualized practices of bereavement vary considerably across social groups and different cultures. Attempts to define a uniform standard of bereavement ignore these cultural differences. Prolonged Grief Disorder was not included in the main body of the DSM-5 when it was published in 2013. However, as you read in Chapter 3, it was included in the revised version of DSM-5 that was released in 2022.

Diagnoses in the Practice of Mental Health Care

The initial aim of the DSM-I was to provide a common vocabulary that would enable mental health workers to communicate with one another about their patients. This remains an important goal, but today, the DSM serves a broader range of functions as well. An up-to-date copy of the DSM is nearly indispensable in the day-to-day work of mental health practitioners in many Western high-income countries. Practitioners rely on the terms set out in the DSM to conceptualize their clinical work, to communicate with colleagues, patients, and family members, and to provide the proper language and billing codes required by payment systems such as insurance companies and government agencies.

In the US, DSM diagnoses also serve many functions in many arenas beyond the treatment of individuals who have been diagnosed with psychological disorders (Rogler, 1997). For example, psychiatric diagnoses may figure in legal deliberations regarding divorce and child custody, child abuse and incest, as well as criminal culpability. Moreover, whether in medical training for physicians, training programs for mental health practitioners, or entry-level courses in psychopathology for college students, textbooks are usually organized around the DSM's medicalized category system. Furthermore, the language used in the texts is largely that of biomedicine.

From 1980 onward, subsequent revisions of the DSM have retained the medicalized frame of reference that was instituted in the DSM-III. However, objections to many aspects of psychiatric diagnoses have mounted among practitioners, researchers, and theorists. For example, Steven Hyman (2010), a former director of the US National Institute of Mental Health, dubbed the DSM diagnostic system an "epistemic prison." As the work of producing the fifth edition of the DSM got underway, critical appraisals of the DSM and of the psychiatric profession spilled out beyond professional journals and conferences onto the public stage. Acrimonious criticisms appeared in the news media and in several polemical books. The titles of a few of these books and essays (published in North America and the UK) indicate both the flavor and the ferocity of the criticisms: *The Book of Woe: The DSM and the Unmaking of Psychiatry* (Greenberg, 2013), *Cracked: Why Psychiatry Is Doing More Harm Than Good* (Davies, 2014); *Unhinged: The Trouble With Psychiatry – A Doctor's Revelations About a Profession in Crisis* (Carlat, 2010); *Drug Companies & Doctors: A Story of Corruption* (Angell, 2009); *The Illusions of Psychiatry* (Angell, 2011); *Psychiatry Under the Influence* (Whitaker & Cosgrove, 2015); *The Emperor's New Drugs: Exploding the Antidepressant Myth* (Kirsch, 2011); *Saving Normal: An Insider's Revolt against Out-of-Control Psychiatric Diagnosis, DSM-5, Big Pharma, and the of Ordinary Life* (Frances, 2013).

Mental health professionals in some other Western countries also expressed strong concerns over the DSM and the forthcoming revised edition. For instance, as deliberations and field-testing for the DSM-5 were underway in the US, the leaders of the British Psychological Society (BPS) composed a lengthy document expressing strong objections to the foundational premises of psychiatric diagnoses (BPS, 2011). The BPS statement argued that consumers of mental health services, as well as the public at large, were negatively affected by the pathologization of natural and normal responses to difficult life experiences. Although such responses might be distressing, the BPS argued that they should not be regarded as psychiatric illnesses. Moreover, a larger concern was that the DSM-5 – like previous editions of the DSM – continued to locate the causes of personal distress wholly within the individual. This amounted to a version of what we have previously labeled *internalism* (see Chapter 6) – a thinking style that causes practitioners to overlook the relational context of much psychological distress, as well as the possible larger societal causation of such distress. The BPS also posted an open letter to the DSM-5 Task Force and the American Psychiatric Association as an online petition (www.ipeti tions.com/petition/dsm5/). The petition, which includes a lengthy rationale, remains online. As of this writing, it had been signed by roughly 15,650 individuals and endorsed by over 50 professional organizations, including several sections of the American Psychological Association.

As the scrutiny of psychiatry continued, critical attention was directed to the undue influence of pharmaceutical corporations on the psychiatric profession in the US and to corrupt practices by several prominent research psychiatrists. *The Emperor's New Drugs: Exploding the Antidepressant Myth* (2013), a book written by US psychologist Irving Kirsch, pointed out that certain pharmaceutical companies had greatly misrepresented the efficacy of antidepressant medications and suppressed the negative results of treatment outcome studies. Kirsch also refuted the claim, which had appeared frequently in advertising by pharmaceutical companies, that a "chemical imbalance" in the brain was the cause of mental disorders such as depression and anxiety. A few years later, Robert Whitaker and Lisa Cosgrove provided an in-depth account of US psychiatry's multiple financial relationships to the pharmaceutical industry. In *Psychiatry Under the Influence: Institutional Corruption, Social Injury, and Prescriptions for Reform* (2015), they detailed how the pharmaceutical industry sponsored conferences, special symposia, and continuing education events, all laced with misleading information about disorders and drug treatments designed to enhance corporate profits.

The extent of US psychiatrists' financial ties to the pharmaceutical industry cannot be overestimated. Indeed, when the editors tasked with revising the DSM-IV sought psychiatrists qualified to serve on several of the editorial work groups, it proved impossible to find a sufficient number of psychiatrists who did not have financial relationships with the industry. Moreover, several prominent US psychiatric researchers were formally charged with research misconduct and academic dishonesty (Scull, 2022; Whitaker & Cosgrove, 2015). Some had concealed negative results of studies on the efficacy of drugs. Others had accepted substantial sums of money to pose as the authors of fraudulent research manuscripts that had been produced by medical communications companies. Moreover, as Scull (2022) noted, the academic institutions that employed these researchers often let them off with little more than a slap on the wrist. Even after being found guilty of serious research misconduct, some researchers continued to move up the career ladder with impunity.

Whither Diagnoses?

The debates and controversies that erupted during the preparation of the DSM-5 also brought to light a consensus among expert psychiatric researchers that few of the categories of disorder contained in the DSM had scientific validity.[3] Furthermore, the discussions revealed a consensus that the causes of most mental disorders remained unknown, despite millions of dollars spent on scientific research. In the opinion of Steven Hyman (2021), a former director of the National Institute of Mental Health, the field's reliance on the DSM categorization system had impeded progress in research about psychiatric disorders. At its best, in Hyman's view, the DSM could provide clinical practitioners with a common language, so that practitioners who evaluated the same patient would arrive at the same diagnosis. (This, of course, is the standard of inter-rater reliability that had never been achieved by any prior edition of the DSM.) Similarly, Thomas Insel (writing in a widely quoted blog in 2013), who was then the director of the US National Institute of Mental Health, argued that the DSM should be thought of as a dictionary, but not as a scientific document. Echoing Hyman, he claimed that such a dictionary – if it were well done – would be useful in providing a lexicon to enable mental health professionals to communicate accurately with one another. Furthermore, a group of leading psychiatric researchers in the US voiced doubts that the existing DSM categories offered a useful basis for scientific investigations (Schatzberg et al., 2009). Acting on those critiques, the NIMH would no longer fund research projects that were designed around DSM diagnoses. Despite the array of criticisms voiced by highly respected psychiatric practitioners and researchers, the DSM-5 was released in spring of 2013 with considerable fanfare.

Since the publication of the DSM-5, some mental health researchers in the US, the UK, and elsewhere have devoted considerable effort to developing better alternatives for conceptualizing psychological distress and dysfunction. One example is the Research Domain Criteria (RDoC) project, which was initiated by researchers in the US NIMH in 2009. The goal of the project was to develop a framework for research on

---

[3] The expression "scientific validity" is used, for instance, to denote how well a study can rule out alternative explanations for its findings.

psychiatric conditions that did not make use of symptom-based diagnostic categories. The developers of the RDoC proposed to devise a category system based on dimensions that were simultaneously defined by observable behaviors (using quantitative measures of cognition and emotion) and neurobiological measures (Cuthbert, 2020). Unfortunately, although 16 years have now passed since work on the RDoC commenced, it has not yielded a diagnostic system that has been taken into use.

Another effort to reconceptualize psychiatric diagnoses is the Hierarchical Taxonomy of Psychopathology (HiTOP). The development of the HiTOP has been the project of a large international consortium of researchers, which includes a strong representation of psychologists with expertise in quantitative data analysis (Hagerty, 2023). The HiTOP project, which is still a work in progress, makes use of large data sets to assess patterns of covariation among measures of disordered behavior and maladaptive traits. The first step is to develop and refine a set of dimensional constructs, as well as corresponding treatment targets.

A third project, based in the UK, aims to reconceptualize psychological suffering in ways that differ sharply from typical psychiatric diagnoses. Project members seek to make personal meanings and lived experiences central to diagnoses of psychological suffering. This would, of course, involve dramatic departures from the dominant biomedical ways of conceiving of emotional distress, unusual ways of thinking, and troubled or troubling behavior. The project members are both experienced clinical psychologists and activists with lived experience of psychological distress (Cromby, 2022; Cromby, Harper, & Reavy, 2013; Harper & Cromby, 2022). Their alternative approach to diagnosis is called the Power Threat Meaning Framework (PTMF). The group sought an alternative to conventional psychiatric diagnoses that would avoid explanations of mental disorders in terms of hypothetical biological deficits, as well as the medicalization of treatment. The PTMF features a contextual understanding of psychological distress. That is, it presumes that psychological distress and dysfunction are bound up with difficulties in the person's life situation and social and relational context. Advocates of the PTMF often sum up the Power Threat Meaning Framework by noting that it does not ask "What is wrong with you?" but rather asks "What has happened to you?"

The PTMF offers a perspective on psychological distress that embeds distress in the context of a person's experiences, relationships, material resources, and personal values. In that way, it departs radically from the DSM diagnoses, which are set within a medicalized frame of reference, and typically focus attention on the person set apart from the context. In doing so, DSM diagnoses imply that the causes of psychological difficulties are "inside" a person, in line with what we earlier termed biomedical internalism. The PTMF, by contrast, opens the way to considering how oppressive or abusive relationships, societal inequities, and oppressive belief systems might contribute to distress or difficulties in functioning. This approach to psychodiagnosis is compatible with the view of persons as culturally and socially situated that this book has presented.

Cultural Variations in Disorders and Diagnoses

Important though it is to challenge the "epistemic prison" of the biomedically oriented thinking, there are further limitations of DSM or other biomedical-style diagnoses that also deserve critical attention. For example, anthropologists and cultural psychologists have long noted that the DSM has had little to say about cultural differences in the expression of psychological distress (which Nichter, 1981, has usefully called "idioms of distress"). For example, there is strong and consistent evidence that schizophrenia typically has a more benign course in India than in most Western societies. Even though access to treatment is often quite limited in the Indian context, the duration of acute episodes of schizophrenia in India often is shorter, and fewer relapses occur (Hopper et al., 2007).

Moreover, expressions of dysfunction may take different forms in different cultural settings. For example, in the US, auditory hallucinations (typically, hearing voices) are regarded as a paradigmatic symptom of schizophrenia. In the US, the content of such hallucinated voices is usually disturbing, negative, or threatening. In India, by contrast, the content of hallucinated voices may be benign or even playful (Luhrmann et al., 2015). In some parts of the world, psychological distress may be expressed as a range of physical symptoms such as pain, fatigue, nausea, or a burning sensation in the soles of one's feet. At the urging of culturally attuned clinicians, the editors of recent revisions of the DSM have made some efforts to amend its Western-centric focus. However, much work remains to be done.

Diagnosis Talk in Perspective

In high-income Western societies, the vocabulary of diagnoses and distress is now part of everyday discourse. People in these societies rely on this vocabulary to make meaning of others' actions as well as their own. They may speak, for example, of being "triggered," "traumatized," "stressed out," "spaced out," and so on. They may label certain individuals as "psychopaths" or "narcissists." Moreover, when people seek psychological treatment for themselves or their family members, they may have already embraced a self-ascribed psychiatric diagnosis. For example, currently, many US teenagers declare themselves to be "on the spectrum" (a reference to Autism Spectrum Disorder). Others may describe themselves as being "triggered" (a reference to a key symptom of Post Traumatic Stress Disorder) by certain situations or experiences (Bonilla, Lamb, & Anantharam, 2025). Such mundane uses of diagnostic labels and their relational and societal consequences are a prominent part of contemporary meaning-making in some social groups.

As you read before, many experts have emphatically pointed out that the DSM is not a scientific inventory of mental disorders, nor does it provide a coherent conceptual framework. With the addition of a hodgepodge of new diagnoses over the years, the DSM has become a patchwork of heterogeneous categories. In some cases, the inclusion of a new diagnosis or the modification of an existing one was the result of political bargaining among the members of the DSM's editorial board. In other cases, categories of disorders were included or excluded in response to shifts in cultural values. In 1974, for example, following a lengthy period of activism by gay men, lesbian women, and their "straight" allies, the American Psychiatric Association's board of trustees agreed to conduct a referendum of its members regarding the question of whether to eliminate homosexuality as a category of mental disorder in the DSM (Drescher, 2015). The issue was a contentious one; 58 percent of those who voted supported the recommendation of "de-classifying" homosexuality. In more recent years, some other proposals for new or revised diagnostic categories have sparked controversy. These include female sexual dysfunction, masochistic personality disorder, paraphilic rapism, and gender identity disorder.

Though the current approaches for categorizing psychological distress and dysfunction may leave much to be desired, could we do without such categories? Are there important functions that such categories accomplish? Most people can expect that at some point in their lives, they will encounter situations that lead to anxiety, sadness, demoralization, or deep confusion. Reliable information about the signs, symptoms, and likely persistence of such difficulties would help them make decisions about whether such situations require professional care. Diagnostic categories also provide a shared language that may enable sufferers to seek and obtain appropriate care. Moreover, informal care – such as support, compassion, understanding, and perhaps a respite from normal obligations – may be more available when a person can make a claim to a socially intelligible form of distress. Many years ago, the US sociologist Talcott Parsons coined the term "sick role" to call attention to the socially agreed rights and duties that a society accords to a person who is deemed to be "sick" (Parsons, 1951). The rights include a release from many of one's usual duties and obligations. Obligations of the "sick role" include following medical advice for getting better.

Diagnosis Talk in Popular Discourse: Naming and Norming
In the US, references to psychiatric diagnoses pepper everyday conversations, social media, and political discourse. Such talk may involve negative judgment about another's behavior and perhaps an implicit or explicit moral judgment, as when someone is labeled a "narcissist" or a "psychopath" or a "hysteric." Such talk may contribute to the "hyperinflation" of diagnoses that worried Allen Frances, whom we mentioned earlier. Social media also play an important role in promulgating diagnosis talk. A quick scan of the internet yielded several examples: Compulsive Buying Addiction, Post-Abortion Trauma Syndrome, Narcissistic Abuse Trauma, Fawning Syndrome, Imposter Syndrome, and Internet Gaming Disorder. (None of these diagnoses have yet appeared in any version of the DSM, and none are under active consideration.) Speculations run rife about possible psychiatric diagnoses of celebrities, politicians, and other public figures.

Another common type of "diagnosis talk" involves unsubstantiated and often exaggerated claims in pop psych and self-help materials concerning the incidence or prevalence of mental disorders. For example, a brochure distributed to school counselors falsely claimed that "one in every five" school students in the US suffers from ADHD or a learning disability. Also, a recent article in the *Networker* (a popular magazine read by some 55,000 mental health workers mainly in the US) claimed that "one in four" adolescent girls suffers from Major Depression, and that 50 percent of these girls are "suicidal." No research citation for this claim was made, nor was any description of the evidence given. Whatever intentions the authors may have had, exaggerating the incidence or prevalence of psychological disorders runs the risk of turning everyday difficulties or problems in living into diseases, akin to what Moynihan, Heath, and Henry (2002) termed "disease-mongering."

Relief for Psychological Suffering: Caring for Those with Mental Disorders

The historical record of mental health care depicts a dismaying array of failed and sometimes brutal attempts to alleviate severe mental disorders. Early attempts included exorcism, fasting and prayer, applying leeches to induce bleeding, purging, ice baths, physical restraints such as strait jackets, and surgical removal of various parts of the body.

In many Western countries, from the 1920s until the late 1960s, various kinds of "shock therapy" were used to treat patients with severe mental disorders. The medical rationale is unclear, but it seemed to be the idea that a shock to the body, often one that led to a coma, might somehow jolt patients out of their condition. Metrazol shock therapy, which was used in the 1930s and 1940s, involved an injection of Metrazol, a convulsant that could produce *grand mal* seizures and a coma. Insulin coma therapy was used from the late 1920s until the late 1960s to treat patients diagnosed with schizophrenia. Patients who received insulin coma therapy would be injected with insulin sufficient to induce a hypoglycemic coma nearly every day for some weeks. Evidence of the effectiveness of insulin coma therapy was limited, and the risk of cardiac and pulmonary complications was substantial. Nonetheless, insulin coma therapy continued to be used until other treatments (notably, neuroleptic drugs) became available.

Electroconvulsive therapy (ECT or electro-shock therapy) involves inducing a seizure in the brain by administering very brief, controlled electric current to a patient who is under anesthesia. It was first used in 1938 as a treatment for schizophrenia by two psychiatrists in Italy who had observed that shocks to the brain induced seizures in laboratory animals. Today, ECT is seldom used to treat schizophrenia. However, it is often an effective means of providing temporary relief from depression or mania. A course of ECT usually involves a series of shock treatments over three or four weeks. Some patients undergo repeated series of treatments over the course of their lives. Some patients report some problems with their long-term memory after multiple shock treatments. Despite its long history as a psychiatric treatment, the mechanism of action of ECT is not understood.

A lobotomy (or leucotomy) is a surgical procedure that severs connections in the brain's prefrontal cortex. First performed in 1935, the procedure was initially proclaimed to be highly successful in treating mental disorders. Tens of thousands of lobotomies were performed in Europe and the US during the mid-1900s. Indeed, in 1949, its originator, Antonio Egas

Moniz, a Portuguese neurologist, was awarded a Nobel Prize for his invention. Eventually, however, the surgery was shown to cause devastating damage to the brain, leaving patients with greatly reduced self-awareness and severe cognitive and emotional impairments. Lobotomies ceased to be performed in most countries by the middle of the 1960s.

In sum, during the first half of the twentieth century, the options offered to patients with severe psychological disorders were almost exclusively drastic physical interventions that were risky and largely ineffective. Moreover, viewed from the present standpoint, it appears that these interventions were not well regulated, nor were there adequate evaluations of their safety or effectiveness.

Talk Therapies

The beginnings of "talk therapy" can be traced to the 1880s. Josef Breuer, a physician practicing in Vienna, stumbled onto a way to help a young woman whom he had diagnosed with hysteria. Anna O. (the pseudonym by which Breuer and, later, Freud identified her) experienced a shifting array of physical complaints. These included a nervous cough, occasional disruptions in her eyesight, loss of the ability to speak, transient paralyses, sleepwalking, and visual hallucinations. Breuer noted that Anna's symptoms diminished when she was able to talk at length about them. Anna called this talk "chimney sweeping."

Initially collaborating with Breuer, Freud carried the idea of a "talking cure" forward, ultimately developing not only a model of psychotherapy, but also elaborate and enduring theories regarding the psychological development of children, the role of unconscious motives, male–female psychological differences, and an expansive theory of psychopathology. The corpus of work that Freud produced during his lifetime laid the foundation for the development of diverse variants of psychoanalytic theory and therapeutic approaches for the next several decades.

The field of psychotherapy has come a long way since Anna O.'s "chimney-sweeping" talks. Today, psychotherapists and counselors are drawn from a wide variety of professional backgrounds, such as psychology, psychiatry, social work, and counseling. Many have received extensive training. In some locales, they may be required to be licensed by a government agency. Professional associations often have codified standards of ethical conduct; some of those associations adjudicate complaints of ethical violations by their members.

Psychotherapists and counselors offer professional assistance for such conditions as anxiety, depression, or post-traumatic stress disorder. They may also help clients resolve personal challenges or manage difficult life events, such as a life-threatening illness. Many theories of psychotherapy and behavior change have been put forward. Therapy may assist people to strengthen their coping skills, develop greater self-knowledge, and make decisions that enhance their well-being.

Psychotherapy involves meetings between a therapist and a person who is seeking help. Psychotherapy may sometimes involve couples or families, depending on the problems for which help is sought. The sessions are private and strictly confidential. Typically, the therapist and the client meet regularly for a period of weeks or months, with the length of time mutually decided. During the therapy sessions, the focus is on the patient's thoughts, feelings, experiences, and behaviors. The sessions may be augmented with "homework assignments" or reading material.

The Drug Revolution

The discovery of drugs to treat serious mental disorders marked a turning point in mental health care. The antipsychotic effect of chlorpromazine was discovered in the early 1950s. Its discovery was serendipitous: chlorpromazine was being tested as a possible cold remedy; psychiatric patients were the guinea pigs. In many parts of the world, chlorpromazine quickly became the mainstay of treatment for patients with psychotic disorders. Indeed, chlorpromazine and similar drugs changed the landscape of care for people with serious mental disorders. No longer need they be confined to "insane asylums" and reformers began to envision and implement alternate possibilities. Today, there are some forty drugs available for treating psychotic disorders, many of which are chemically related to chlorpromazine. The first antidepressant medications came on the market in the late 1950s. In the same period, lithium carbonate, a mineral salt, came into use as an effective mood stabilizer for people with bipolar disorder.

There is no doubt that psychiatric medications can change the lives of persons with mental disorders. However, many psychiatric medications may also carry side effects. These may include weight gain, nausea, dizziness, constipation, sexual dysfunction, loss of appetite, and sleep disturbances. Antipsychotic medications may produce emotional blunting and over-sedation. Their long-term use can lead to tardive dyskinesia, a neurological disorder that produces involuntary movements of the face and body. Surveys carried out in the US estimated that the number of patients who modified or discontinued their use of antipsychotic medications – sometimes because of side effects, sometimes because of their expense – was between 50 and 75 percent.

Psychological Disorders in Sociopolitical Context

Social Policies, Deinstitutionalization, and Mental Health Care

The wide availability of anti-psychotic and other medications made it possible to imagine a social order in which long-term hospitalization of persons with severe psychological disorders was no longer necessary. This prompted a movement in support of deinstitutionalization. Many who supported deinstitutionalization wished to ensure the civil liberties of mental patients, to promote their autonomy, and to reunite them with their families and communities. They sought to replace institutionalization with the more humane alternative of community-based care. Such community-based care would provide treatment and support in clinics close to patients' homes; clinic staff would facilitate the integration of formerly hospitalized patients into their families, churches, and other social groups.

Such deinstitutionalization movements have had varying outcomes, depending on the political will to allocate financial and other resources needed for such movements to succeed. In some countries in Europe, mental health care for severely impaired people was reconceived as small, home-like residences located in community settings and supported by public funding. By contrast, in the US, the conditions (and financial resources) needed to support such community-based care seldom materialized. Instead, the closure of mental hospitals left many people with severe and chronic psychological disorders with little support unless family members were able to provide it. Today, many such individuals have no alternative but to live on the streets. The psychiatrist Nicholas Rosenlicht (personal communication, October 3, 2025) has described this as the broadscale abandonment of institutional and societal responsibility for members of society who cannot care for themselves.

Community-Based Movements

Community-based movements have played important roles in securing better care, legal protections, and increased public responsibility for care. Some offer ongoing support groups for individuals with mental disorders and their families. In locales where public funding for mental health care is minimal, these groups have crucial roles to play. There are many such organizations. Here, we briefly describe three of them.

NAMI

The National Alliance on Mental Illness (NAMI) is the largest grassroots mental health organization in the US. NAMI was founded in 1979 in response to the dramatic deterioration in the care and living circumstances of large numbers of people with serious mental disorders. Its founders were families who had a member with a serious psychological disorder. Responding to the crisis in social care, the founders' goal was to provide advocacy, education, support, and public awareness so that all individuals and families affected by mental illness could build better lives. NAMI is not against psychiatry, nor does it claim to offer an alternative to psychiatric biomedical treatment. NAMI serves as the umbrella organization for some 650 local affiliates. These affiliates offer trainings and events for people living with serious mental disorders, their families, members of the community, and mental health professionals. In some cases, these trainings are conducted by individuals who are living with serious mental disorders. NAMI also supports a national telephone helpline, as well as a yearly nationwide Mental Illness Awareness Week.

The Hearing Voices Movement

The Hearing Voices Movement (HVM) was founded in 2010 in the Netherlands by Marius Romme, Patsy Hage, and Sandra Escher. It is a patient-centered movement that promulgates a less stigmatized view of voice-hearing. The HVM deliberately substitutes the neutral term "voice-hearing" in place of the stigmatizing term "hallucination." Voice-hearing is seen as an unusual behavioral variation; it is not automatically assumed to be a symptom of mental disorder. This change in language and meanings allows for a range of possible responses to such voices. Those who participate in HVM activities may or may not have a psychiatric diagnosis. There are Hearing Voices Networks in several countries, including the Netherlands, Canada, the United Kingdom, and many states in the US. These are organizations of people who identify themselves as voice-hearers, family members of voice-hearers, activists, or mental health practitioners. The HVM sponsors ongoing support groups for voice-hearers who seek better ways to understand and manage their voices.

The Recovery Movement in the US

In the US, the term "Recovery Movement" came into use in the early 1990s. The term referred to the long-term experiences of individuals who had been diagnosed with serious mental disorders. The Recovery Movement aimed to offer an approach that was radically different from traditional psychiatric care in its goals and its emphases. When anti-psychotic drugs first came into use, their positive effects led practitioners to anticipate that patients with serious mental disorders would fully recover. However, it soon became apparent that a substantial number of patients continued to experience some difficulties that prevented them from resuming their previous work or social roles. Moreover, in the US at present, publicly funded mental health care is typically limited to brief meetings with caregivers, which often are focused on drug-prescribing. As Andrew Scull (2022, p. 374) pointed out, *"The rise of the DSM and of psychopharmacology reduced the psychiatric encounter to brief consultations that revolved around the prescription of medications and management of side effects."* There is little opportunity for patients to express their concerns about problems in everyday living, nor to explore ways to minimize stigma and exclusion.

The Recovery Movement is an effort to rectify these shortcomings. The movement does not focus narrowly on symptom reduction. Rather, the term "recovery" refers to the processes by which people find ways to lead meaningful lives. This may involve a full recovery from mental disorder, but it may also involve learning how to live with the disorder. Ongoing peer support usually plays a key role in a person's recovery. Larry Davidson, a US psychologist, has had a long-term dedication to community-based supports for persons with serious mental disorders. Davidson (2016) conceives of recovery as a continuing process of accommodating to serious mental disorder and addressing its consequences. In this process, the help of a supportive community is essential. Central to the Recovery Movement is the principle that people with serious mental disorders are entitled to a life in the community, as well as to control over their lives.

In Conclusion: Thinking Styles and Vocabularies

We end this chapter with some thoughts on the medicalized vocabulary that is used to talk about psychological distress. As we noted, much of the vocabulary of psychiatry is borrowed from biomedicine. Think of words such as patient, disorder, symptom, relapse, prodromal, remission, co-morbidity, course of the disorder, and so on. A common vocabulary enables practitioners to communicate meaningfully with their colleagues; it also enables them to share new scientific knowledge. Also, a common vocabulary serves prosaic but crucial bureaucratic necessities; it provides the standard labels, descriptors, and billing codes necessary for medical records and for healthcare payment systems. Moreover, adopting the language of biomedicine has aided psychiatrists' quest to solidify their status as "real" doctors.

There are, however, less positive aspects of this vocabulary. It sets boundaries on the ways in which practitioners can talk about and think about the people they serve. Adopting the vocabulary associated with biomedicine restricts speakers to thinking about psychological suffering as if it were equivalent to a biomedical illness or perhaps actually a biomedical illness. Ludwik Fleck's description of a thinking style helps us to think about this (see Chapter 2). For Fleck, a thinking style is "the entirety of intellectual preparedness or readiness for one particular way of seeing and acting, and no other" (1935/1979, p. 64). When a person enters a field (such as psychiatry or clinical psychology), they must master the field's ways of seeing and acting, including its ways of speaking. One consequence is that novices in the mental health field quickly come to adopt the collective's ways of talking and thinking about psychological suffering. The words that they use, and their ways of speaking and writing are not matters of choice. Rather, they are parts of a tightly regulated set of practices that follow from the biomedical and internalist thinking style of the professional thought collective of psychiatry.

In our view, the biomedical thinking style is not adequate for a full understanding of psychological suffering, particularly its embeddedness in the cultural, social, and political surround. This embeddedness points to the need for more attention to the relational, social, and cultural contributions to psychological distress and to the relief of such distress.

CHAPTER 9

Critical Perspectives on Psychologists' Research Practices

Debates about psychological research methods are nothing new. Since the early days of the academic discipline of psychology, psychologists have discussed and disagreed about the best ways to conduct psychological research (about the last half century, see, for instance, Rosenthal, 1968; Gergen, 1973; McGuire, 1973; Meehl, 1978; Cohen, 1994). The most recent debates started just after 2010, when the psychology discipline was hit by what came to be called *the replication crisis*: large numbers of established psychological research findings proved impossible to replicate. Not surprisingly, different debaters identified different research practices as the causes of the inability to replicate earlier findings. And consequently, they suggested different kinds of remedies. The disagreements among debaters about what the problem was, and how to solve it, provide insights into the existing views of the strengths, weaknesses, and problems of contemporary psychological research. These insights go well beyond the specific issues that were raised during the replication crisis, though. The many writings about the replication crisis are therefore good sources of knowledge and questions for general critical reflection on contemporary psychological research practices.

The replication debates are an indication that there are many psychologists who are deeply interested in the foundations of psychological theory and research practices. The debates also indicate that many psychologists are prepared to put serious efforts into correcting misunderstandings and amending mistaken practices in the discipline. There are few disagreements on that level. The disagreements appear between different analyses of the replication problems, and therefore between the suggestions for how to remedy them. In what follows, we describe and discuss these different analyses and suggestions for remedies.

In the first section of the chapter, we give a brief description of the contemporary replication crisis. In the following three sections, we give voice to some of the scholars who examine the sources of the crisis and the analyses that they have offered. Not surprisingly, psychologists disagree about the causes of the failures to replicate. Some claim that questionable research practices by researchers were the main culprits. Others claim that intrinsic problems, especially in the conventionally used methods for testing research hypotheses, were the source of the problems. Still others suggest that much psychological research is built on conceptual misunderstandings originating in untenable assumptions about psychology's object of study, that is, humans.

In the following sections we draw on the insights of Ludwik Fleck (see Chapter 2) to examine some of the assumptions underpinning common methodological practices in psychology. We focus especially on the aspects of psychology's empirical methods that have been criticized as problematic. We also consider the assumptions underlying those methods and ask whether they may also be problematic.

What Is the Replication Crisis and Why Did It Hit Psychology?

Why is it so important to replicate research findings? It is important, because among scientific researchers, a single research finding is hardly ever taken as definitive proof of a thesis. The finding has to be repeated, preferably by independent researchers. Such repetitions of studies are called *replications*. They are sometimes performed in a setting and with procedures that are as similar to the original as possible, and sometimes in settings that differ from the original in systematic and theoretically meaningful ways. However, in the recent history of the psychology discipline, research that repeats other researchers' studies has often been regarded as an unimportant type of research compared to research that produces new findings. As a result, replication studies became difficult to publish. Eventually, some psychologists grew worried about these disciplinary trends and exhorted their colleagues to take seriously the need to replicate studies. Those who did found that many findings in psychological research could not be replicated. One early example was a failure to replicate the findings of a well-known study of priming, a type of unconscious influence on behavior (Doyen et al., 2012).

The first large investigation of replicability in psychology brought together several hundred researchers and sought to replicate the studies that had yielded one hundred well-known and supposedly well-established research findings (Nosek & Lakens, 2013). This project found that only 39 percent of the original results were replicated. Moreover, even when findings seemed to be replicated, the effects were markedly more modest than what had been reported in the original studies (Open Science Collaboration, 2015). Replication failures like these led to vigorous debates about the likely causes of the failures. And not surprisingly, the replication failures have also led to worries about the credibility of psychology as a scientific endeavor. If psychological research has so often produced flimsy and unstable findings that cannot be replicated, why should people trust what psychologists say? In what follows, we describe three different critical approaches to the replication crisis.

Questionable Research Practices and p-hacking

Several of those who debated the replication crisis adopted what we might call a "disciplinary-political" perspective on the replication crisis. They focused on the prevalence of research practices that lead to large numbers of spuriously significant test results. These practices are often denoted by the acronym *QRPs*, that is, "*Questionable Research Practices*," or by the expression "*p-hacking*" (see Nelson, Simmons, & Simonsohn, 2018; Nosek et al., 2022). Both expressions refer to illicit manipulations of the data from a study that had originally not achieved significant results, aiming to present seemingly significant results. Here are some examples.

Researchers have sometimes (without acknowledging it) added or removed variables from their reporting, in order to make their results reach statistical significance. Sometimes researchers whose studies did not achieve statistical significance for a hypothesis, have added or removed some data from their analysis, such that the results reached statistical significance. Sometimes researchers have mathematically transformed raw data in such a way that the results were made to reach statistical significance. And researchers have sometimes added one or more hypotheses after they have completed their study and seen the results, but reported the added hypotheses as if they had been proposed in advance. Some researchers have excluded from their reports all tests of hypotheses that had not reached statistical significance, which means that they "cherry-picked" only significance test results that supported their hypotheses.

Researchers who were engaging in practices such as these may have reported significant findings, while violating the rules for hypothesis-testing psychological research. If so, it would not be surprising if, when their findings were tested in stringent replication studies, those replications did not reach statistical significance.

As a prevention against questionable research practices, reformers have suggested mandatory pre-registration of research studies, including the hypotheses to be tested and the statistical tests to be done. Reformers have also suggested that scholarly journals should require researchers' reports to disclose all the measures and manipulations that have been used. They should also describe all measures and variables that they decided to exclude, and the reason why they were excluded. And they should give the rationale for their chosen sample sizes (Nelson, Simmons, & Simonsohn, 2018).

Some of the reformers have argued that some QRPs were embedded in the culture of the institutions where researchers work. They pointed to the incentive structure in these institutions, as well as the practice of scholarly journals to require statistically significant results in order to publish articles. This so-called "file-drawer problem" was noted as early as in the 1960s (Rosenthal, 1968). Under these conditions, researchers are rewarded with career advancement if they quickly publish large numbers of articles that report statistical significance, rather than if they conduct well-crafted, seriously considered, and thoughtful research that includes replication efforts. Many reformers claimed that this incentive structure was responsible for the existence of questionable research practices among researchers (Leys, 2024).

Problem-Ridden Research Practices in Psychology, Such as Statistical Testing

Adopting a more theoretical approach to the replication crisis, other debaters have argued that QRPs and p-hacking account for only a small portion of the replication problems. These critics instead claim that the real culprits are some of the established practices of psychological research. In the view of these critics, many common ways in which researchers in psychology use statistics are unsound and do not, in fact, have a grounding in statistical theory. Given the dominance of these practices, the critics argue, it was inevitable that a replication crisis would erupt sooner or later. One of the main targets of the critique has been null hypothesis significance testing (NHST) as it is commonly used in psychological research. For instance, one of the commentators argued that "*NHST is a poor criterion for scientific truth,*" and that "*the sheer mechanics of NHST, even when computed and applied correctly, could explain the bulk of the failed replications*" (Green, 2021, p. 178, 180; see also Gigerenzer, 2018). Because null hypothesis significance testing is such a central feature of psychological research, we take a closer look at the contemporary critique of it in Chapter 11.

Other critics who focus on conventional practices in psychological research have scrutinized the types of measurements that psychologists use and argued, for instance, that *"problematic measurement and inattention to measurement error are likely culprits in limiting the replicability of research findings"* (Wiggins & Christopherson, 2019, p. 208). Going beyond sheer "inattention," Lilienfeld and Strother (2020) pointed to what they see as serious misunderstandings in much psychological research of what measurement actually entails. Because quantitative measurement is such a staple in psychological research, we provide a review in Chapter 10 of the historical developments that led to the dominance of quantitative methods in psychological research (Michell, 1999).

The overall message of these suggested remedies was that psychologists should reform their research practices to make them conform better to the standards in more established sciences (Leys, 2024). For example, the commentators often referred to what has been called "the new statistics," which dismisses the use of null hypothesis testing and p-values, and instead turns to effect sizes and confidence intervals, and sometimes Bayesian statistics (Cumming, 2014). Psychologists, according to these critics, need to learn statistical theory beyond what is typically taught in methods courses in psychology departments.

In the eyes of some of these commentators, psychologists also need to think more seriously about the weaknesses (and often fatal vagueness) of the *psychological* theories that they are testing. Many psychological theories, according to these critics, are so vague and unspecific that the researcher must complement the theory with a forbiddingly large number of added assumptions and specifications in order to achieve an operationalization that can be studied by experimental or other quantitative methods (Oberauer & Lewandowsky, 2019). The following quote from the German psychologist Klaus Fiedler summarizes the messages in this kind of critique: *"No statistical analysis can be better than the design of a study, and no research design can be better than the rationale of the underlying theory. The logic and the purpose of scientific inquiry often are neglected in the current discourse on quality of science, which is almost totally centered on statistics and compliance rules"* (2017, p. 57).

In the discussions about the need to improve many psychological theories, some critics have pointed to problems connected with the pervasive internalism (or "intrapsychic-ness") of, for instance, much theorizing in social psychology (such as the use of individuals' motives, attitudes, and explicit and implicit goals as the *causes* of behavior). One particular target of this critique has been the subfield of social cognition. In a review of such research, Fiedler (2014) points to the scarcity of inclusion of contextual factors in research on priming, stereotype threat, confirmation bias in decision-making, and other common research topics in social psychology. Fiedler and other critics, therefore, emphasize that, in order to achieve ecological validity and objectivity – and thereby replicability – psychological research needs to include interpersonal and other contextual variables to a much greater extent than has hitherto been common.

Conceptual and Epistemological Critiques

Very different discussions of the replication crisis, and very different suggestions for remedies, have come from researchers situated outside the usual settings of psychological research institutions. These commentators are typically critical of the above-mentioned suggestions for reforms, arguing that they miss, or in the worst case may inadvertently conceal, questions that psychologists ought to deal with before they begin to construct their theories and design their studies. These necessary questions are based in the history and philosophy of science; and many psychologists have too little knowledge about these fields, the critics argue (Morawski, 2019). To quote one of the critics: "*There is a big discrepancy in how they* [psychologists] *discuss those epistemological questions, and how such questions are debated among historians and philosophers of science. So much so that the reform debates* [in psychology] *seem to be completely out of tune with contemporary history and philosophy of science*" (Flis, 2019, p. 159). According to the critics, psychologists need to scrutinize, and quite likely fundamentally revise, both their epistemological assumptions and their methodological habits. This would necessarily mean revising their ideas of what psychological theory and research should be like. And this would, to use the vocabulary of Ludwik Fleck (see Chapter 2), amount to reconsidering their thinking styles. As Fleck noted, this is usually not an easy task.

One question that these commentators raised has to do with the nature of the psychological *concepts* and the words for the psychological phenomena that have been studied in the research that has failed to replicate. The questions about concepts that the commentators asked are, for instance: Does it make sense for psychologists to aim to define the psychological concepts, and thereby phenomena, that they study in the same detail and with the same aim to achieve universality with which natural scientists define their basic concepts (Maiers, 2022)? Is that even possible to achieve in psychology? Should psychologists instead assume, and accept, that psychological concepts are inherently vague and that their meanings vary depending on historical and contextual factors? Contextually dependent concepts and phenomena clearly cannot be nailed down in detail once and for all or be taken to be valid everywhere. These questions and conclusions also imply that context-dependent phenomena and concepts, such as those typical of psychology, are not amenable to research based on hypothetico-deductive schemes (see Debrouwere & Rosseel, 2021, for an enlightening discussion of why psychological phenomena may be especially ill-fitted for such research methods).

Fabian Hutmacher and David Franz (2024), two German psychologists, have provided examples of psychological concepts that have vague and varying meanings: stress, cognition, theory of mind, memory, learning, intentions, and forgiveness. Similar vagueness is also found in several concepts used in neuroscience and psychiatry. Hutmacher and Franz pointed out that part of the reason for this vagueness is that the phenomena psychologists want to study ultimately have their origin in people's every-day experiences. Everyday experiences are clothed in everyday words, whose meanings are always the result of (usually tacit) agreement among people in a social setting. An agreed meaning may be vague, and it can change. Further, if researchers want to communicate their findings to people, they need to at least partly use everyday words, with their varying, context-dependent, and intrinsically vague meanings. In the words of Hutmacher and Franz: "*Psychological phenomena are fundamentally linked to psychological concepts and are, therefore, as dependent on cultural norms, institutions, and manners of speaking as psychological concepts are*" (2025, p. 225). Taken together, these observations invite the conclusion that the psychological phenomena that psychological researchers seek to pinpoint are seldom, if ever, static. They are always "*on the move*," to quote the Canadian philosopher Ian Hacking (1999, p. 108). Also, when people use specific psychological concepts and words (such as diagnostic categories), they may, through their use, introduce new meanings. Such changes may contribute further to the variations and vagueness of the meanings of words and concepts (for a dramatic illustration, see Hacking, 1995). See also Chapter 11, where we discuss the uses of the term "concept" in psychology, and Chapter 13, where we describe conceptual analysis.

To quote Hutmacher and Franz again: "*. . .the different meanings and rules for application cannot simply be reduced to some kind of context-independent core meaning because getting rid of the context would result in losing at least a part of the meaning*" (2025, p. 224). Not everybody would agree with their conclusion. According to Robert Wilson, the idea of context-independence is one of the governing assumptions in much psychological research:

> [the assumption] that the psychological abilities of interest are those that can be assessed by probing an individual in abstraction not only from her real life, social environment, but from any substantial social environment. (2004, p. 44)

In another type of conceptually-oriented approach to the replication crisis, the German psychologists Roland Mayrhofer, Isabel Büchner, & Judit Hevesi (2024) applied arguments from three prominent philosophers of science (Karl Popper, Thomas Kuhn, and Imre Lakatos) to discuss what can be learned from this crisis. One of their conclusions was that there may be a serious mismatch in much contemporary psychology between that which is being studied (psychological phenomena as such, i.e., the onto-logical level) and the methods that are usually used in such research (the ways to create knowledge, i.e., the epistemological level). Mayrhofer et al. proposed that the nature of the human psyche may be such that it *"at least partially resists access through a quantitative perspective and approach"* (p. 3). If there is some truth in this, it should perhaps not be surprising if some findings about psychological phenomena that have been studied with quantitative methods are difficult to replicate. And therefore, they sug-gested, *"as a consequence, improvements in quantitative methods cannot resolve or mitigate the problems of the replication crisis"* (p. 7).

Mayrhofer and colleagues are not the only ones who have suggested that there is a mismatch between human experiences and behavior, on the one hand, and quantitative research methods on the other. This has been a contentious issue from well before the beginnings of modern psychology. At least until the end of the nineteenth century, most thinkers were convinced that psychological phenomena were nonmaterial and therefore not quantitative in nature, and consequently not accessible by quantitative measurement. And in fact, as the Australian psychometrician Joel Michell has argued, psychologists have yet to prove that human psychological characteristics have a quantitative nature (Michell, 1999). If these charac-teristics do not, perhaps quantitative methods should not always be the first (or default?) choice for psychologists who want to study humans? In Chapter 10, we discuss the historical origins of the reliance on quantitative methods in psychological research in more detail.

The discussion of the replication crisis by the German psychologists Julia Schnepf and Norbert Groeben points in the same direction as Mayrhofer et al. They pointed to the frequent occurrence in psychological research of what they call *anthropological oversimplification* of the human research subject. By this they meant the lack of attention to *acting*, that is, people's planned-intentional actions. In such actions, individual and social meaning and meaning-making play central roles. But, Schnepf and Groeben noted, psychologists often study *behavior*, in the sense of "*a more or less involuntary reaction to situational cues, without the organism engaging in more complex intervening meaningful activities*" (2024, p. 5). Schnepf and Groeben saw this as a consequence of the quantitative methods that dominate in psychological research. They argued that these methods invite, or perhaps even prescribe, the study of "behavior" in the sense of reactions to stimuli, rather than of planned-intentional acting.

We end this section by quoting the conclusion by Ivan Flis, a Croatian historian of psychology, that "*the kind of problems opened up by the replication crisis go deeper* [than just 'method' – our comment], *to the fundamental historical and philosophical definitions of the rationality and the science psychologists use to guide and construct those methods*" (2019, p. 171). In the next section, we address Flis's suggestion that there are some "deeper" issues involved in the replication crisis. In particular, we scrutinize the assumptions that underpin different kinds of psychology and psychological research methods.

Active Assumptions and Their Passive Consequences in Psychological Research

In Chapter 2, we took up a discussion of thinking styles in psychological research, and the importance of the *active assumptions* that underpin theories or research traditions. Such assumptions are not always explicitly spelled out; rather they are often basic notions that are taken for granted, and therefore seldom discussed. We also described Ludwik Fleck's argument that such assumptions have what he called automatic or "*passive*" *consequences*, not the least of which are the methods by which a particular discipline studies its objects of research. This means that, given a certain set of active assumptions, certain ways of gathering and analyzing data follow automatically. That is, it will feel natural for researchers to use them. Fleck even argued that the connections between the active assumptions and the passive consequences are so strong that it is possible to discern, from a set of passive consequences (such as research methods), some of the active assumptions that shaped the research tradition and theories of the thought collective that uses those research methods.

One reason why an interested reader might need to make this type of indirect inference is that research articles in psychology very seldom declare the active assumptions that form the base of the study that is being reported. Rather, these assumptions are usually taken for granted by the researchers. This means that if one wants to find out about the images of human beings that are at the base of a research tradition, one is often left with Ludwik Fleck's advice to read them indirectly, from the methods and techniques that are used. This is what we do in the next section.

We begin by sketching typical methodological characteristics in quantitative psychological research and theory, followed by our suggestions about the assumptions on which they are based – explicit as well as implicit or "active" assumptions, in Ludwik Fleck's terms. Note that what follows is not a complete account of the assumptions underlying psychologists' research methods. Rather, we give examples that may perhaps lead readers to do their own investigations.

Some Characteristics of Contemporary Psychological Research Methods

Observers have sometimes suggested that what unites psychology as a *discipline* is, first, a shared allegiance to a certain set of method practices, and second, the avid policing of those method practices. See, for instance, the historical study of psychological research writings between 1950 and 1999 by Flis and Eck (2018). Also see Hutmacher and Franz, to whom we referred earlier, who concluded, after their discussion of the vagueness of psychological concepts, that " . . . *researchers seem to seek refuge in the belief that quantitative-experimental methods can serve as a unifying basis for the discipline*" (2024, p. 8).

Whether the goal of unifying the discipline is realistic or not, it is certainly true that most contemporary psychological research uses quantitative, and often experimental, methods. Most psychological research also uses parametric statistics for analysis and testing of the significance of results. Confirmatory research is very common, often in the form of hypothetico-deductive designs. Most psychological researchers treat the groups they study as samples drawn from some population, to which they aim to generalize the findings. It is also common to average data across groups of people but draw conclusions about the characteristics of individuals. And it is very common in psychological research to define variables by operational definitions, that is, in terms of the measures used to study them. In most psychological research, the researcher controls the design of the situation in which data are collected and decides which responses are to be taken into account. Finally, especially in experimental research, it is often "behavior" that is being studied, rather than people's considered actions (in the sense noted by Schnepf & Groben, 2024, that we described previously).

Common Assumptions in Quantitative Psychological Research

In this section, we examine the practices that we described earlier by reflecting on the assumptions that must be in place for each of them to make sense. To begin, a researcher who uses quantitative methods for data collection must assume that the phenomena that are being studied really have quantitative properties. Ludwik Fleck might class this as one of those "active" assumptions that are inherited from one's predecessors and never brought out into the open to be scrutinized. It may be because quantitative methods are so common today that this assumption is hardly ever made explicit. In Chapter 10, we take a closer look at how the assumption of quantitative attributes came to be integrated into most of modern psychology; we also consider some of the critiques of the assumption.

The practice of using parametric statistics to test research hypotheses builds on the assumption that the group studied by the researcher constitutes a (in the ideal case, random) sample drawn from a specific population, and that the variable under study is normally distributed. On this basis, the distribution of data points found in the studied group is assumed to be an approximation of the population distribution. This is the major assumption that motivates the use of parametric statistics. One consequence of this assumption, that is, one of its "passive consequences" in psychological research, is the frequent use of null hypothesis significance testing. However, since the beginnings of such testing, there has been serious critique of the reasonableness of the assumptions underlying this practice. In recent years, especially in the wake of the replication crisis, such critiques have increased. In Chapter 11 we present the debates about null hypothesis significance testing in some detail.

We noted in the previous section that many psychological research methods, such as experiments, study "behavior" in the sense of fairly simple (and in some cases "automatic") responses, rather than people's considered actions (Schnepf & Groeben, 2024). A psychological experiment in which the experimenter exposes participants to a manipulation of some kind and then reads off a reaction from the participants' behavior exemplifies this kind of method. What assumptions could be at the basis of such methods? Think back to Robert Wilson's (2004) conclusion earlier in this chapter about the common assumption of context-independence. It may be pertinent here. And could there be some still lingering assumptions from the S-R paradigms of psychology's behaviorist era? In some cases this could well be so. See, for instance, Ruth Leys's (2024) discussion of the simplified images of humans, combined with assumptions of the automaticity of behavior, which she found to characterize much of psychologists' priming research. In other cases it could perhaps be that the available methods themselves prevent psychologists from studying complex things such as people's considered actions. This implies that using such a method – the method being, in Fleck's terminology, a "passive consequence" of certain active assumptions – can unwittingly impose those particular assumptions on the researcher. It is therefore worth noting that many of the data collection methods in use today were developed in a period when behaviorist ideas informed the dominant "active assumptions" (in Ludwik Fleck's terms) of many psychologists. Should we therefore expect that some behaviorist active assumptions could still be at large in psychological research through being built into psychological research methods?

Operational definitions of variables are often used in psychological research. They are described, for example, as "*a description of something in terms of the operations (procedures, actions, or processes) by which it could be observed and measured*" (American Psychological Association, 2024). The assumption on which this type of definition is based is that the chosen operation (such as measuring anxiety by scores on an anxiety inventory) gets at the meaning of the phenomenon one wants to study. However, though operational definitions are popular and their use dominates in many settings, there is no unanimity among researchers about their value. First, there is disagreement about whether the underlying assumption is credible. Second, the use of operational definitions has been criticized by psychologists and epistemologists for encouraging (or even creating) simplistic versions of psychological theory. In Chapter 10 we describe the historical beginnings of the use of operational definitions and the ongoing discussions about their value.

What If . . . ? Questioning Assumptions and Methods

What if there is some validity in the conceptual and epistemological critiques that we have just described? To recapitulate briefly: What if many (or even most) psychological phenomena really do not have quantitative properties? What would this imply for the relevance and value of quantitative psychological research? One implication might be that the development of more and more sophisticated quantitative methods does not necessarily lead to better psychological knowledge. And what if psychological concepts really are unavoidably vague, changeable, and context-dependent, and therefore not possible to pinpoint universally and in detail through psychological experiments? And what if certain psychological research methods are based on erroneously oversimplified images of humans? Could it be that research using such methods risks producing ecologically invalid results? And on that basis: Could it be that the methods used in the research that was implicated in the replication crisis were based on oversimplified images of humans? And could it be that this research therefore had been producing ecologically invalid results? Finally, and on a general note: as some commentators argued, perhaps psychologists need to become more conceptually and epistemologically sophisticated. Perhaps they should more carefully scrutinize and question conventional assumptions and methods in psychology.

If there is something of value in questions and suggestions such as those we just listed, perhaps psychologists should consider entertaining assumptions about humans, and research methods other than the ones that have hitherto dominated, at least for some kinds (perhaps several kinds) of psychological questions. These are suggestions that an increasing number of psychologists, including us, are taking seriously today.

CHAPTER 10

Disagreements and Debates in Psychology's History

Can we learn anything about today's discipline of psychology by studying its history? Yes, of course. Historical investigations help us gain insight into where psychology and psychological researchers have been, and thereby indirectly why they are where they are now. At all points in time, researchers' ideas will have been embedded in sociocultural settings and shaped by the prevailing styles of thinking in these settings. On this basis, one can examine, for instance, which research topics and questions psychologists in different eras have regarded as important, and which questions they instead saw as trivial, "too political," or even "not psychological." One can find out which methods of study, which background assumptions, and which ways of drawing inferences were regarded by earlier psychologists as sound, and which were disparaged as unscientific. A historical perspective also leads to an awareness of the dominance of certain theoretical frameworks in particular time periods and in different regions of the world. And knowledge of psychology's history leads to an interest in when theoretical and practical frameworks changed, why and how they changed, and the social or scientific forces that led to change (Danziger, 2003).

Some examples from the history of psychology serve as cautionary tales, because they alert us to methods, theories – and therefore thinking styles – that have had ethically or politically problematic consequences. One well-known early example is early psychologists' interest in the eugenics movement, with its insistence on racial and ethnic differences in intelligence. Recent history provides other kinds of cautionary tales, such as the retrospective investigations of a number of canonical studies in psychology. Several of these studies have turned out to be either deliberately misreported or even fraudulent (Cahalan, 2019; Le Texier & Kazak, 2019; Reicher, Van Bavel, & Haslam, 2020; Scull, 2019). The history of the "replication crisis" that we described in Chapter 9 can also serve as a cautionary tale.

The historical topics we have chosen for this chapter illustrate the power of thinking styles in the discipline. In some cases, they also illustrate how thinking styles are influenced by forces in the surrounding society. The first section in the chapter concerns the history of the eugenics movement among early psychologists, triggered by evolutionary theory and political conservatism in the second half of the nineteenth century. In the second section, we review the history of the measurement of psychological properties. This history includes debates about whether such properties are quantitative or not, and also the enduring imperative in large parts of the discipline to use only quantitative methods in psychological research. The third section discusses the origins and uses of operational definitions in psychology, including the debates about whether such definitions are meaningful or not. In the fourth section, we look at the origins and development of some of the most prominent "psychological" words in the recent history of the discipline. In the final section, we describe the history and development of psychological research and theorizing about women and gender. This topic has been of especial interest to us as female psychologists with longstanding interests in gender and gender equality (see Magnusson & Marecek, 2012).

Psychology, Eugenics, and Evolutionary Theory

Modern humans, or *Homo sapiens sapiens*, is one of the species that have evolved from the first simple forms of life. This means that modern humans are, in varying degrees, genetically related to all other existing species. For instance, most (actually, very nearly all) of the human genetic material overlaps with that of humans' nearest living relatives, chimpanzees and bonobos. Still, there certainly are genetic differences between humans and apes, such as species-specific variations within the genes that are shared, in addition to the genes that are not shared. And as we know, there certainly are both behavioral differences and differences in habitats between humans on the one hand, and chimpanzees and bonobos on the other.

What conclusions, if any, should a psychologist draw from these facts? This has been a contentious question from the very beginning of the academic discipline of psychology (though the early psychologists obviously did not have access to today's knowledge of genetics, nor to today's knowledge about the impact of variations in cultural settings and living conditions among humans).

The nascent field of psychology, in the latter half of the nineteenth century, was contemporaneous with Charles Darwin's evolutionary theory and was deeply influenced by it. In a quirk of history, a cousin of Charles Darwin, Francis Galton, was especially eager to bring evolutionary thinking into psychology (Michell, 2022; Richards & Stenner, 2023). Galton's aim was to determine the genetic origins of differences between individuals in various abilities, especially intelligence. In his search for these origins, he developed methods and ideas that became the basis of modern differential psychology. He also established the *eugenics* movement (Richards, 1997). The word "eugenics" is a combination of the two Greek words *eu* (good) and *genos* (kind, lineage, or race).

When the proponents of eugenics developed their ideas, a hierarchical view of society and of humans had long been dominant in Western thought: People in high societal positions were, as a matter of course, valued more highly than those in lower positions. The hierarchical view of humans was so taken for granted by the eugenicists that it qualifies as one of the *active assumptions* of a thinking style, in Ludwik Fleck's terms. The assumption invited a hierarchical interpretation of evolutionary theory (though, in fact, such an interpretation need not have been read into the theory), leading to what we could call an *eugenicist thinking style*. Consistent with this style, eugenicists claimed that people in different social layers of society were, in Darwinian terms, either more and better evolved (the highest class) or less and worse evolved (the lower classes or "races"). On this basis, many eugenicists wanted to improve the "quality" of humankind by selective breeding of the "higher" classes.

The eugenicists were worried that, in modern societies where the conditions of the lower classes were improving and their numbers increasing, there would be a high risk of degeneration of all of humanity. Based on this supposition, eugenicists urged governments to encourage marriages between what they saw as genetically favorable individuals, and to discourage or prevent marriages between supposedly genetically unfavorable individuals. Eugenicists also urged governments to enact involuntary sterilization laws in order to prevent people whom they saw as degenerate from reproducing.

Eugenic ideas, because they were commonplace, also colored the views of many early psychologists after Galton, influencing their opinions of what the psychology discipline's role should be. For example, the development of IQ tests at the beginning of the twentieth century was based partially on eugenic interests. And eugenic versions of evolutionary theory influenced early psychologists' views on madness, women, children, crime, and "race" questions (Richards, 1997; Richards & Stenner, 2023). As a result, it was not unusual for psychologists of that era to regard women, non-whites, people with psychological disorders, and criminals as existing on lower levels of the evolutionary ladder than white men (Rowold, 1996; Taylor & Shuttleworth, 1998).[1]

Today, most psychologists would agree that these ideas have no basis. However, we should keep in mind that it has taken a long time to erase the traces of eugenics in the discipline. In fact, ideas based on eugenics were influential in large parts of the Western world, including psychology, at least until the Second World War (Richards, 1997).[2] Furthermore, some ungrounded ideas about innate differences persisted even longer among some psychologists. For example, in the 1960s, when the number of women in the discipline began to increase, female psychologists sometimes had to battle some male colleagues' crude "evolutionary" ideas about women's and men's "natural abilities" (Bohan, 1992; Scarborough & Furumoto, 1987). Indeed, in those days, and in many (maybe most) countries of the world, a woman's wish to pursue higher education or a career outside the home might well have been regarded by psychotherapists as an indication of psychopathology, and therefore as an aberration that ought to be treated and corrected (Chesler, 1972; Friedan, 1963).

Much has changed since then. However, discussions, and even inflamed debates, about evolution and human psychology (including views of the abilities of women and of people who are not white) have raged off and on in the ensuing decades. Especially controversial have been the nativist and implicitly (and sometimes explicitly) racist and sexist propositions by sociobiologists and early evolutionary psychologists. By now, modern evolutionary theorists have thoroughly dispensed with those early propositions (Heintz & Scott-Phillips, 2023; Heyes, 2018; Kendal, Tehrani, & Odling-Smee, 2011; Plotkin, 2004, 2011; Waring & Wood, 2021).

Modern Evolutionary Theory: Genes and Culture in Context

An emphatic message from contemporary evolutionary theorists is that to understand how evolution influences humans in the short run as well as the long run, one must take the social and cultural surroundings into account

---

[1] Quite a few thinkers, including several psychologists and psychiatrists, therefore argued that women, and people of "lower races," should be kept out of well-paying professions and higher education, and should not be given the right to vote (Lewin, 1984; Rowold, 1996).

[2] For instance, National Socialists in Germany in the 1920s and 1930s built much of their race ideology on the writings of eugenicists in other Western countries.

as much as the physical surroundings. Further, one must take cultural forces into account, not just biological forces (Heyes & Moore, 2023; Plotkin, 2011; Uchiyama & Muthukrishna, 2021). This means that one cannot assume, as had been assumed earlier, that culture is primarily an *effect* of genetic evolution, but rather, as is the contemporary view, that culture is an active factor in enabling or even *causing* evolutionary change. One pertinent example is "niche construction." This expression denotes that humans can modify their local environments in ways that can then be *culturally* inherited by their offspring through teaching and imitation (Kendal, Tehrani, & Odling-Smee, 2011). We touched briefly on niche construction in Chapter 7, about language.

Modern evolutionary theorists also warn against some common misunderstandings of what evolution is (Olofsson & Örestig, 2015). The first misunderstanding is the notion that evolution is about "the survival of the fittest" in an ongoing fight with competitors, especially for access to food. In actuality, evolution is about random mutations and gradual change over eons, taking place in often-changing environments and often-changing cultural contexts, and therefore requiring a variety of behaviors. A second misunderstanding is the mistaken belief that if a trait fits well into contemporary environments, this should be taken as proof that the trait evolved for that purpose. In fact, such a trait may be an evolutionary byproduct of an original process that had nothing to do with the contemporary functionality of the particular trait (Such traits are sometimes called *spandrels*; see Gould & Lewontin, 1978.) A third mistake is to think of evolution as completely random. While there is randomness in the appearance of new gene material through mutations, the consequences of mutations are not random. Whether a certain genetic change in humans contributes to survival is determined by historical and ecological contexts, including culture, and such contexts do not vary randomly. A fourth mistake is believing that whatever has developed during evolution is "natural" and therefore good and useful. On the contrary, there are many "natural" and evolved traits that are far from perfect and not very well fitted for their supposed purpose. A fifth mistake is to think that evolution was a matter of the past and that it has reached an end state. But evolution continues. It is happening right now. In fact, there are signs that culture and cultural changes play increasingly central roles in evolutionary change today (Waring & Wood, 2021). So, evolution is complex. Something of the complexity comes across in this quote from the UK-based language researcher Kenny Smith:

If we are interested in how culture shapes the evolution of cognition (for language or other behaviors), we need to understand both how cognition shapes culture, and how this in turn allows culture to reshape cognition, either through gene–culture co-evolution or acquired biases in learning. (2020, p. 707)

Psychologists and Evolutionary Theory Today

In recent years, inspired by recent developments in evolutionary theory, genetics, epigenetics, and linguistics, some psychologists are approaching questions of evolution and human psychology anew. These psychologists share a skepticism about early nativist and eugenic ideas among psychologists. Beyond this basic stance, there are differences, for instance, in which abilities they see as foundational for the evolution of human culture. Different scholars also have different ideas about whether these foundational abilities were the products of genetic evolution or of cultural developments (Heyes & Moore, 2023). In one view, the tools, techniques, and norms of today's humans have been culturally inherited, but the cognitive processes that made this cultural inheritance possible were genetically inherited (Henrich & Muthukrishna, 2021). In a second view, social interactions during childhood play a more substantial role in cognition than in the first view, but genetic inheritance is seen as the leading force in shaping cognitive processes and abilities such as shared intentionality (Tomasello, 2020). In the third view, social interaction contributes more to the cognitive processes that enable cultural development than in the first two views, and genetic inheritance contributes less. In this view, interactions during individual development use and re-purpose previously inherited mechanisms for learning, motivation, and attention that humans share with other vertebrates. This view refutes the ideas of very specific genetically inherited programs for abilities such as mentalizing, shared intentionality, or language (Heyes, 2018, 2019, 2024; see also Chiao & Blizinsky, 2019). The third view has received support from recent studies of the relations between cognition and behavior on the one hand, and gene expression on the other hand. On that basis, one international team of researchers concluded that "*. . .cognitive and behavioral traits are massively polygenic (depending on hundreds or thousands of genes) and are driven by complex gene-by-environment interactions. . . . Genetic contributions to behavior are often socially contingent and more probabilistic and interactive than deterministic*" (Brick et al., 2022, p. 495).

Psychology, Science, and the Problem of Measurement: The Quantitative Imperative

Most psychologists use quantitative methods in their research. In fact, using quantitative methods is so common in psychology that reliance on them may seem self-evident: for many psychologists, "method" has come to mean *quantitative* methods. However, in the earliest period of the discipline's history, this was not the case. Many kinds of methods were used. What caused the change? To answer that question, it is necessary to look at the budding discipline of psychology in European and American universities in its historical context.

While philosophers and others had been writing treatises on psychological topics for many centuries, it was not until the very end of the nineteenth century that psychology became its own academic discipline. This meant that psychology was a newcomer in university settings compared to the natural sciences, which by then were well-established and notably successful. Therefore, many academic psychologists were made to feel that they needed to prove that psychology deserved to be called a science. To understand how they sought to prove this, we need to do a short detour to the early history of science.

One of the effects of the scientific revolution of the seventeenth century was a consensus that the natural world consisted solely of matter, that matter had a quantitative structure, and that anything material could, therefore, be measured and counted. There was also a consensus that mental phenomena (i.e., psychological phenomena) were not part of the natural material world. They were seen as a distinct nonmaterial kind that was nonquantitative and, therefore, not measurable. This view gave rise to *the quantity objection* (also called the *exclusionist* tradition) that many scholars used to refute early attempts to develop quantitative theories about mental phenomena or quantitative measurements of such phenomena (Michell, 1997, 2006). The quantity objection to the possibility of measuring mental phenomena held sway, with somewhat varying force, throughout the nineteenth century.

We now look at the intellectual context in Europe during the second half of the nineteenth century, which was the time and the place in which the academic discipline of psychology began consolidating. Because of the immense successes of the natural sciences since the eighteenth century, and the many technological and practical uses of scientific discoveries, there had been a significant change in worldview among scholars as well as in large parts of the general public. It may be difficult for us today to appreciate the immensity of the move from the traditional worldview to the modern "scientific" worldview that took place across the nineteenth century in large parts of the Western world. It was in this period that the natural sciences acquired their high status in the academy and in society at large. *Being scientific* became a badge of honor eagerly sought after in the new disciplines that were established.[3] Among them was psychology.

In the natural sciences, "being scientific" had become increasingly, and more explicitly, synonymous with being able to measure; a *quantitative imperative* had been in force more or less since the scientific revolution. Constantly refining their measurement methods had become an important activity for natural scientists (Hacking, 1983). The high value given to quantification and measuring in the natural sciences influenced early psychologists in their strivings to have their discipline accepted as a real science. Considering the high status of the natural sciences, this is not surprising. Could overcoming the quantity objection, and making much more use of quantitative measurements, lead to acceptance of psychology as a real science? Many of the psychologists of the day were prepared to bet that it would.

This belief was reflected in psychologists' publications at the end of the nineteenth century (Michell, 2004). Quotes from two of the most influential early psychologists illustrate this: Francis Galton (in the UK) stated that, "...*until the phenomena of any branch of knowledge have been submitted to measurement and number, it cannot assume the status and dignity of a science*" (1879, p. 147). And James McKeen Cattell (in the US) observed in 1893: "*The history of science is the history of measurement*" (p. 316). Cattell saw the developmental state of the psychology discipline in the 1890s as akin to the state of biology and chemistry 200 years previously, and he concluded, "*If material science* [biology and chemistry] *once consisted of definitions, anecdotes, and speculations, it is no wonder that these make up a large part of psychology at the present time*" (1879, p. 318). Since then, Cattell noted, chemistry and biology had progressed from their undeveloped state to their contemporary status as real sciences. They had done so by becoming increasingly able to quantify, and measure, their objects. On this basis,

---

[3] It may be of interest to reflect for a moment on a difference in terminology between the English language and other European languages such as German and the Scandinavian languages. In English, the word "science" is generally taken to mean only *natural* science. In German and Scandinavian languages the corresponding words, "Wissenschaft" and vetenskap/videnskap, have a wider meaning: they include more than just the natural sciences. The social disciplines and the humanities are usually also called Wissenschaften/vetenskaper. In that intellectual context, for a discipline to be called a Wissenschaft or vetenskap did not require the same strictures of quantification and measurement as it did in the English-speaking academic world to be called a science.

Cattell expected a similar progression for psychology, but he thought it would take time: *"...mental phenomena are more multiform, complex, transient, and obscure than those of the living body. It is natural, therefore, that psychology should be the last of the sciences"* (1879, p. 319). To decide if psychology could become a real science, he concluded, *"... we have to consider [...] whether there are mental magnitudes analogous to those of the physical world, and, if so, whether they may be measured and correlated"* (1879, p. 321).

Only a few decades later, in the 1920s and 1930s, most academic psychologists, especially those in North America and the UK, had become convinced that mental magnitudes existed, and that they were measurable. From then on, psychologists increasingly favored quantitative methods.[4] Many psychologists even imported the natural sciences' *imperative* to use quantitative measurements. In the same period, the quantity objection faded from view, and it did so without much discussion (Michell, 1999).

The verdict by historians of psychology who have studied this period is that the psychologists of the day did not, in fact, produce a convincing rationale for assuming that psychological predicates were measurable, nor for adopting quantitative methods (Hornstein, 1988; Michell, 1997). In Joel Michell's words, *"scientific measurement requires confirmation that the relevant attribute is quantitative, which means evidence of internal ordinal and additive structure"* (Michell, 2023, p. 662). Such confirmation of quantitative properties was not forthcoming in psychology. That is, and as was also noted by critics at the time, psychologists did not resolve the basic issues of the quantity objection. If so, why did they adopt the measurability thesis and the almost exclusive use of quantitative methods? Further, why did they almost across the board begin to enforce a quantitative imperative? After all, assuming measurability and preferring quantitative methods would not necessarily have led psychologists to enforce an imperative to use *only* quantitative methods.

One possible partial answer comes from the work of the German psychophysicist Gustav Fechner. In the second half of the nineteenth century, Fechner argued that because the senses were part of the body, they were material, and therefore sense data had to have a quantitative structure (Hornstein, 1988; Michell, 1997). Many psychologists – though far from all in those early days – were convinced that Fechner's claim made

---

[4] In continental Europe and the Nordic countries this development was slower, possibly because for several decades to come, research and teaching of psychology was typically part of philosophy departments or departments of education.

it safe to assume that psychological properties generally should be seen as "material" and therefore quantifiable.

Another possible answer is practical and perhaps political. Using quantitative methods produced data in the form of numbers, and the fact that researchers were able to produce numbers was, in itself, taken as support for the quantitative view (Danziger, 1985; Gigerenzer, 1991; Stevens, 1946). And in the eyes of many, this made psychology seem scientific. It is worth noting, though, that the methods used to produce measurements of psychological phenomena were constructed in such a way that they could produce only quantitative results. There was no way for such methods to "find" that psychological phenomena were nonquantitative. Logically, this also means that there was no way for these methods to "find" that psychological phenomena were quantitative. Because the measurement methods presupposed a quantitative structure, they could not help but produce quantitative data, thus strengthening the belief that psychological phenomena have a quantitative structure. In Ludwik Fleck's terms (see Chapter 2), we would see this as an example of how an *active* assumption became built into the methods and practices of large parts of the discipline of psychology. In this case, what became built in was an unproven assumption that the psychological phenomena that were studied had quantitative properties. Over time, the fact that no one had answered the theoretical question of whether psychological phenomena were really made up of quantitative units came to seem more and more irrelevant (Hornstein, 1988).

Yet another kind of practical answer can be found in the common (though false) equation of numerical data with precision and objectivity (Porter, 1995). Being associated with precision and objectivity conferred social and economic advantages, as well as an increase in status in society, to the young psychology discipline (Michell, 1999). The same was true for politics within universities. Finally, the use of quantification and measurement, combined with increasingly advanced statistical techniques, helped professional psychologists to create a sharp distinction between the academic ("real") discipline of psychology and popular psychology.

As the US-based psychologist and historian Gail Hornstein has noted, many psychologists in the early days just ignored the opposition to the quantitative imperative. Others used a debating strategy that split apart theoretical issues about measurement from methodological practices. Those who used the latter strategy talked about methods as being "just techniques" and claimed that they were therefore theoretically neutral. Ludwik Fleck would have objected to the validity of such arguments because, in his (and several other writers') view, a method always has its basis in some theory (see Chapter 2). However, for many psychologists, talking about methods as atheoretical "...*made it seem possible to proceed with the work despite the ongoing debates*" (Hornstein, 1988, p. 7).

As time went on, many psychologists went further and began using adherence to quantitative methods as *the* criterion of good research. This meant that "...*the more quantitative a line of research, the more plausible its results were seen to be*" (Hornstein, 1988, p. 22). Adhering to the quantitative imperative also simplified the researcher's choices when designing a study, because psychologists soon developed a number of standardized quantitative techniques for researchers to apply. This standardization relieved researchers of many complex decisions about their research, because those decisions were already made in the approved methodological packages. Using Ludwik Fleck's terms, we would say that the quantitative imperative functioned as part of a powerful thinking style, carried by an active thought collective and making it unlikely for a psychologist to even consider other ways of doing psychological research.

In conclusion, it is fair to say that a quantitative imperative has been active in large parts of the academic discipline of psychology in many, or even most, Western countries for most of the twentieth century. Most of the time, there was little discussion about this imperative. However, in recent years, the debates about quantitative characteristics and measurement in psychology have reemerged, and the quantitative imperative is not quite so dominant today as it used to be. We refer interested readers to discussions between psychologists about questions such as whether psychological inventories and rating scales really *measure* anything psychological at all (Uher, 2021, 2022); whether psychological phenomena should be imagined to have quantitative properties or not (Michell, 2022, 2023); whether this question is one that could ever be answered empirically (Trendler, 2022); and whether it even makes sense to ask the question about quantitative psychological properties (Franz, 2022a, 2022b; Mayrhofer & Hutmacher, 2020; Slaney et al., 2024; Tafreshi, 2022; Uher, 2021).

Operational Definitions and Operationism

Our third historical example concerns a question that is connected to the issues surrounding quantitative measurement in psychology: How should a psychologist *define* that which is to be studied? Ideally, a definition of a thing describes the principal features, or the structure, of that thing: the "what-it-is-to-be *that kind of thing – its principal features or structure*" (Hibberd, 2019, p. 31). In order to describe these features and structures, the researcher obviously must be able to observe them. However, psychologists typically study phenomena (such as cognitions, emotions, and so on) that cannot be directly observed and described. Therefore an ideal definition is seldom possible. To get around this problem, experimental psychologists in the 1930s began using *operational definitions* (Leahey, 1980; Stevens, 1935, 1946). A common description of an operational definition is "*a description of something in terms of the operations (procedures, actions, or processes) by which it could be observed and measured*" (APA, 2024). Some examples are: scores on an anxiety inventory as the definition of anxiety; increases in heart rate as the definition of anxiety; increases in cortisol levels in the blood as the definition of stress; an IQ test as the definition of intelligence; the number of hours since the last meal as the definition of hunger; and Major Depression Disorder defined as comprising a particular set of symptom criteria in the DSM.

The practicing researcher uses operational definitions in order to make it possible to study unobservable psychological phenomena. To decide on an operational definition of a phenomenon, a researcher may begin by perusing the research literature for existing operational definitions. The next step is to either adopt one of those operations, or, if none are satisfactory, to construct a new operational definition. Using operational definitions helps communication between researchers: If two researchers have used the same operational definition of a concept, they tend to feel certain that they are studying the same thing.

The time and place to look for the beginnings of operational definitions in psychology is the 1930s and the United States, when many academic psychologists were inspired by the logical positivist movement and by the physicist Percy Bridgman's "operational attitude" to science (Leahey, 2001; Rychlak, 1983). Operational definitions were soon adopted as the main definition strategy in large parts of the psychology discipline. The word "operationism" (or sometimes "operationalism") came into use as a summary term for the practice of using operational definitions.

However, even from the beginning, there was disagreement about these definitions. Those in favor of their use asserted that operational definitions are theoretically neutral methodological tools, and that their use, therefore, implies no specific epistemological assumptions (Stevens, 1946). Those who were critical argued, to the contrary, that operational definitions are not neutral tools; like all methodological tools, they are built on certain assumptions about that which is being studied (Danziger, 1985;

Green, 2001; Hibberd, 2019; Leahey, 1980, 2001). The critics, therefore, concluded that an "...*attempt to detach operationism from its philosophical context merely smuggles that context into psychology unexamined*" (Leahey, 1981, p. 343). This critical conclusion is akin to how Ludwik Fleck reasoned about thinking styles. He described how some of a thinking style's active assumptions (i.e., the "philosophical context" in the quote) may sometimes be "smuggled" in via the use of a particular research method.

Think back to the general idea of a definition that we quoted earlier: A definition describes "*the* what-it-is-to-be *that kind of thing – its principal features or structure.*" If we take that idea to heart, then in order to accept the use of operational definitions, we must assume that the measuring *operation* that we have chosen really describes "*the what-it-is-to-be*" of the psychological phenomenon we want to study. This is not an assumption that everybody would accept (though it would be one of the active assumptions, in Fleck's terms, that underpin the use of operational definitions). Critics have argued instead that by describing complex psychological phenomena in terms of a measurement procedure, researchers may end up with theories in which those psychological concepts have lost their original meaning (Mayrhofer & Hutmacher, 2020). The German psychologists Fabian Hutmacher and David Franz (2025) summarize this critical position:

> Since the meaning of psychological concepts and the rules for their application are dependent on their relations to other terms, to actions, to social norms, to institutions, and to culturally shaped and shared worldviews, technical conceptualizations (e.g., as achieved by an operational definition) will not be sufficient for theorizing about, explaining, and understanding a psychological concept, or for using the concept in a meaningful way in scientific or ordinary discourse. (p. 225)

Critics have also pointed to the risk of conflating the *measurement* of a variable or property with that variable or property *itself*. According to these critics, operational definitions have a logical error built into them: an operational definition " ... *confuses the activity of manipulating and/or measuring a variable with what that variable is (or with what the term referring to the variable stands for)*" (Hibberd, 2019, p. 45). In a similar vein, others have noted that operational definitions confuse the *process* of measuring with the *quantity* that is the object of the measuring process (Michell, 1999). This means that there may be a risk that researchers take the *measure* of a dependent variable as being the same as the *phenomenon* that they want to study. A researcher who does so is arguing in a (vicious) circle, which would insert an irreparable error (Danziger, 1985). We take up the risk of such methodological circles in Chapter 11, about contemporary critique and disagreements among psychologists.

Another twist on this critique is that "*If operations literally* define *concepts (i.e., the concept is* nothing but *the operation by which it is defined), then each operation defines a new concept*" (Green, 2001, p. 46; emphasis in the original). Here we can think about the long-lived debates about what intelligence "really is." These debates had their origin in the different operational definitions that were used by different psychologists, who, not surprisingly, disagreed about what the real *phenomenon* "intelligence" is.

Critics both inside and outside psychology have claimed that the operationism that early psychologists such as Stanley Smith Stevens and Edward Tolman developed was a philosophical mistake with very practical-scientific consequences. The critics argue that, by excluding practically all other ways of doing and thinking about research from the discipline, operationism hampered progress in psychology in the following decades (Green, 1992; Hibberd, 2019; Leahey, 1980, 2001). The US psychologist Thomas Leahey has summarized this critique: "*Operational definition – even in Bridgman's ur-operational definition – is not the pure theory-neutral methodological technique that psychologists think it is, because it endorses some forms of psychological theory and forecloses others*" (2001, p. 54; see also Green, 1992).

Several critics argue that psychologists should stop using operational definitions in their research. Other critics think psychologists are entitled to keep using operational definitions, provided that they stay aware of the traps and shortcomings connected with that use, such as the ones we have mentioned here. The second group of critics especially urges researchers to stay vigilant about how they conceive of all parts of the triad of their *concepts*, their *operationalizations* of their concepts, and their *validations* of them. Researchers should, above all, not allow themselves to lapse into the routine use of operational definitions found in the research literature. They have to be aware of the timebound nature of psychological knowledge, and the culturally induced changes that continually affect many psychological topics and questions (Feest, 2005; Slife, Wright, & Yanchar, 2016; Vessonen, 2021). And researchers must, above all, be aware that there are no neutral definitions. All definitions are based in some interest, theory, or ideology, and all definitions *do* things with our view of that which is being defined. Michael Billig reminds us that:

... definitions have a rhetorical, or argumentative, meaning, for the academic definition of a commonly used term is not merely an elaboration of internal meanings, but is an argument against other definitions. The function of such a definition is to locate the essence of the matter in a direction which accords with the theoretical leanings of the writer, and to move it away from those of rival theoreticians. (1996, p. 178)

We noted Thomas Leahey's argument that an "*. . .attempt to detach operationism from its philosophical context merely smuggles that context into psychology unexamined*" (1981, p. 343). Is there a risk that such "smugglings" occur today? It would certainly seem so. In contemporary textbooks for beginning students of psychology, including methods textbooks, operational definitions are typically described merely as methodological tools and often as the paramount, and therefore the best (or the only), method for definitions. Discussions about critical questions about operational definitions tend to be conspicuously absent.

The History of Psychology's Words

In this section, we take a look at the words that psychologists use. Where did the common "psychological" words come from? And how, and for what purposes, and in what social and political circumstances did they get the meanings and uses that they have for psychologists today? Have the words always had those particular meanings and uses, or have their meanings changed in significant ways? If so, why and with what consequences, if any? To explore the history of a psychological word, one looks for how particular historical circumstances and cultural contexts may have shaped the meaning and use of that word (Danziger, 1997).

As we noted in Chapter 9, many psychological words are part of everyday language. This fact is due to two historical "migration" processes. First, when psychologists began theorizing about the human psyche, what they had to work with were ordinary people's words for describing their experiences and actions. That is, many or even most psychological categories (and in some cases the exact words for them) were part of language long before psychologists began studying them. Kurt Danziger provides an example of such a word, "emotion": "*Psychologists did not invent the concept of 'emotion,' for example, to account for certain empirical findings; they obtained certain empirical findings because of their desire to investigate a set of events which their culture had taught them to distinguish as 'emotional'*" (1997, p. 6). That is, psychological theorizing did not start from some empirical zero, as it were; it began in linguistically expressed, already existing everyday understandings of that which psychologists wanted to study. On the basis of these everyday words, psychologists developed a terminology that became the kernel of psychological theory and practice. Note that this process is quite different from that of the natural sciences, where researchers typically invent new words and new concepts.

Could the use of commonplace words to theorize psychology create problems for the discipline of psychology? On that question, opinions vary. However, if the use of commonplace words leads to a lack of stringency in psychologists' usage of words, this can have problematic consequences. It will inevitably cause conceptual confusion, which, in turn, will lead to confusion about the meaning of empirical research results, and perhaps even about theoretical conclusions. To counteract such confusions – conceptual as well as empirical – psychologists need to look carefully at the words they use, to make sure that they use them consistently, and with meanings about which there is consensus. One way to achieve this is to engage in what is usually called conceptual analysis. We describe such analysis in Chapter 13, in which we present strategies for becoming a discerning reader of psychology.

In a second, reverse migration process, as psychologists studied, treated, and wrote about humans, they used their psychological terminology to communicate their findings. In this process, some of the newly minted psychological words migrated from the ranks of psychological scientists and clinicians to become part of everyday language. Some examples are stress, depression, attitudes, group processes, trauma, personality, and variable. There are many more.

These migrations show that psychological words do not (as do many words in the natural sciences) live their lives in a scientific sphere far away from people's everyday lives. Rather, as we noted in Chapter 8, in many countries, people eagerly deploy these psychological words in their daily lives, using them to make sense of their own and others' experiences and behaviors in their daily lives (Hacking, 1995; Kleinman, 1988).

Through another type of migration, mainly since the Second World War, the vocabularies of academic psychology and clinical psychological practice in many parts of the world have been heavily influenced by the vocabulary of North American psychologists, particularly those based in the United States (Danziger, 1997; Richards & Stenner, 2023). Note that the point here is not that psychological publications are written in English (though they often are). The point is that many of the words, concepts, and categories used by North American psychologists have found their way into the vocabularies and theories of psychologists in other countries.

These words, etc., are likely to be influenced by the values, norms, and life forms of the North American cultural settings in which they were first elaborated and promoted. And, of course, those values and norms might not be consonant with those of other cultural settings, such as non-Western parts of the world, but also other parts of the Western world. In recent years, this migration has led to counter-movements, such as decolonial psychology (Bhatia et al, 2024; Garcini et al., 2025; Hook, 2025).

There are two different dimensions to consider here: First, there is the dominance of a psychological vocabulary, concepts, theories, and research results that have been developed in one cultural setting and might be ill-fitted for other cultural settings (Henrich, Heine, & Norenzayan, 2010). Second, there is the long-lived conviction of *universality* in much of Western psychology. This is the assumption that the standard Western psychological vocabulary is applicable everywhere. But, as Kurt Danziger noted nearly three decades ago: "*Contrary to common belief, these categories do not occupy some rarefied place <u>above</u> culture but are embedded in a particular professional sub-culture*" (1997, p. 5, emphasis in the original).

How did the notion of a vocabulary that stands apart from culture come to be common in Western psychology? A dip into disciplinary history can provide some clues: As we saw in the discussion about the problems of measurement in psychology, when the discipline of psychology began to establish itself in universities in Europe and North America, a primary ambition of many pioneers was for psychology to become accepted as a natural science. This meant, to quote the British historians of psychology Graham Richards and Paul Stenner, that "*Psychology, in establishing itself as a 'Natural Science', began accepting the orthodox scientific assumption that its technical language referred unambiguously to naturally occurring phenomena, reflecting an 'objective' reality*" (2023, p. 255). Thus, many early psychologists assumed that psychological words like "intelligence," "personality," "emotion," "attitude" denoted – were the names of – objectively existing and naturally occurring phenomena, just as physicists took physical words like "atom" and "mass" to denote objectively existing and naturally occurring phenomena. In this view, what psychologists do in their research is – in analogy with the natural sciences – discovering universal facts about objectively existing, naturally occurring human properties (Danziger, 1997, 2006; Hacking, 2007a). Someone who regards psychological knowledge as analogous to knowledge of the physical world will assume that a psychological word will have a single universal meaning regardless of where it is used. Using Ludwik Fleck's terminology, we would say that this assumption formed part of a *universalist* thinking style in psychology.

Over recent decades, the conception of psychological knowledge as akin to physical or "natural" knowledge, and therefore universally valid, has been increasingly challenged. Jeff Sugarman (2009), a Canadian psychologist, has provided a helpful overview and discussion of the related philosophical positions. He also relates these positions to conventions in the psychology discipline. And in a recent article, Brick et al. (2022) provide a thorough discussion of the problems connected with the essentialist background assumptions that are at the base of universalist thinking in psychology. They argue that such assumptions make it tempting to see psychological concepts as representing natural categories, in line with those of the physical sciences. See also our discussion about the nature of psychological concepts in the section "Conceptual and Epistemological Critiques" in Chapter 9. In the section "Psychological Categories – Natural or Human-Made" in Chapter 12, we discuss the character of psychological properties in more detail.

But do *words* really matter that much? Yes, there are in fact good reasons to think that words *really* matter; that it matters greatly which words psychologists use, and how they think about these words when they use them. We end this section by once again quoting Graham Richards and Paul Stenner:

> . . . in symbolising our experiences, language by definition transforms them. Language is not all there is, but however "natural" or "universal" some human psychological phenomena may be, it is only via its mediation that we can refer to them, reflexively affecting them, to a greater or lesser degree, in so doing. This means that the world in which we actually live is a world mediated by language. (2023, p. 254)

The History of the Psychology of Women and Gender

In this section, we take up the history of the psychological study of gender. This research was influenced by, and also engaged with, the late twentieth-century social movements that challenged the gender order. Several of the psychologists who were active in driving changes in gender studies within psychology were also activists in the political women's movements in their countries. We have chosen North America as our main focus. However, very similar changes were happening, at varying speeds, in much of the Western world.

The academic discipline of psychology formed itself in Europe and North America at the end of the nineteenth century – a fact that is central to understanding many early psychologists' views on women. The nine-teenth century contained the long Victorian period with its intense societal focus on differences and hierarchies among humans; especially between women and men, but also differences between people of different ethnic groups (called "races" in those days). This focus was strengthened by the evolutionary thinking at the end of the nineteenth century (see the first section of this chapter), which heavily influenced neighboring fields such as medicine, biology, and psychology.

The first psychologists came of age in an era in which a view of white males as the superior representatives of the human species was taken as self-evident. When early psychologists wanted to study humans, they therefore studied men. In those days women, as well as other categories of people, were seldom studied except when they were compared with men, often in order to "prove" the inferiority of these categories to men. In fact, for much of its history, even long after its beginnings, general psychology remained "womanless" (Crawford & Marecek, 1989). Women appeared, when they appeared, for instance in studies of certain psychiatric disorders that were assumed to be caused by women's biology. By the middle of the century, women were still largely excluded from psychologists' experiments about "normal" psychology. The discipline thus tacitly maintained the early understanding that men were the prototypical humans. For similar reasons, members of minoritized or marginalized social groups were also excluded from research studies. Not surprisingly, therefore, few women were permitted entry into the profession of psychologist, or as researchers or teachers of psychology.

Within the context of disciplinary male-centeredness, many psycholo-gists developed a preoccupation with differences between the categories "women" and "men." In parts of the discipline, thinking about women and men in terms of differences between them became routinized and acquired the characteristics of the almost automatic "active assumptions" that in Ludwik Fleck's terms form the basis of a thinking style. One can see this in the practice of turning questions that concerned women[5] into research on differences between men and women (cf. Terman & Miles, 1936). We call this preoccupation, and the research methods that were used, the *sex*

---

[5] At the beginning of the twentieth century, typically such issues were women's right (or not) to vote, and women's access (or not) to higher education and prestigious professions. Psychological studies of "sex differences" in the assumed necessary abilities soon began appearing. However, these early studies tended to be, as one early feminist critic noted after having surveyed the literature, filled with " ... *flagrant personal bias, logic martyred in the cause of supporting a prejudice, unfounded assertions, and even sentimental rot and drivel*" (Thompson Woolley, 1910).

differences thinking style. It proved both long-lasting and resistant to change.

But is there really anything wrong with studying differences between women and men? In principle, no. However, as many gender scholars in psychology have argued, it was wrong to allow this thinking style to become so dominant that other, perhaps more important, aspects of the lives of women and men (and other sex categories), such as inequality and oppression, long remained below the radar for psychologists. Another unfortunate characteristic of research informed by the sex differences thinking style was that it tended to "homogenize" the sex categories: The focus on comparing women and men, as *groups*, moved attention away from important variations within the groups, such as differences based on social class or ethnicity (Magnusson & Marecek, 2012, esp. Ch. 14).

By the late 1960s, psychologists in some countries were evincing an increased interest in women and gender, as well as the first signs of a possible move beyond the sex differences thinking style. These changes coincided with, and were likely caused by, the increase in the number of women studying psychology at universities. This, in turn, was an effect of the general increase of women in the paid labor force and the parallel increase in women's educational attainment from the 1960s. These developments led to more women having work roles and responsibilities that had previously been reserved for men. And this led to discussions and comparisons of the abilities of women and men: Were women perhaps as good as men in the professional positions that they were now entering? Such questions were among those studied by psychologists in this era who were interested in gender.

These changes in psychology were also, at least partly, a result of the women's movement in Western countries. In the US and elsewhere, feminist activism was based on the aphorism *"the personal is political"* (coined by Carol Hanisch in 1970). This is an aphorism that has maintained its currency into the present. One form of feminist activism was "consciousness-raising": Small groups of women met together over a period of months to examine social and political issues in their lives. The aim was political: to develop a critical consciousness and to produce new knowledge about the societal basis of women's subordination.

Another kind of activism emerged among feminist scholars in many disciplines, including psychology, who brought to light the extent of gender-based domestic violence, rape, and the sexual abuse of girls. These scholars broke with long-standing taboos against speaking about such experiences: until then, women and girls had been well aware that, if they wanted to avoid stigma and further victimization, they should not talk about their experiences of abuse. Feminist activists also established service agencies such as rape crisis centers and shelters for women fleeing abusive relationships. Many of these agencies continue to this day, and several have expanded the scope of their work to respond to new forms of relationship violence. Other feminist activists carried out public education campaigns and promoted social, legal, and cultural transformations in the gender order, including legal activism to promote reforms in the adjudication of divorce, sexual assault, and workplace harassment (cf., Ferree & Martin, 1995; Kravetz, 2004). Further, many feminists in the mental health professions offered critiques of the theories and practices of psychotherapy, and some also developed new forms of interventions (Chesler, 1972; Greenspan, 1983).

In academic settings, feminist scholarship on women, gender, and sexuality burgeoned. The first officially recognized program in Women's Studies in the US began at San Diego State University (in California) in 1970. Many such programs of study soon followed at colleges and universities in many parts of the world. They offered a variety of academic options for students. In many disciplines, academic journals devoted to the publication of scholarly work on women and gender came into being. In psychology, these included *Psychology of Women Quarterly*, which began publishing in 1976, *Sex Roles* (1975), and *Feminism & Psychology* (1991). All these journals remain in publication today.

By the middle of the 1970s, many countries had enacted laws that barred discrimination based on a person's sex category. This opened doors to higher education previously closed to women, with psychology being one of the fields to which women flocked. However, when women sought entrée into academic departments of psychology as graduate students or faculty members, they were not always well-received (Bookwala & Newton, 2022). In some cases, there was outright opposition from some male faculty members who believed that women were incapable of the intellectual work that was required. Others believed that training women was a waste of resources, because they would soon marry, have children, and drop out of the professional work force. Some men believed that women lacked the ability to be competent psychotherapists and did not deserve places in training programs for clinical practitioners. Some voiced their worries that the "feminization" (as they termed it) of psychology would diminish the discipline's prestige, along with psychologists' earning potential. However, many men in the discipline were open to training female students and to working alongside female colleagues. It is worth noting that in these early discussions concerning women's place in the discipline, little or no attention was paid to the circumstances and obstacles faced by women who were not White.

As the cohorts of psychologists who had been steeped in the feminist movements of the 1970s took up academic positions, a substantial number of them turned their scholarly attention to re-assessing the claims regarding women's intellectual abilities, inclinations, and preferences, as well as their proper (or "natural") roles in the family, marriage, and public life. That is, these feminist psychologists began seriously questioning the long-standing *sex differences* thinking style in psychology. In some instances, the reevaluation took the form of historical inquiry. Stephanie Shields (1975), a US psychologist, for example, examined the ways in which scientific psychology of the late nineteenth and early twentieth century was shaped by the culture of that era. She described in detail the androcentric and sex-difference-oriented bias in psychologists' thinking that was a product of early evolutionary theory and conservative politics. Shields went so far as to argue that the psychological discipline of that era had played "*handmaiden to social values*" (1975, p. 753).

Against this historical background and the long life of the sex differences thinking style, it is not surprising that, as psychologists' attention turned to women, many still framed their research questions in terms of comparisons between men and women. For example, Eleanor Maccoby and Carol Jacklin, two US developmental psychologists, undertook an exhaustive review of the English-language corpus of empirical studies of sex differences. Their book *The Psychology of Sex Differences* (1974) assessed empirical studies on a wide range of social behaviors, intellectual abilities, motivations, and aspirations, asking in what ways and to what extent boys and girls, men and women, differed. Maccoby and Jacklin's review led them to two broad conclusions: First, they noted that there was only a handful of consistent findings of male–female differences, and those differences were quite small. Second, they noted that much of the research was methodologically flawed in such fundamental ways that firm conclusions could not be drawn (Jacklin, 1981; Maccoby & Jacklin, 1974).

Many feminists in psychology in this period studied sex differences in order to re-examine and disprove longstanding stereotypes about male superiority. However, several feminist psychologists soon called for replacing these efforts with research focusing on women in their own right, and also with research aimed at understanding the disparities in social power afforded to members of different sex categories (cf. Crawford & Marecek, 1989; Hare-Mustin & Marecek, 1988; Kessler

& McKenna, 1978; Parlee, 1979). As critical analyses of the gender order circulated through academia as well as public culture, many feminists in psychology turned their attention to the study of women's day-to-day lives. This involved setting aside disciplinary norms such as studying behavior in the laboratory and using males as the proper subjects for research. Furthermore, some feminist psychologists posed questions about experiences such as menstruation, childbirth, breastfeeding, sexuality, and abortion that had rarely been studied. Others pursued investigations of gendered power differences in marriage and family roles, in workplaces, in educational settings, and so on. Moreover, the many forms of gender-based violence that affected the lives of women and girls became an enduring focus of interest.

In the 1980s, many feminists in psychology were influenced by developments in the sociology of gender, such as Candace West and Don Zimmerman's (1987) suggestion that gender could be understood as something that people *do* in their daily lives; that is, it is in daily interactions that a person's sex category acquires its cultural meanings. Other feminist psychologists were influenced by the "turn to language" in academic scholarship in the same period and pressed for a close focus on how language powerfully shapes people's understanding of the world, including gender issues (Hare-Mustin & Marecek, 1989).

How has the discipline of psychology been changed by the efforts of feminists? In many parts of the world, the accomplishments and ideas of women in academic psychology have achieved a good deal of acceptance. Few, if any, academic psychologists today dismiss questions concerning women and gender as unworthy of study. Further, as a corollary, scholarly attention to masculinities and to boys' and men's life experiences has been growing, and queer perspectives are receiving increased attention in psychology. Moreover, women in clinical practice are no longer relegated to the margins of the discipline, nor are they regarded (as was common earlier) as capable only of working with children.

Today, the psychological study of gender relations and people's everyday lives is more multifaceted than before. For instance, the US legal scholar Kimberlé Crenshaw's writings on intersectionality directed researchers' attention to the need to devise ways of capturing the experiences and meanings of the intertwined social categorizations that are always active in an individual's life (such as gender, race, ethnicity, and social class) (Crenshaw, 1989). There is now more scrutiny of the Western-centric elements of psychological theories, concepts, and research approaches, coupled with increased recognition of and respect for cultural particularities of human thought and action, and calls for an increase in cultural humility among psychologists (Christopher et al., 2014).

Psychologists nowadays – both researchers and practitioners – in several parts of the world are increasingly attuned to the emergence of new categories pertaining to sex and gender. They are open to people's adoption of new categorizations to describe their gender (e.g., genderqueer, agender, genderfluid, nonbinary) and are prepared to support those who experience deep unease because their physical appearance does not match their identity. Also, a good deal of knowledge has accumulated regarding services and practices to help survivors of gender-based violence. However, little is still known about ways to curb intimate violence. Gender-based violence remains a key social problem across the world, despite over fifty years of activism and research.

As a finish, we should note again that most of the content of this section describes the historical contexts of the psychologies of women and gender in the US. In the rest of the Western world, somewhat different issues have been at the forefront, and there have been different timescales of social changes. Were we to examine the emergence of feminist social movements and scholarship outside Western countries, the differences would be even more striking. However, in many (perhaps most) parts of the world where psychology in the Western style is being taught and practiced, things have changed in somewhat similar ways, and they have changed mainly due to social movements such as those we described in this section.

Learning from History

We began this chapter with a question: Can psychologists learn anything from studying the history of their discipline? In the introduction, we asserted that they can, and after our descriptions of a few historical periods and processes in the discipline, we hope that readers agree. We should also emphasize that the examples we have given are only a handful of the many fascinating – and sometimes deeply problematic – developments and debates in the history of the discipline and practice of psychology. In the next chapter, we move forward into contemporary times and present some of the foremost debates and disagreements among psychologists today.

CHAPTER 11

Contemporary Debates among Psychologists

Psychologists have always quarreled among themselves about the best ways to do psychology, and about what kind of endeavor "psychology" really is. This is as it should be. The worst that could happen to psychology as a discipline and a professional practice would be that psychologists just sat back in contentment and stopped bothering about foundational questions. In this chapter, we take up some issues that have been debated in recent decades. We focus on issues that have some bearing on the views of humans as socially contextualized persons that we have described in this book.

In the first section, we point to the inseparability of method and theory in psychology, and the consequences that follow if a researcher is unaware of this connection. In the second section, we examine problems with the practice of relying on group averages to draw conclusions about individuals. In the third section, the focus is on variables, and especially the historical changes in how variables have been thought about and used in psychological research. In the fourth section, we look closely, and critically, at the uses (and sometimes misuses) of tests of statistical significance. In the final section, we take up psychologists' understandings of the term "concept."

Methodological Circles in Psychological Research and Theory

In many settings, the word "method" conveys the idea of something strictly procedural, freed from theoretical assumptions – just something one *does.* However, a method is much more than just something one "does." In Chapter 2, we described Ludwik Fleck's view of methods as the *passive or automatic consequences* of the active (or theoretical) assumptions that form the basis of a thinking style. A certain set of active assumptions about those who are being studied leads researchers to use methods that are consonant with those assumptions. This means that research methods inevitably have certain assumptions built into them: they can never be "theory-neutral."

To quote Kurt Danziger, a research method "*is the repository of explicit and implicit theoretical assumptions*" (1985, p. 1). Danziger further noted that such inbuilt assumptions can have far-reaching consequences that he named "methodological circles."

> We have here the possibility of a *methodological* circle where methods based on assumptions about the nature of the subject matter only produce observations which must confirm these assumptions. Within such a circle theoretical change would be limited to the set of theories which share the assumptions incorporated in the methodological rules. (1985, p. 1, emphasis in the original)

It follows from this quote that methodological circles can limit the possibilities for theoretical development about research topics. Could such limiting via methodological circles be a problem in psychology? Perhaps. In the sections that follow, we discuss some practices, and some problem areas, in contemporary psychology that might contribute to methodological circles. We prefigure these sections with another quote from Kurt Danziger. It echoes Ludwik Fleck's arguments about thinking styles and thought collectives and warns psychologists of the dangers of remaining within the "charmed circle" of their own conventions:

> It is clear that the theoretical assumptions which are built into the standard methodology can never be refuted by the use of this methodology. The fundamental features of the data base are predetermined by the methodology that produces it. . . As long as the methodology enjoys overwhelming social support within the scientific community these features are protected from the effects of contrary evidence because no evidence from outside the charmed methodological circle is accepted as valid. Within the circle no anomalies can arise, at least not with respect to the forms that the method necessarily impresses on the evidence. (1985, p. 10)

Danziger continued: "*A more fundamental theoretical change would surely depend on a fundamental change in methodology*" (1985, p. 10). In other words: No thoroughgoing theoretical change will be possible unless a researcher looks critically at the "charmed circles" created by the assumptions that underpin their methods. We therefore argue that it is necessary for psychologists to occasionally step outside their own "charmed circles" and scrutinize both the origins and the consequences of the theories and methods they espouse. In the following sections, we take up some such origins and consequences, and recent debates about them.

Psychological Research Is Often Based on Group Averages. Is This a Good Way to Create Knowledge about *Persons*?

In a common form of psychological research, the researcher measures some property or activity (such as reaction time or personality traits) of participants who have been assigned to two or more groups that are hypothesized to differ in some theoretically interesting way. The groups are then compared by the aid of calculations based on the arithmetic means and standard deviations of each group's measurements. These procedures are so commonplace in psychology that they tend to be taken for granted. Indeed, it may seem strange to even bring them up for scrutiny. The principle is that the individual participants provide the data needed to construct an aggregate for each research group, and it is on the basis of these aggregates that researchers then form their generalizations (Wilson, 2004).

However, since their inception in the early twentieth century, these practices have been criticized for committing the *ecological* fallacy of using *group* characteristics (means, standard deviations, correlations, and so on) as the basis for theorizing about the psychology of *individuals* (Lamiell, 2019, 2021). The mistake is that the *distribution* of data across the groups is used to draw conclusions about the meaning of the concept for the *individuals* who are being studied. This, in turn, implies the theoretical claim that individual *differences* (as measured across a group) can be equated with *individuality*, that is, with the properties of individual persons (Uher, 2022). In other words, the researcher assumes *"that the structure of psychological processes in individuals is isomorphic, or at least essentially comparable, to the structure of group data"* (Danziger, 1985, p. 6).

The assumption of isomorphism between individuality and group averages is one of the bases for the psychology of individual differences and, thereby, for much of personality psychology (Uher, 2021). However, the soundness of this assumption has been questioned on the basis of the arguments above (Lamiell, 2021). The critics point out that, although psychological studies that compare groups can provide demographic data that can be useful for making policy decisions, such studies tell us nothing about the individuals who participated (Lamiell, 2019; Speelman & McGann, 2016). Further, statistical inferences drawn from group data (such as averages) are defined to be valid only for *aggregates* of individuals, that is, for groups (Grice, 2015; Grice et al., 2020; te Meerman, Freedman, & Batstra, 2022; Piantadosi, Byar, & Green, 1988). In fact, group averages can mask great variations among the participants in a study (Speelman &

McGann, 2016). This, in turn, can have theoretical consequences, because research that is limited to analyses at the group level will, again by definition, be unable to produce descriptions of real individuals (Uher, 2022).

Assuming isomorphism also implies accepting the *homogeneity* premise: The idea that changes in psychological functions that are measured on the group level are caused in exactly the same way in all participating individuals. The homogeneity premise has been called into question, first, because individuals' life experiences vary considerably; and second, on the basis of the plasticity of the human nervous system in the face of these variations in experiences (Richters, 2021).

To highlight the details of the problem of using group averages for theorizing about individuals, Aaron Fisher, John Medaglia, and Bertus Jeronimus (2018), three US psychologists, compared group data, such as averages, with individual data points in six different studies. They found that there were large discrepancies between the *estimates* of individual values made from the group data and the *actual* individual data points. This means that the individual level and the group level in a study are not necessarily related, that is, one cannot uncritically assume a group-to-individual generalizability. On the contrary, such generalizability is something that needs to be proved in each case.

There have been some attempts at devising methods for avoiding the ecological fallacy of using group data as the basis for conclusions about individuals. Grice et al. (2020) have suggested a statistical method for analysis in which persons are the focal points of analysis, instead of the usual group averages. They argued, by the use of illustrative examples, that this method makes it possible to go beyond averages and find out how many, and which, of the participants in a study who responded in the theoretically expected ways. Another method that has been suggested is to complement the use of conventional statistics with a coefficient of centrality (Trafimow, 2019a).

Variables in Psychology

Today, "variable" is a central term in psychological research and theory, but it was not always so. The story of variables in psychology is the story of how a word that began its life as a purely statistical-technical term was gradually incorporated into the discipline's vocabulary and eventually was also used to refer to the internal processes of those whom psychologists study. By the middle of the twentieth century, using the word variable with this "inside" meaning had become firmly established in psychologists' vocabulary. We devote the main part of this section to the establishment of this meaning of the term. At the end of the section, we briefly discuss a use of the term that is problematic in another way – when social categories such as class, "race"/ethnicity, gender, age, health status, and so on are made to serve as "independent variables" in research.

Early psychologists encountered the word "variable" only as a term in statistics, for example when using statistical *test variables* such as *Student's t* and *F*. This was soon to change. The change began in the 1910s and 1920s, as behaviorists introduced stimulus-response language. In behaviorists' experiments (and in contrast to the earlier introspection experiments), the theoretical concepts that were studied were described in "stimulus" (S) and "response" (R) terms. Using S-R terms in research eventually became the norm in much of psychology. It was not long, however, before many psychologists began to take exception to the behaviorist and even mechanistic associations of the words *stimulus* and *response*. In the 1930s, *variable* was suggested as a more neutral word to use, and it soon became common as a substitute at both the "stimulus" and the "response" ends. This was a *conceptual transformation* – it meant that the word "variable" went from being used to denote statistical test variables such as *t* and *F*, to denoting what went on in the experimental situation. This transformation took place during the 1930s and 1940s, and it happened in several steps (for many interesting details of how the uses of "variable" increased during this period, see especially Danziger, 1997; Danziger & Dzinas, 1997).

In a first step, expressions such as "manipulation of variables" became common as a description of the experimenter's actions at the stimulus end of an experiment, which typically consisted of varying the strength or frequency of the stimulus. The stimulus that the experimenter manipulated soon became called the "independent variable." The change from "stimulus" was fairly straightforward: the experimenter *varied* the stimulus that was presented, and so the word "variable" made some sense.

In a second step, "variable" began to be used as well for what the experimenter would read off at the response end: the subject's response. This was named the *dependent variable* because its values were assumed to *depend* on the variations of the independent variable (Danziger & Dzinas, 1997; MacMartin & Winston, 1990). For the dependent variable, the change also seemed straightforward: it was used for the R in the S-R model, indicating the subject's *overt* responses, and the fact that they *varied*. The experimenter registered changes in these responses, such as a measurable change in social behavior or reaction time by a human subject, or a change in the frequency of bar pressings by a rat. These changes were taken as measures of the specific dependent variables.

Then, in a third step, the term "dependent variable" was expanded to be used also for the *internal* property that was assumed to cause the overt responses that were measured. And soon this new kind of assumed internal dependent variable was labeled an "*intervening* variable," to distinguish it from the overt dependent variables. The word "intervening" signaled that it was assumed to be an organism-internal variable that *intervened* in some way to cause the subject's overt response. Intervening variables were assumed to be "...*causally active entities that have a real psychological existence independently of the psychologists' investigative practice*" (Danziger & Dzinas, 1997, p. 45). That is, the intervening variable was assumed to be in place already before the experiment began. And in contrast to the overt dependent variables, intervening variables are unobservable; they can only be assumed to exist.

The number of articles and reports that invoked such assumed causally active "intervening" variables increased in psychological research journals from the Second World War onwards (Koch, 1959). An example can illustrate this. The expression "personality variable" had originally referred to a person's *scores* on a personality inventory (i.e., something observable). Now it came to be increasingly used to denote the inner traits (i.e., something unobservable) that were assumed to be *causing* those scores.

In a further step, some psychologists began using the expression "personality variables" also when talking about aspects of people's personalities that had not yet been studied. This removed any anchoring to the previous meaning of *overt* "dependent variables" such as scores on personality inventories. This step was taken in several subfields of psychology, not just personality psychology. Here are some examples: assumed aspects of emotion, of which a researcher had no measurement, could be talked about as "emotional variables," or as "variables that influence projection," or (more specifically) as "the impulsivity-inhibition variable." The expression "clinical variables" was sometimes used as a general reference to unmeasured "clinical" (usually meaning psychiatric) features of individuals. Motivation was sometimes written about as (unmeasured) "basic variables that govern behavior."

Historians have found that by the end of the 1950s, psychologists often used the word "variable" for the attributes of people's inner psychological reality that they wanted to investigate (as in the previous examples). And, to quote Danziger and Dzinas again, this led to "... *a temptation to assume that all such events already exist preformed in the shape of variables before the intervention of psychological research practice*" (1997, p. 45). This assumption was often accompanied by "*. . .an assumption that everything that exists, exists as a variable*" (Danziger & Dzinas, (1997, p. 46).

However, as Danziger and Dzinas also noted, "*. . .statements about variables entail theoretically freighted assertions about the constitution of psychological reality*" (p. 45). One such "theoretically freighted" assertion that was especially important was the assumption that what psychological research techniques do is simply hold up a mirror or magnifying glass to allow the researcher to read a pre-existing internal variable structure in each research participant. However, this is not the only way to think about research results. A critic would argue that finding variables by doing research that is built on the "variable assumption" of psychological reality is not *proof* that psychological reality is organized as variables. At this point, it is helpful to remember that research methods are always built on the foundational assumptions of some theory (or thinking style). Derek Edwards has formulated the consequences of this fact succinctly:

> . . .it may be that outside of the lab (and perhaps inside it too), meaningful human actions are simply not organized on a factors-and-variables causal basis. It could be that experiments do not *reveal*, but rather *make it so*, that human actions can be fitted to predictable causal formats. (1997, p. 4, emphasis in the original)

That is, if you use methods that are designed to study variables, you will inevitably "discover" variables, whether people's actual psychological reality is organized in the form of variables or not. Edwards here also touches on a theoretical assumption that we mentioned briefly before: a tendency to assume and assert the causal efficacy of the hypothesized "intervening" variables. We can think about statements such as that a certain personality variable *causes* a person to behave in a certain way. We discuss causal explanations in more detail in Chapter 12.

At this point, one might want to ask what drove psychologists to move "variables" from outside persons to their insides, thereby transforming "variables" into internal causal agents. However, there is, as yet, no fully convincing answer to this question.

The word "variable" continues to be common in psychological publications, often in its use as denoting internal properties of persons. To get a sense of how this meaning of "variable" is used by psychologists today, we searched through a large number of articles in prestigious scholarly psychology journals published between 2018 and 2024 to examine their uses of the term "variable." Here is a selection: The dominance variable; the prosocial prestige variable; motivational variables; aggression variables; trauma-related personality variables; the self-efficacy variable; individual difference variables; the resistance-to-peer-influence variable; maternal personality variables. We observed many cases in which the word "variable" was used even though it was obvious that no measurements had been made. That is, no variable had been defined or measured; these "variables" were simply assumed to exist.

What should one make of the changes in the uses of the word "variable" in psychology? Might there be some deleterious theoretical or practical consequences? We take up some aspects of these questions in Chapter 13, about being a discerning reader, where we describe conceptual analysis of the words and terms that psychologists use.

Can Social Categories Be Independent Variables?

It is not unusual for research to compare the behavior or attitudes of people in different social categories, such as social classes, ethnic categories, "race" categories, and so on. And it is not unusual to use these categories as *independent variables*. Here, we ask whether it is reasonable to conceive of social categories as variables, and even as *independent* variables. To answer, we look at the requirement for something to qualify as an independent variable. In the previous section, we noted that the term "independent variable" is defined as something that the researcher manipulates (i.e., gives different values, strengths, or intensities, and so on) within a research situation. The purpose is to study the effects these manipulations (i.e., the experimenter-induced variations in the independent variable) have on a dependent variable. Different manipulations of the independent variable are expected to cause different outcomes in the dependent variable.

How does the manipulation requirement fare in research that uses social categories as independent variables? The experimenter certainly cannot manipulate (i.e., vary) each participant's social category inside the research situation, because each participant's category positions are already in place before the participant meets the researcher. Clearly, therefore, social categories cannot be independent variables in the same sense as the independent variable in an experiment. Instead, when social categories are used as independent variables, the researcher typically compares the responses of participants who belong to different social categories. This means that the researcher must assume that a comparison between groups of people (people in different social categories) is equivalent to having manipulated an independent variable for each individual in a study. Is this assumption justified? The social category has not been varied for each participant. And it would seem illogical to talk about "variables" (varying what?) when one compares people who belong to different *stable* social categories.

Based on these arguments, some researchers have claimed that it is problematic to think of social categories as independent variables. We have found that researchers working within a social interactionist framework analyze this problem in a helpful way. Such researchers begin by noting that the way social categories work is not analogous to how factors or independent variables work (Grills & Prus, 2008). An independent variable that an experimenter manipulates has (or is at least expected to have) a causal effect, *in itself*, on a research participant's behavior. It *acts* on the participant in some way. This is not the case with a social category: A social category is, by definition, the result of social and cultural negotiations, and it gets its meaning only in human interaction. That is, a social category is a creation of human interaction and human collective life; it therefore has no existence or meaning outside of social life. Further, in real life (and therefore also in research), categories do not have independent meanings. This means that the meaning-giving does not occur one category at a time; rather, the meaning of a certain social category is influenced by the other social categories to which that person belongs. This makes it even less plausible to regard social categories as independent variables. The US legal scholar Kimberlé Crenshaw (1989) labeled this interaction between the meanings of categories *intersectionality*.

Some would disagree with the arguments here. They would argue that even though social categories are the result of social negotiations, the resulting categories still have consequences that must be based on some kind of causal powers. There are, after all, distinct differences in many behaviors between people belonging to different social categories. Aren't these differences *caused* by the social categories? To this objection, a social interactionist would answer, for instance, that

> we are not denying the linkages (commonly expressed as correlations) of social categories with other aspects of community life that surface in quantitative research, but we do contend that these correlates represent comparatively superficial reflections of the much broader underlying sets of social processes that characterize social life. Moreover, it is these sets of humanly engaged social processes rather than the categories that epitomize variable analysis ... that constitute the more authentic subject matter of the social sciences. (Grills & Prus, 2008, p. 20)

For readers interested in studying such "sets of humanly engaged social processes rather than the categories that epitomize variable analysis," the research approaches that we describe in Chapter 14 offer some strategies.

Null Hypothesis Significance Testing in Psychology

Significance testing using *t*-tests, analysis of variance, regression analysis, and so on has a long history in psychological research. Many psychologists, perhaps, would not know what to do about their research if they could not test for statistical significance. However, since the introduction of significance tests, there have been vigorous discussions about the statistical theory, and logic, behind the tests, and about what kinds of conclusions the tests allow (Cohen, 1994; Gigerenzer, 2004, 2018; Green, 2021). As a result of these debates, recent decades have seen an increase in criticisms of the practice of significance testing. This is true for psychology as well as for other disciplines (Hubbard, 2019; Nickerson, 2000; Stunt et al., 2021).

The inventors of statistical testing constructed the tests to indicate whether a result warrants further scrutiny, thus *not* as tests of the "significance," in the sense of the scientific importance, of a result. These early theorists also stated explicitly that *statistical* significance is not synonymous with *scientific importance*. A "statistically significant" *p*-value, in fact, says nothing about the scientific meaning or importance of a particular result. But as several contemporary critics have noted: this crucial distinction between "statistical" and "scientific" is all too often forgotten. That is, it is not unusual for psychologists to use a statistically significant *p*-value as proof, or a strong indication, that their findings are *scientifically* important. These misunderstandings suggest that not every psychologist knows what a "significant" *p*-value means.

The following quote from a policy text about statistical testing issued by the American Statistical Association (ASA) provides the statisticians' answer: A significant *p*-value "*is a statement about data in relation to a specified hypothetical explanation, and is not a statement about the explanation itself*" (Wasserstein & Lazar, 2016, p. 131). That is all. A *p*-value is *not* a measure of the probability that a hypothesis (that is, an explanation) is true; it is *not* a sign of the probability that one's results were produced by chance; and it is *not* a statement about whether the null hypothesis is true. The ASA policy text goes on to discuss what the misunderstandings of statistical significance imply for the practice of scientific research:

The widespread use of "statistical significance" (generally interpreted as "p < 0.05") as a license for making a claim of a scientific finding (or implied truth) leads to considerable distortion of the scientific process... By itself, a p-value does not provide a good measure of evidence regarding a model or hypothesis... No single index should substitute for scientific reasoning. (Wasserstein & Lazar, 2016, p. 133)

A few years later, the journal *The American Statistician* published a special issue about significance testing, in which the editors felt that they had to resort to exhortations such as these: "... *'statistically significant' – don't say it and don't use it ... Regardless of whether it was ever useful, a declaration of 'statistical significance' has today become meaningless"* (Wasserstein, Schirm, & Lazar, 2019, p. 2). Note that the problem is not the use of probability reasoning as such; such reasoning is an integrated part of the scientific process. The problem is the misunderstanding of what statistical testing is, and especially the misuse of "statistically significant" as if it were a scientifically legitimizing cut-off.

To illustrate, we provide a number of *corrected* common misunderstandings of statistical significance: Statistical significance (such as "$p < 0.05$") does *not* mean that there is less than 5 percent likelihood that the result of a study is due to chance. Statistical significance does *not* mean that there is less than 5 percent likelihood that the null hypothesis is true. Statistical significance does *not* mean that there is a greater than 95 percent probability that the research hypothesis is true. A statistically significant p-value does *not* confirm the research hypothesis. Statistical significance does *not* mean that the study one has done is of good quality. And a statistically significant p-value does *not* indicate the effect size in a study (Kline, 2009).

In contrast to these misunderstandings, here are two things that a statistical significance *can* tell the researcher: The first: statistical significance ($p < 0.05$) indicates that, if the null hypothesis were true, and if one were to perform a very large number of repetitions of the same study, then a very small number of the results (usually fewer than 5 percent) would be as extreme as that in the current study (Spence & Stanley, 2018). The second: in the ideal case of a randomized sample and experiment, the p-value gives the likelihood of achieving the observed result of the experiment if the experimental manipulation had no effect. In less ideal cases (which many or most cases in psychological research are), not even this conclusion may be warranted (Nordin, 2020).

Do psychologists know these facts about null hypothesis testing? Actually, it seems that many do not, at least not until quite recently. A few years ago, a study of the 30 most commonly used introductory psychology textbooks in Europe and North America found that 27 of the books provided incorrect descriptions of what statistical significance tests tell a researcher (Cassidy et al., 2019). And recent overviews of the teaching of statistics to psychology students have found that similarly incorrect descriptions are used (Sestir et al., 2023; White & Gorard, 2017). Further, despite the increasing critique of the use of null hypothesis testing (here shortened to NHST), a survey of psychological research journals a few years ago found that the use of NHST (including many cases of misuse like the ones listed earlier) had actually increased in recent decades (Hubbard, 2019). The use of NHST is so widespread and, if we are to believe its critics, so automatic that it may qualify as "the null ritual" (Gigerenzer, 2018). And, as we noted in Chapter 9, some psychologists have suggested that such ritualistic use and misuse of NHST may be one of the factors that precipitated the replication crisis in psychology.

A number of statisticians and statistically knowledgeable psychologists have published advice on how researchers can move from the discredited uses of NHST to more adequate testing methods (e.g., Grice, 2015; Normile et al., 2019; Trafimow, 2019a, 2019b). Has this advice reached its audience? And if it has, are there signs that it is being taken up? The answer may still be "no" to both questions.

To illustrate, we use a study of NHST use among academic researchers, lecturers, journal editors, and program leaders at universities and funding agencies (in medicine, health-and-life sciences, and psychology) in the Netherlands (Stunt et al., 2021).[1] Stunt et al. wanted to find out why researchers continue to use NHST methodology in the face of repeated and recently increasing criticism. To study the question, Stunt and colleagues did semi-structured interviews, followed by focus group discussions. They asked about the participants' views on the benefits and drawbacks of null hypothesis testing. They also asked about the participants' familiarity with the ongoing debates about NHST and about alternative "new statistics" procedures. One of the most pervasive findings of the study was the participants' experiences of powerful barriers – in their workplaces, in their disciplines, and in academic journals – against abandoning NHST. Many participants were afraid of negative consequences (such as having their research articles not accepted for publication) if they were to use other methods. Also, most of the participants did not see

---

[1] This study was done in the Netherlands and there is every reason to believe that its conclusions are valid in many other countries as well. Its conclusions align well with the earlier-mentioned studies of textbooks and methods teaching in other "Western" countries.

themselves as agents who could initiate change; they referred to (and deferred to) the hierarchical structure of academic workplaces and organizations and waited for others to initiate change. Those among the participants who were teachers of methods argued that the conventions of the academic system made it impossible for them to change their teaching to include alternate methods. Stunt et al. summarize their results as showing that "*a circle of interdependency arises that is difficult to break*" (Stunt et al., 2021, p. 16).

It is tempting to draw parallels here with Ludwik Fleck's ideas about *thinking styles* and *thought collectives.* To begin, Fleck's ideas about the constraining power of academic thought collectives seem confirmed by this study: the participants did not seem to see themselves as agents who could institute change in the practices. Further, one could ask whether certain (misconceived) statistical assumptions and habits were so thoroughly ingrained in these researchers' thinking style that they did not dare to change their habits. Or could it be that these researchers would not be able to change them? Had the assumptions at the basis of their statistical habits become so self-evident and "active" (in Fleck's terms) that the researchers were not able to move outside their bounds? Here we can think of what Fleck said about how thinking in the terms set by one thinking style may make a researcher unable to think in the terms of other styles. See also Gigerenzer (2018) about "the null ritual," and Simmons, Nelson, & Simonsohn (2011).

Concept Use in Psychology

Psychological reasoning, explanation, and theory-construction all are dependent on the use of concepts. So, what is a concept? This question has long been debated among philosophers, linguists, and psychologists without arriving at an answer that is agreed upon by all. The main divide is, to put it very simply, about whether concepts should be seen as symbols, such as mental representations in individual minds, or whether they should be seen as culturally shared linguistic entities that are symbolized by the words that express them (Glock, 2009, 2010). In the psychology discipline, the first answer is the most common. So, for instance, psychologists working within the representational framework (see Chapter 6) have developed several definitions of "concept," such as: the classical definitional approach, prototype approaches, exemplar-based approaches, theory-based approaches, essentialist approaches, and grounding or simulation approaches (Gilhooly et al., 2022). Philosophically inclined psychologists have instead adopted linguistic and usage-based definitions of concepts from analytic philosophy (Slaney & Racine, 2011). In this section, we present, discuss, and contrast the *representational* view and the *usage-based* view of concepts.

Before we continue, we should note that in their daily lives, people use concepts effortlessly, seldom reflecting on how concepts should be used, and reflecting even less on what kind of "things" concepts are. Accurate concept *use* does not require explicit or formalized knowledge of what concepts *are*, or of the *rules* for using a particular concept. Children easily learn their own community's conceptual landscape in the process of learning their native language. Children's surroundings provide ample and sufficient feedback about the correct and incorrect uses of the words for each specific concept that is being learned. Becoming able to use concepts in daily life is an integrated part of children's language-learning. But, of course, being able to *use* concepts correctly in daily life does not mean that one has knowledge about what kind of *things* concepts are. To acquire such knowledge, one may have to engage in theoretical reflection of the kind we do below. We begin with theories about concepts as mental representations.

Concepts as Mental Representations

A common view of concepts in cognitive psychology is that they are "*mental representations of broad classes or categories of things, actions, and relationships*" (Gilhooly et al., 2022, p. 294). This view places concepts squarely as entities (mental objects) in the mind (see also Chapter 6 about mental representations). Concept formation is described as "*an inevitable result of how brains react to stimulation, in that similar stimuli evoke similar activation patterns and by association will arouse similar memories and activation tendencies*" (Gilhooly et al., 2022, p. 294). Concepts are typically taken to be structures in the mind (or the brain, depending on the choice of theory) that are independent of, and may precede language. Learning a new word is a process of associating the new word, via similarity, to a preexisting mental conceptual structure. This means that concepts are seen as a kind of mental "placeholders" that symbolize specific classes of objects, events, or relations and their properties. These placeholders contain information that enables a learner to notice if a thing or event, and so on, is similar enough to a certain category to make it belong to that category rather than another (Slaney & Racine, 2011).

Note the word "category" in the previous sentence. It is fairly common in psychological research to see the terms "category" and "concept" as equivalent, in the sense of taking a concept to be the mental representation of a category. Thus, researchers who subscribe to the representationalist view of concepts often study how people learn to sort objects or pictures into groups or categories based on one or more shared characteristics. Such sorting is often used as an illustration of the typical processes in humans' concept formation. However, a problem with this view is that it is doubtful whether sorting into groups (i.e., categories) is part of all kinds of concept formation. In everyday life, far from all concepts that people use depend on sorting objects or phenomena into categories.

On the general representational base that we briefly described just above, psychologists have developed several approaches to concepts: what they are, how they are represented, and how they are formed by individual learners. All these approaches have been subjected to critique from within the representational framework, and none can satisfactorily account for all kinds of concepts, all kinds of concept use, or all kinds of concept development (Gilhooly et al., 2022).

A great deal of critique has been directed at this use of the term "concept." The French philosopher Edouard Machery (2009), for instance, while accepting the general framework of categorization, argues that psychologists should stop using the term "concept" and instead specify what they are looking for in each specific case. And there is no lack of critique from those who reject the representational framework. For instance, because representational views of concepts conceive of concepts as representations in the mind, these views have been subjected to the same type of critique as that leveled at the representationalist view of the mind (Glock, 2009; Hacker, 2013a; Sprague, 1999; see also the discussion about mental representations in Chapter 6). One central part of this critique goes roughly like this: concepts, by definition, must be shareable entities if people are to be able to use them; that is, people in the same language community share certain concepts (such as the concept CAT). Mental representations, on the other hand (in this case symbolized as "cat"), are, by definition, individual and non-shareable. This creates a logical contradiction: if concepts are taken to be mental representations in individuals' minds or brains, they cannot at the same time be culturally shared entities (Glock, 2009). Further, the view of concepts as containing knowledge or information has been criticized as incoherent on the basis that knowledge as well as information can only be *expressed* in concepts. For knowledge to be possible, people must have concepts with which to express it: both knowledge and information *presuppose* concepts (Slaney & Racine, 2011).

Concepts as Usage-Based Elements of Language

The second view of concepts that we present, we call the usage-based view. Here, concepts are taken to be elements of language that people use for understanding their world and for talking about how they understand it (Slaney & Racine, 2011). These elements (i.e., concepts) are seen as human cultural creations that are created, used, and shared in language communities. By growing up in a language community, children will acquire concepts through learning the correct use of the words that express each concept. In this sense, concepts can be seen as *abstractions* from the uses of words (Glock, 2006). Therefore, in this view, concepts are not symbols – they are among the kinds of things that are represented by symbols such as words or pictures (Glock, 2009).

As an example, we can take the concept CAT, which is expressed by the words "Katze" in German, "katt" in Swedish, and "cat" in English. The *concept* CAT, then, is the abstraction that captures the uses of these three words. This means that there is what philosophers call an internal or *logical* relation between a concept and a word that expresses the concept. But how can one know that it is the concept CAT that is expressed by those three words? One can best find out about this by studying how the three words are used in the respective languages. If one finds that the words Katze, katt, and cat are repeatedly used in similar or identical contexts, and with similar or identical functions, one can be fairly sure that they express the same concept. Expressions of concepts can vary; a concept can be expressed not just by a word but also, for instance, by a picture (of a cat, for instance), provided that an explicit connection has been made between the picture and the concept.

To *possess* a concept is, first, to be able to correctly use a word or phrase that expresses the concept; second, to be able to explain what one means when using the concept; third, to respond correctly to somebody else's use of the concept; and fourth, to understand how the concept in question relates to other concepts (Bennett & Hacker, 2022). But note that, as we wrote earlier, in everyday speech, people effortlessly and correctly use and master concepts and the words for concepts without worrying about whether they possess them, or whether they are dealing with "concepts" or not. This, of course, is how it should be. That is how language functions.

There are correct and incorrect ways to use concepts: that is, their use is rule-governed. And it is in people's language communities that the rules for using concepts are formed, upheld, and taught (Maraun & Peters, 2005). This means that concepts, as well as concept formation and the rules for the use of concepts, are the products of people's interactions in their language communities. The usage-based view of concepts is, therefore, incompatible with the view we described in the previous subsection, in which concepts are taken to be mental representations in individual minds.

In the usage-based view, to *analyze* a concept is to investigate different uses of a particular word for a concept, including correct and incorrect uses of the word. This means studying the language practices connected to particular concepts, that is, studying how people in a specific language community use a concept, and often also studying how the concept evolved, and how it may be changing, and why. A psychologist adopting this understanding of concepts would, for instance, be interested in how people's – including psychologists' – uses of particular concepts, such as their concepts about the person, the mind, reason, thought, desire, mental health, and so on, shape their ways of thinking about themselves. When studying psychologists' concept use with this approach to concepts, one's interest would be directed at how their uses shape both psychological theories and clinical practices.

For a psychologist who has adopted the view of persons as situated in culture that we have described in this book, the usage-based view of concepts and concept formation has the greater appeal of the two approaches we have discussed. It is the approach that most consistently facilitates the development and study of research questions of interest to such a psychologist.

Encountering Concepts in Psychological Texts

We end with some advice to readers of psychological research articles or textbooks. When encountering the term "concept" in such a text, it is a good idea to ascertain the author's view of what concepts *are*, and also to investigate whether the author uses the term "concept" in a consistent way. And if so – in which of the ways we have described (Machado & Silva, 2007; Racine, 2015; Slaney & Racine, 2011)?

One can then also ask questions like these: Has the author provided a proper definition of the term "concept"? If not, can a meaning of the term be discerned anyway? Is the definition that is used stringent enough (for instance, in terms of the discussions in this chapter)? Are several meanings of the term "concept" being used in the same article or study? Do these meanings conflict? Could such conflicted meanings "infiltrate" the research questions or the conclusions and compromise their validity? If a specific definition of "concept" is used, do the researcher's conclusions stay within the frame of that definition, or does the researcher extend the conclusions to other meanings of "concept"? If so, does that extension seem warranted?

Questions such as these are part of what philosophers and psychologists call *conceptual analysis*. Because it is a helpful tool for psychologists, we describe the practice of conceptual analysis in Chapter 13, "Being a Discerning Reader of Psychology."

CHAPTER 12

Explanations in Psychology

Much of what psychologists do, whether as scholars, teachers, or practitioners, is geared toward formulating explanations – of psychotic breakdowns, conflicts at work, failure at school, marital discontent, or of positive psychological change. Arriving at an explanation of a problem is an important step toward being able to do something about that problem. In this chapter, we describe the kinds of explanations that are common in psychological research and practice. We also discuss which of these explanations are most compatible with a view of humans as socially and culturally contextualized persons. Further, talking about explanations inevitably raises a number of related issues: reification, determinism, and the nature of psychological categories.

We begin with a discussion of different ways of conceiving of the psychological phenomena that psychologists seek to explain. We then take up the nature of the categories that are often used in psychological explanations. In the sections that follow, we describe the most common explanatory strategies in psychological practice and research: explanations based on reason-giving, causal explanations, explanations that reduce, and the explanatory strategy of abduction, also called inference to the best explanation. The chapter ends with a discussion of issues connected to deterministic explanations in psychological theory and research.

Psychological Phenomena and the Reification Trap

Many psychological phenomena are *activities*: a person thinks, reasons, solves problems, persuades, cooperates, and so on. And people in groups solve problems, cooperate, negotiate, or quarrel, and so on. Many other psychological phenomena are *abilities*, such as the ability to ride a bicycle, to read, or to understand a language. Yet other psychological phenomena are durable *dispositions* to act in certain ways, or to feel certain emotions, for example to act courageously, to be timid, to be cheerful, to be tactful, or to be irritable.

These psychological phenomena are usually well expressed by verbs: to *do*, to *experience*, to *be able* to do, or to *tend to* do. Even so, in everyday language as well as in academic psychological language, it is common to use nouns rather than verbs to talk about psychological phenomena. Think about these examples: when someone is depressed, it is not unusual to say that they suffer from *depression*. When someone is anxious, it is not unusual to say that they suffer from *anxiety*. When someone believes something, it is not unusual to say that they *have* a *belief*. And when someone experiences something, it is not unusual to say that they *have* an *experience*. In this way, an abstract noun, such as those in the examples, can often be a practical shorthand for a longer expression that uses verbs (Uher, 2022).

However, certain ways of using such "shorthand" abstract nouns can cause conceptual and theoretical problems or even confusion. This happens when the use of an abstract noun instead of a verb leads one to *reify* the psychological phenomenon that is being talked about. The verb *to reify* comes from the Latin verb *facere* (to make) and noun *res* (a thing), so the literal meaning of *to reify* is "to make a thing." Reifying a psychological phenomenon, that is, "making" that phenomenon into "a thing" or an entity, proceeds in two steps. The first step is the one we encountered just above, that is, talking about phenomena such as *to act* or *to feel depressed* by using nouns like "*action*" or "*depression*." As we said then, this is an unproblematic step that is built into how everyday language functions.

The problematic part of the reification, that is, the actual "thing-making," happens in the second step, when abstract nouns are seen as the names of things or entities that exist independently of the activity or state they denote (Sprague, 1999). Think of going from talking about "feeling depressed" (using a verb) to "suffering from depression" (using an abstract noun). If one then concludes that the noun "depression" is the name of some *independently* existing entity inside the suffering person – "the depression" – one is reifying the state of feeling depressed into a "thing." In sum: *to reify* is to conclude that an abstract noun that stands in for an activity or a state is the name of an independently existing entity, when one has no basis for assuming that such an entity exists.

In psychology, the second reifying step may consist of assuming that phenomena such as the mind, consciousness, personality traits, emotions, abilities, depression, and so on are independently existing *inner entities*, and making this assumption solely on the basis of knowledge about people's activities and experiences (Vessonen, 2021). Reification in psychology and other disciplines, such as psychiatry, has been much discussed and criticized in recent years (cf. Boag, 2011, 2018; Hyman, 2010, 2021; Kendler, 2016, 2017; te Meerman, Freedman, & Batstra, 2022; Schleim, 2020, 2022; Uher, 2013; Vessonen, 2021).

Sometimes the reification involves a further step: To ascribe agency to the assumed inner entities by claiming that they have the power to cause certain behaviors, that is, claiming that they can *explain* those behaviors: "*We might, for instance, develop a term initially describing <u>performance</u> and then forget the term's descriptive use and later mistakenly use it to <u>explain</u> what was initially described*" (Boag, 2011, p. 226, emphasis added). The problem here is that the term used to explain the performance is not independent of that performance, because it was originally *derived* from a description of the performance in question. For something to *be* a cause, it must be describable on its own terms, by its own intrinsic properties, not in terms of that which it is supposed to cause. Because unwarranted reification in psychology can have unfortunate consequences, we provide a few examples of analysis and critique.

Simon Boag (2011, 2018), an Australian psychologist, investigated the consequences of reification in personality psychology. In particular, he scrutinized the logic and assumptions underlying the Big Five factor model of personality, a common model in contemporary personality psychology (McCrae & Costa, 1995). Boag began by noting that the model is built on the claim that people have distinct psychological traits, such as extraversion and neuroticism (viewed as the "independently existing entities" that we defined earlier), and on the further claim that such traits cause certain consistent ways of thinking, feeling, and behaving, including people's scores on personality inventories (corresponding to the ascription of agency above). However, as Boag noted, the proponents of this model have provided no independent evidence for these claims. This means that those who administer the Big Five personality inventory to people have access only to the participants' scores on the inventory (corresponding to the verbs above). They do not have access to any independently existing inner entities inside each participant which might have caused the scores. Boag drew the conclusion that the assumption that trait measurements reflect inner entities with the power to cause the trait scores on the inventory is an example of "…*reification, such that the performance to be explained is misconstrued as a faculty causing that same performance*" (2011, p. 227).

Writing about personality psychology in general, Jana Uher, a German psychologist, agreed with Boag about why it is problematic to treat traits as independently existing entities. As she argued, because of the way that personality traits are assessed, what personality theory takes as "traits" (i.e., independently existing inner entities) are no more than *"categorical summary statements about a person's behaviour"* (the behavior being scores on the inventory) (2013, p. 25). And, Uher continued, if one uses such summary statements to explain and predict behaviors, what one is doing is using a *description* of a behavior as an *explanation* for the same behavior. And then one is in a vicious circle.

Boag's and Uher's examples show that reification often leads to circular explanations. And circular explanations, by definition, do not explain anything at all. This is akin to the methodological circles that we discussed in Chapter 11.

In another example, the Dutch psychologist Stephan Schleim (2018, 2022) scrutinized research on biological causes of psychological suffering (see also Meerman, Freedman, & Batstra, 2022). Schleim focused on Major Depressive Disorder and Attention Deficit Hyperactivity Disorder (ADHD) and concluded that much of the search for biological causes of these disorders has been built upon premature reification:

> The idea of a biological taxonomy for psychology and psychiatry then always carries the risk of prematurely reifying definitions of psychological processes or classifications of mental disorders, that is, the risk of treating them as things while they are in the first place pragmatic constructs to help scientists, clinicians, and patients fulfill their needs. Such a premature reification would also be at odds with, first, the history of changing definitions of mental disorders, ... second, the introduction of new disorders, and, third, the removal of others. (2022, p. 4)

In our final example, Kenneth Kendler, a US psychiatrist, pointed to problematic consequences of reification in the DSM-5 (the *Diagnostic and Statistical Manual of Mental Disorders of the American Psychiatric Association*, Fifth Edition). Kendler argued that the approach taken in the DSM-5 was based on a conceptual error: the reifying mistake of *"taking an index of a thing for the thing itself"* (2016, p. 771). He drew on the example of the symptom criteria for Major Depressive Disorder, for which the DSM uses a *constitutive* definition. With a constitutive definition, the criteria that have been specified for a disorder are seen as definitively defining (i.e., constituting) the disorder. That is, those who meet those criteria are assumed to *have* the disorder.[1] This definition makes it tempting to reify the disorder that one "has" as if it were an independently

---

[1] In a comment that touches on other issues than the one we are discussing here, Kendler criticized the use of constitutive definitions in psychiatry, because, "[t]he constitutive model locks in our

existing thing-like entity: the depression. Kendler concluded that this is what has happened with psychodiagnosis: " ... *our field has undergone a 'conceptual creep' in which our criteria have mistakenly become our disorder*" (2016, p. 779). He also noted that this reifying conceptual creep is not the result of scientific research or of any kind of scientific deliberation. Rather, and in Kendler's words, "*I suggest that the mental health field has confused a social process – whereby DSM criteria have become 'official' – with an ontological and scientific one*" (Kendler, 2017, p. 2058). Here Kendler referred to social processes within a thought collective consisting of the working groups of psychiatrists in the US which are convened to make decisions about diagnoses and diagnostic criteria in the DSM. We would add that these working groups were influenced by social processes that, over many years, had been shaping the framework of the larger collective of psychiatrists to which they belonged.

Further, reification may lead one to conceive of individual psychology as consisting of several separate *subpersonal properties*, each with some specific agency of its own. Taking reification this far therefore also means that one is committing "*[t]he conceptual mistake of breaking persons down into psychological parts*" (LaVine & Tissaw, 2015, p. 35; also think back to Chapter 11, where we discussed the problems connected with thinking about human psychology in terms of separate variables).

Psychological Categories: Natural or Human-Made?

The examples in the previous section are related to another crucial aspect of psychological explanations: How should psychologists best conceive of the psychological categories that they use in their explanations? For instance, are these categories natural or are they human-made? Natural categories are "*categories of things existing in nature that are well bounded and have stable, cohesive causal structures, as is the case for chemical elements*" (Hyman, 2021). Further, natural categories exist and function independently of what humans say about them, and independently of whether humans even know about them. We need to ask, therefore, whether *psychological categories* (such as extroversion, ADHD, or Major Depression Disorder) existed, as natural categories, before psychologists and others defined them and began using them. Were these categories, at some point, *discovered* by psychologists or others? Or are psychological

definitions. It is premature and reflects a definitiveness about the underlying nature of our disorders, which is far in advance of our current knowledge" (2017, p. 2059).

categories instead the products of psychologists' and others' efforts to understand people? That is, are psychological categories perhaps *human-made* (Smith, 2005)?

To illustrate the category problems, we can first think of the category of automobile. It is an example of a human-made category: The category did not exist before the first automobile was produced by humans. As an opposite example, blue whales are not made by humans and are usually taken as constituting a natural category, because whales did not depend on humans for coming into existence. However, while the blue whales themselves existed before humans began calling them "blue whales," there is no agreement about whether the *category* "blue whales" existed before that moment of naming. As these examples show, the general questions concerning human-made vs. natural categories, and the kinds of creatures they are usually taken to denote, are far more complex than we can make them seem here. For more elucidation, see, for instance, Hacker (2007).

These questions are closely connected to an old bone of contention in the discipline of psychology: The question of whether psychology should be seen as a natural science or as a social science – the idea being that natural scientists *discover* facts about independently existing entities or categories in the natural world (Brick et al., 2022). As we noted in Chapter 10, many early psychologists, especially those in the Anglophone part of the world, wanted psychology to be accepted as a natural science. Others did not. This discussion is still ongoing, and no consensus is in sight.

Now let us turn our attention back to psychological categories. A category is a set of "somethings" that have important characteristics in common. We can think of the category "cat" as encompassing individual animals that share a certain genetic makeup. Categories need to be distinct enough from one another to enable observers to decide which individuals belong to which category (e.g., to the category "cats" vs. the category "dogs"). It seems logical to think of those two categories as existing in nature, independently of whether humans had discovered them. For many psychological categories, things seem less obvious. Should such categories be seen as existing in nature, whether or not they have been labeled yet? Here are a few examples to consider. We return to the examples of reification from the previous section.

Did ADHD exist before the diagnostic category "ADHD" was put forward? That is, should we think of the diagnostic category "ADHD" as a *natural category* – a category that exists in nature, independently of whether humans have yet discovered it and labeled it as a category? We can, of course, be certain that the behaviors and experiences that today are regarded as criteria for this diagnosis did occur earlier, even though they were not bundled together in the "ADHD" diagnostic box and defined as criteria. And we can be certain that any underlying brain processes occurred before the diagnostic category was invented.

Some thinkers argue that not just the behaviors and brain processes but also the *category* ADHD existed before the diagnosis was invented, but that it was mislabeled (e.g., as the earlier diagnostic category MBD, or Minimal Brain Damage). Others argue that the diagnostic *category* ADHD is the result of *human acts of categorization.* This would mean that ADHD did not exist *as a category* before "ADHD" was described by humans (even though the behaviors taken as criteria for ADHD did occur) (see Schleim, 2018). On this view, we should not mistakenly assume that occurrence of the indices (i.e., the behaviors that are used as criteria to diagnose ADHD) proves the independent existence of the category (in this case, the ADHD category) as a natural category. These thinkers would agree with Kenneth Kendler's warning against *"taking an index of a thing for the thing itself"* that we quoted earlier. (See also the study by te Meerman, Freedman, & Batstra, 2022, which we describe in the later section on causal explanations in this chapter.)

These and other complications haunt many categorizations that psychologists and others use. One instructive and dramatic example from recent history is the diagnostic category "multiple personality disorder," now renamed "dissociative identity disorder" (for a detailed discussion, see Hacking, 1995). Another example with gendered social and cultural ramifications is the diagnostic category "hysteria" which was common in the nineteenth century (see Scull, 2009).

Now let us consider one of the personality traits (i.e., categories) identified by the Five Factor theory and several other personality theories: extroversion. Did the psychological *category* "extroversion" exist before psychologists defined it in terms of a certain response profile on a personality inventory? That is, is extroversion a natural category? Clearly, there were people who behaved in ways that today are called "extroverted" or outgoing before personality inventories were created. The existence of such behaviors is not in question. What is in question is the explanation of the behavior: a typical trait explanation would conclude that the person has a trait – "extroversion" – that *causes* "extroverted" behavior. However, as we discussed earlier, this is a circular argument, and circular arguments have no explanatory power. Further, using this kind of circular explanation of the behavior also risks reifying the behavior (see the previous section). Here, we need to heed

Kendler's warning once more: we should not assume that a score on a personality inventory can be identified with "the thing itself."[2] It may instead be that the notion of such agentic inner entities was invented by humans. Perhaps we should conclude that the *category* "extroversion," understood as an inner psychological property with agentic force, is actually human-made.

One indication that this conclusion may be accurate comes from the observation that categorization schemes for psychological categories do not seem to be universal (Henrich, Heine, & Norenzayan, 2010; Hornstein & Star, 1990). If psychological categories were natural (like the categories cats and dogs), one would expect to find identical or nearly-identical psychological categorization schemes everywhere. Consider here also what we wrote in Chapter 3, "Culture, Communities, and Persons," about culture-bound syndromes and other culture-specific psychological properties. We should also take into account the fact that no psychological categorization schemes last indefinitely; rather, such schemes are revised repeatedly (Brinkmann, 2024).

Another aspect of categorization that must not be overlooked is that psychological categories used about humans have dynamic power. That is, people are influenced by the categorizations to which they are subjected: many categories that are used about humans are *interactive*. When subjected to such a categorization (e.g., being told that one is extroverted, has ADHD, or has depression), humans *react* to this categorization, often by developing new ways of thinking about themselves, and possibly also new behaviors, all of which reaffirm the categorization (Hacking, 2007b). This means that after receiving a diagnosis and subsequently learning about typical characteristics of people with that diagnosis, a person may become more "diagnosis-typical" in their behavior and experiences than before receiving the diagnosis. The fact that many psychological categories have such interactive powers should perhaps make one think twice before applying such a category to a person.

Psychological Explanations

Before selecting the type of explanation to use in psychological research or clinical practice, one should be aware that the choice of explanation is a *philosophical and conceptual* choice. This means that the *kind* of

---

[2] Here, we should note the parallels to the problems surrounding the use of operational definitions. See Chapter 10.

knowledge the researcher or clinician wants to achieve should determine the choice of explanation. Neither routine nor social pressures in a thought collective should be allowed to determine the type of explanation to use (Franz, 2022).

As a background to our descriptions of the different types of explanations, we step back for a moment to consider which psychological research practices may provide the best conditions for explaining phenomena of interest to psychologists who want to study people as *persons*. We begin with the US psychologist and philosopher Daniel Robinson, who provided an illustration of the need for such consideration, when he noted, "*Once a memory drum[3] is used to present experimental participants with pairs of words, it is inevitable that memory will prove to be an associative process strengthened by repetition*" (2016, p. 328). Robinson here reminded us that the research method that a researcher chooses (such as a memory drum) will, by its very design, determine which kinds of responses, response patterns, and explanations are possible. Using a memory drum that juxtaposes pairs of nonsense syllables is one method among many other possible methods to study memory, and it may say little about how memory functions in settings outside the laboratory. Robinson therefore warned that if researchers are not careful, they may allow their research methods to determine how they understand the character of the phenomena they want to explain. He warns researchers to avoid the temptation " ... *to require of explanations that they address events the character of which is determined by the mode of inquiry rather than by the conditions under which such events typically take place*" (2016, p. 328). The message here is that a psychological explanation of a phenomenon should be relevant to the conditions in which people usually go about their lives, not just to the methods (experimental or other) used by the researcher to study the phenomenon (see also Feest, 2017, for similar arguments).

Further, as has surely been apparent throughout this book, psychologists who base their research on different views of the people they study, such as the views we have described in several chapters of this book, will ask different kinds of research questions. Different kinds of research questions will lead researchers to look for different *kinds* of explanations. Some psychologists may ask questions about the biological (for instance, brain) determinants of a particular behavior or emotion. Such psychologists are fairly likely to look

---

[3] The use of "memory drums" and the study of learning and memory by having subjects associate meaningless syllables that are repeatedly presented by such "drums" was initiated by the German researcher Herman Ebbinghaus (in the second half of the nineteenth century). This method came to shape most early theories of memory (Richards & Stenner, 2023).

for causal, and therefore determinist, explanations. In such explanations, the explanatory traffic typically goes only in one direction: from the biological cause to its behavioral effect (Edwards, 1991). Other researchers may ask questions about the social determinants of the same behavior or emotion. For them, the explanatory traffic will also go in one direction, but in this case, it goes from causes in social forces to their behavioral effects. Yet others may ask questions about how individuals in different social positions interpret the demands made on them, as well as about their related experiences, emotions, and behavior. These researchers are likely to look for explanations in terms of reasons and interpretations. In such explanations, the explanatory traffic may move in more than one direction, especially when people act (as they often do) to change the very conditions under which they are acting.

Reasons and Contextualized Explanations

When one asks somebody why they performed a certain action (such as why they went inside), the typical answer contains a word like *because* – for instance, "Because it was too cold outside." Similarly, if one asks somebody why they believe a certain thing (such as why they believe it will rain soon), one also often gets an answer containing the word *because* – for instance, "Because I see dark clouds on the horizon." In both these cases, the word "because" signals that the person is using the reason they mention after the word "because" as the *explanation* for the action or belief. This meaning of the word "reason" is captured by the Oxford English Dictionary as "*a fact or circumstance forming a motive sufficient to lead a person to adopt or reject some course of action, belief, etc. . . . often followed by why, that, of, for, to do.*"

Note here that when people explain an action or belief by providing a reason for it, they point to some fact or circumstance. These facts or circumstances are often external to the person, but they could also be internal, as in: "The reason why I went inside was that I was feeling cold," or, "I went inside because I was feeling cold." These examples of reasons illustrate something else that is important, namely, that reasons are connected to a context of some kind. In our examples, the context was physical: the temperature had dropped below comfort level, or dark clouds were looming. In another case, the context might be a social situation that was making certain demands on the speaker.

Explaining by giving the *reason* or motive for an action is quite different from explaining by providing the *cause* of that action. A reason is not a kind of cause (Tanney, 2013). In fact, explanations in terms of motives and reasons are not, not even in principle, replaceable by causal explanations.

That is, it is not that reasons or causes are better or worse at achieving the same kind of explaining; rather, providing a reason and providing a cause achieve different *kinds* of explaining (Bennett & Hacker, 2022; Tanney, 2013). In a much-cited article about social psychological research, the philosopher Rom Harré and the social psychologist Paul Secord further clarified the distinction between the two types of explanation:

> In terms of reasons, the consideration is of an active agent making a decision in a normative or justificatory context; in terms of causes, the consideration is of a passive agent exposed to certain circumstances and conditions, both internal and external. . . . It would be a serious mistake to treat reasons offered in a justificatory context as if they were causes. (1972, p. 161)

Peter Hacker elaborates a little more about reasons and persons:

> Explanation of action in terms of agential reasons . . . enables us to understand the agent's behavior ideographically rather than nomothetically.[4] Knowing his reasons for doing what he did, we may come to know what kinds of things weigh with him in his deliberations, and what kinds of considerations move him to act. We can see the extent of his rationality and the degree of his reasonableness, as well as the values for the sake of which he is prone to take action. Such explanations enable us not only to judge the agent and evaluate what he did, but also to judge his character. It enables us to understand our fellow human beings as persons. (2007, p. 232)

Note here Hacker's emphasis on understanding human beings as *persons*. Keeping these things in mind is important for a psychologist, because there are wide areas of human life where it is necessary to know an individual person, and also that person's reasons, in order to explain their actions and beliefs. These are areas where explanations in terms of causes would simply not apply (Sprague, 1999).

There is more to say about what it means to take into account that human beings are active agents who act in normative and justificatory contexts and give reasons for what they do and believe (see also Fuchs, 2023). To begin, mature human beings have the faculty of reason and rationality.[5] And they have a will – they can *deliberate* about and choose

---

[4] The term "ideographic" (or "idiographic," from Greek *idéa*, form or semblance) has been used to denote research based on an interest in the individual and the individual's unique life history in the social and cultural context of each individual. The term "nomothetic" (*nomos* is the Greek word for "law") denotes research studying classes of individuals with the purpose of deriving laws that explain phenomena on a general (class), not individual, level. The individuals who are studied are seen as representing the population (class) from which they are drawn, rather than as unique persons.

[5] The word "reason" and the word "rational" both stem from the Latin word *ratio*: reckoning, calculation, reason.

between alternatives, and they can act *for a reason*. They have cognitive powers that usually enable them to foresee the effects of their behavior. Humans see themselves as able to make certain things happen and to prevent other things from happening, and so on. And they see themselves as doing these things intentionally. All this means that explanations based on reasons can be either backward-looking, as when one acted *for a reason*, or forward-looking, as when one is acting *with* some *purpose*.

It is characteristic also of human body movements (apart from reflexes and twitches) that they "...*are actions of which it makes* sense *to say that they are voluntary, intentional, made or done deliberately or on purpose, for a reason or out of a motive*" (Hacker, 2007, p. 145). Likewise, it is characteristic of human emotions that they are warranted by some reason (rather than being caused by some cause). Moreover, it is usually the case that an emotion may change if the belief that prompted it turns out to have been false. Further, humans are usually (if not always) *reasonable* in their reason-giving; that is, they usually do not go beyond what is seen as reasonable in their social context, such as the need to take the interests of others into account, and to avoid making extravagant demands.

In sum, people exercise the faculty of reason when reasoning about some issue, when giving reasons for their own actions and beliefs, and when discerning others' reasons for actions and beliefs. These reasoning activities are verbal; they take place in language, often as a reply to a "why" question. To appreciate the reason that a person gives for a particular action, belief, or emotion, one therefore needs to take the details of that person's choice of words into account.

Further, one needs to know the meaning of those particular words in that person's social and cultural context. To fully identify and appreciate a person's reasons for, say, performing a particular action therefore requires placing both the reason and the action (and, of course, the person) in their proper context (Wilson, 2004). Only in this way can one achieve a properly *contextualized explanation* of the person's action and choice to act in a particular way (Alvarez, 2018; Tanney, 2013, 2022).

We have borrowed the British philosopher Julia Tanney's example of a contextualized explanation of an action as an illustration: imagine someone writing the letters c – a – t – on a blackboard. If one does not know the context, one can have no idea of *why* this person wrote those particular letters, nor what would be the next letter after *t*. But then add the contextual information that the writer is a chemistry teacher and that those observing her are chemistry students during a chemistry lesson.

Knowing these things about the context, one realizes that the letters c-a-t would be quite at home in a chemistry lecture as the beginning of the word "catalyst." If the students were asked why the teacher wrote the letters c-a-t-, their *contextualized* explanation would be that "*she wrote the letters 'c,' 'a,' and 't' because she was writing 'catalyst'*" (2013, p. 157). It would also be correct to formulate the explanation as "the teacher's *reason* for writing the letters c-a-t- was that she wanted to write 'catalyst'." What one can learn from this simple example is applicable also when people explain their actions by giving reasons in a wider and more complex context than a chemistry lesson.

All this means that, to achieve the full explanatory force of a *reason* explanation, one needs to place the action to be explained in its appropriate context. Another way to put this is that an action that is puzzling when seen without its context, or when seen in the wrong context, will in its proper context no longer be puzzling. When an action is seen in its proper context, one usually finds that there was a *good reason* for that particular action. Now, what does it mean to have a *good reason* to act? This is a tricky question, not always fully answered even by successfully identifying the details of a person's reasons or purposes. More may be needed. Daniel Robinson urges us to consider the whole picture and, above all, to realize that the picture cannot be meaningfully divided into different "explanatory" parts:

> Having a good reason to act is, among other considerations, to be disposed in ways dependent on confidence, conviction, satisfaction, highly subjective assessments of costs and benefits, allegiance to moral precepts, estimations based on "all-things-considered," hopefulness – factors scarcely touched by textbook notions of "reasons" and "emotions." To think of these terms as referring to partitionable features of mental life is to think that one can pull out of the cup what is hot, then what is sweet, then what is liquid and then what is brown – all the while accounting for "hot chocolate." (2016, p. 331)

Note the mention of "allegiance to moral precepts" in Robinson's quote. This is a reminder that reasons, as indeed practically every other aspect of human psychology, are always conceived in relation to the norms and rules of conduct in a person's context. A good reason is typically one that adheres to these norms of conduct. And because norms of conduct may vary between locales, so may moral precepts, and therefore what are seen as morally good reasons to act. The possibility of such variations must be taken into account when developing psychological explanations of people's decisions and behavior.

The act of reasoning (for instance, reasoning in the sense of the thinking that forms the basis of reason-*giving*) is probably often taken to be an individual cognitive action. This is sometimes true, but perhaps more often it is not. Reasoning always takes place in a particular context and is influenced by the resources, norms, and boundaries that this context offers (Gastelum-Vargas, Chemero, & Raja, 2024). Moreover, reasoning often takes place in interaction with other reasoners. A moment's reflection will make one aware of how often reasoning – and thereby also reason-giving – is dialogical, taking place in conversations and other kinds of collaborations. See also Chapter 6, on thinking, where we discussed the importance of contextualized and dialogical aspects of thinking. The interactive and, therefore, social and cultural character of reasoning further underscores the need to take the normative context into account when explaining behavior.

Causality and Causal Explanations

What does it mean for something to *cause* something else? This seemingly simple question has been given many different answers throughout human history, and we have space here only for a few answers. One of the clearest cases would be when an agent (such as a cat) pushes an object (such as a cup) off the edge of a table, such that the object falls to the floor. For someone who observes this series of events, there is nothing mysterious about the cause. The connection between the cause (the cat's push) and the effect (the cup falling) is obvious. This is an example of *agent causation*. Agent causation is often taken as the prototype of causation: a substantial *agent* acts on an object (often called the *patient*), thereby making something happen to that object (Hacker, 2007).

However, in addition to the prototype of agent causation, there are other, less clear-cut types of causality. For instance, not only active agents, but also inactive agents or things, may be causes. This means that there are several types of causes, and several types of *causality*, some of which do not involve an active agent. And this means that causes can bring about effects in several different ways. Also, a cause needs not always precede its effect (as it did in the cat example); the effect may be simultaneous with the cause. Think about, for instance, cutting a piece of paper: the cause (the movement of the scissors) is simultaneous with the effect (the cut in the paper). Finally, both in daily life and in science, people's choices of what to think of as causes are highly dependent on context, on their own interests, and on what they see as normal or expected, and so on.

In consequence, one should expect the terms "cause" and "causality" to be used in several different ways. And one should not expect it to be possible to reduce all the uses of these terms to one single form. To quote Peter Hacker, the category, or idea, of causation is *"unruly, multifaceted and frayed at the edges"* (2007, p. 89). This, according to Hacker, is what makes causation "work" in the widely varying everyday conditions of human life. Of course, against this background of unruliness and multifacetedness, any pronouncement about having found *the* cause of something should always lead one to ask which type of cause is implied and which type of causality.

Debates about the concepts of "cause" and "causality" have a long history in philosophy, and the debates still go on (Tanney, 2013, 2022). Can we feel assured that proper attention has been given in all of psychology to these debates and to the unruliness, multifacetedness, and frayed conditions of "cause" and "causation"? If not, might there be problems connected with some of the ways in which psychologists have drawn inferences about causality? These are reasonable questions to ask, considering that a good deal of psychological theory and research aims at identifying causal relationships.

As we noted earlier, there are several definitions of, and kinds of, causality, but we limit our discussion here to *efficient* causality. This is causality with two requirements: to be causal, the action performed by the agent (the cup-pushing that the cat performed) must be (1) necessary and (2) sufficient for the effect (the cup falling to the floor) to occur. When an explanation in terms of efficient causation is sought in a psychological experiment, the experimenter varies the intensity or frequency of an intervention (the independent variable, the assumed cause) and observes the research participant's response (the dependent variable, the assumed effect). If the variations in the independent variable are followed by consistent variations in the dependent variable, with all other aspects kept constant, this is taken to indicate that the changes to the independent variable are *sufficient* for the changes in the dependent variable to occur. Achieving sufficiency will sometimes be enough, as when a researcher, for instance, wants to identify one of several possible causes of a stress reaction.

If a researcher is confident that no other independent variable leads to the same changes in the dependent variable, this is taken to indicate that the chosen independent variable is also *necessary* for these changes. Necessity is, of course, far more difficult to establish than sufficiency. The number of potential independent variables, other than the one the researcher is studying, is likely to be large, and it may not be possible to test all of them. Therefore, in research practice, an independent variable that is sufficient for a certain effect to occur may not be necessary for that effect. There may be many other variables that have the same effect, and if they have not been studied, it is impossible to pronounce with certainty about efficient causality. This means that a full proof of efficient causality is difficult to achieve, even in well-conducted experiments.

And then, of course, to complicate matters, there is the question of deciding the proper *level* at which to look for a cause. We discuss these issues in the next section.

Causal Explanations that Reduce

A reductive explanation is one that fully explains the properties of one phenomenon (such as an atom) by the behaviors and properties of phenomena on another conceptual level (such as the properties of the elementary particles of the atom in question). By this particular reductive explanation, one is able to say that because the properties of the elementary particles *cause* the properties and behaviors of the atom, the atom is, in a sense, *nothing but* the effects of the properties of its parts, the elementary particles. This explanation can, therefore, be said to *reduce* the atom to those effects. In many (but far from all) branches of natural science, reductive explanations are both necessary and valuable. In other sciences, such as psychology, sociology, neuropsychology, and cognitive neuroscience, reductive explanations are also used. For instance, in some parts of psychology and in neuroscience, "downward" reductive explanations in terms of neurological or other biological mechanisms are not unusual.

Another type of reductive explanation is not uncommon in psychology: *metaphysically* reductive explanations[6] (Slife & Williams, 1995). This term designates explanations that refer to a universal, or final, law or principle that is assumed to govern behavior, and beyond which no other cause needs to be sought. Examples of metaphysically reductive explanations can be found in theories that assume the existence of abstract and invisible structures or processes that govern observable behavior. Such theories reduce that which they explain to the effect of this abstract and invisible principle, structure, or process. We can think of the reinforcement

---

[6] The word "metaphysical" is a combination of the Greek words *metá* (after or beyond) and *phusikós* (natural). It is usually used to denote entities or forces that are immaterial or beyond the physical, and that are so basic and self-evident that they are not themselves in need of an explanation. "Metaphysics" is the branch of philosophy centered on fundamental principles which do not have to be explained by anything else (such as a law) and are expected to explain all that exists.

principles of behaviorist, Skinnerian, theory, which were assumed to be universally effective, and to function as "final," that is, metaphysical, laws. An explanation of a particular behavior as the effect of such a general psychological law is a reductive explanation: it reduces the behavior in question to being just an instance of the effects of that law. Several metaphysically reductive explanations are used in psychology and the other social sciences. Explanations in terms of cognitive processes and explanations in terms of psychodynamic defense mechanisms (such as repression or projection) are examples from two subfields of psychology. One consequence of using metaphysically reductive explanations is that the individual whose behavior is explained by a general law or principle (e.g., a reinforcement principle, or a defense mechanism) often will be viewed primarily as the location where the law has its effect, and not always as a person in their own right.

Many psychologists have – perhaps out of routine and habit in the discipline – opted for reductive causal explanations. However, several critics have pointed out that on close scrutiny, many of the explanations that psychologists have put forward have proven to be philosophically and conceptually problematic (Bennett & Hacker, 2022; Robinson, 2016; Sharp & Miller, 2019). For instance, those explanations might not satisfy the criteria we mentioned before.

Quite a few psychologists have also argued that reductive explanations are not as self-evident and valuable in psychology as they are in some of the natural sciences. For instance, Paul Sharp and Gregory Miller (2019), two US psychologists, have pointed out that a causal explanation that reduces to a "lower" level (such as to neural activity) is not necessarily more explanatory than an explanation at a "higher" level (such as explanations that point to social interactions or political events). This is so, they argued, because in psychology, the researcher is dealing not just with "nature" in the sense of atoms, nerves, and so on. There is also "culture" in the sense of human beings who live surrounded not only by natural phenomena but also by other human beings and the products of their activities and those of other human beings. "Culture" includes broader patterns such as social norms and rules of behavior. Could such circumstances as these perhaps invalidate the use of reductive causal explanations in psychological and neuroscientific research? There are many who think so (Frisch, 2022; Robinson, 2016; Sharp & Miller, 2019). These psychologists have been especially critical of the simplistic ways in which such reductionist explanations portray the psychological understandings of those concerned, that is, of the *persons* whose actions are being causally "explained":

> One of the things that all of these reductive strategies share is an attempt to grossly simplify the complex lives of persons understood as embodied, rational, and moral agents interactive within evolutionary and developmental trajectories that include histories of constantly unfolding socio-cultural and biographical traditions, practices, artifacts, and identifications. (Martin & Bickhard, 2013, p. 8)

In her scrutiny of psychological research on priming (see Chapter 9), Ruth Leys identified many examples of such simplifications of people's lives. As we reported in Chapter 9, she found that many psychologists who study priming assumed that most of people's behavior can be explained reductively. In the view of these researchers, psychologists therefore do not need to take people's consciousness into account – neither to explain how people understand their immediate environment, nor to explain people's behavior in that environment. Both can, according to these psychologists, be understood as the result of automatic links between a stimulus and a behavioral outcome. In this view, neither the person who is the seat of those links, nor the context of that person, needs to be entered into the explanation. Leys also found that the use of reductive explanations is not unique to studies of priming but is part of the general logic of much cognitive science (Leys, 2024). Similar criticisms of reductive explanations and their neglect of context and social norms have been leveled at biologically oriented diagnostic practices in psychiatry, on the basis that no disorder in the DSM can be fully described, explained, or diagnosed on the "reductive" neurological level alone (Frisch, 2016, 2022). See also Chapter 5, about brains, where we discuss neuro-reductionism.

A Scrutiny of the Uses of Causal Explanations

When considering complicated psychological questions, such as the origins of psychological suffering, it is especially important to take into account what is required for causality. Though experimental manipulations are obviously not possible in such cases, many causal explanations have been suggested throughout history. Today, several psychologists and psychiatrists are skeptical of the possibility of ever establishing efficient causal explanations of many psychiatric conditions. We provide some examples of such critiques here, focusing specifically on the *necessary* and *sufficient* conditions for causal explanations that we described earlier.[7]

---

[7] It should be noted here that much psychological research, and most of the research on psychiatric conditions, is *epidemiological*. Such research may, for instance, search for co-occurrences of certain

The Dutch sociologist Sanne te Meerman and colleagues (2022) had observed that researchers often use the findings from *group* studies about ADHD to draw conclusions about the *individual* level. This means committing the *ecological fallacy* that we described in Chapter 11: the fallacy of using group characteristics (means, standard deviations, correlations, and so on) as the basis for theorizing about individuals. As part of a review article about several kinds of misunderstandings and misuses of the diagnostic term "ADHD," they closely scrutinized a large study that claimed to have found proof of specific brain-anatomical *causes* of ADHD. te Meerman et al. first noted that the data that had been gathered in the study showed that many of those who had been diagnosed with ADHD in the study did *not* have brains that deviated from "normal" brains in the way assumed to be typical of ADHD. Therefore, the assumed brain deviation from the "normal" could not be a *necessary* causal condition for an ADHD diagnosis. te Meerman et al. also noted that the data implied that many participants whose behavior had not qualified them for an ADHD diagnosis *did* have brains that deviated from "normal" in the expected "ADHD" direction. Therefore, the assumed brain deviation could not be a *sufficient* condition for an ADHD diagnosis. As we saw earlier, efficient causality requires both sufficiency and necessity. Both are needed to establish efficient causality. So, could this particular brain condition be *the cause* of ADHD? The scrutiny by te Meerman and colleagues makes this seem unlikely.

In a recent review article concerning theories of psychiatric disorders, Steven Hyman, a US psychiatrist and neuroscientist, scrutinized contemporary practices of psychiatric diagnosis in the US. He took as his starting point the question of natural kinds that we discussed earlier in this chapter and noted, *a propos* causality:

> If by natural kinds we mean categories of things existing in nature that are well bounded and have stable, cohesive causal structures, as is the case for chemical elements, then the poorly bounded, etiologically and patho-physiologically complex psychiatric disorders are something else entirely. Psychiatric disorders are heterogeneous, with diverse genetic,

---

possible background factors and certain diagnoses in a population. This research can at best establish a *correlation* between an assumed background factor and a certain diagnosis. And a correlation between two items cannot be used to establish causality between them. A correlation can tell the researcher that the two correlating items may have something in common. However, what that "something" is cannot be discerned from the correlation coefficient.

developmental, and environmental etiologies, symptoms, and treatment responses. (2021, p. 23)

Hyman added that clinical and scientific *"observations do not converge to anywhere near the point of suggesting natural kinds"* for psychiatric categories (2021, p. 23). And this, of course, means that all pronouncements about "natural" *causes* of psychiatric disorders should be seriously called into question.

Even in well-controlled psychological experiments, the question of causality may be more complicated than it might have appeared in the discussion of necessary and sufficient causes earlier in the chapter. One should especially be aware of the differences between the context of study and the everyday context to which researchers aim to generalize their research findings. These differences are likely to be extreme in the case of psychological research that involves strictly controlled experimental conditions. Not surprisingly, some critics have questioned whether such studies can ever tell us very much about life outside the laboratory (Frisch, 2022). At this point, we therefore quote Derek Edwards once more:

> . . .it may be that outside of the lab (and perhaps inside it too), meaningful human actions are simply not organized on a factors-and-variables causal basis. It could be that experiments do not *reveal*, but rather *make it so*, that human actions can be fitted to predictable causal formats. (1997, p. 4, emphasis in the original)

That is, the very format of a researcher's study may limit, and often narrowly shape, the responses that it is possible for the participants to produce.[8] If Edwards is right, the format may limit the responses to such an extent that spurious causal patterns of responses are produced. Such patterns, spurious or not, may tell one little about the participants' lives and reactions outside of the study situation. Note that this shaping of participants' responses is not restricted to experimental studies. Multiple-choice inventories, for instance, also limit respondents to certain kinds of responses, specifically, those enabled by the format of the inventory questions and by the response alternatives.

---

[8] This shaping power is based on the contract between the researcher and the participant, in which the participant has agreed to abide by the instructions that the researcher gives. Participants who disobey and behave in ways outside the agreed-upon format will typically be removed from the study. Note that this is as true for nonexperimental research as for experiments. Further, in many types of experiments, such as in neuroscience, the participant's movements and available response repertoires are severely restricted, making such studies even farther removed from normal everyday circumstances.

Perhaps people's everyday psychological lives are not best explained by causal explanations. What a person is disposed to do in a situation may depend on the person's beliefs, desires, and intentions in that specific situation, and on the particularities of the situation. And it may also depend, maybe just as much, on the person's *other* beliefs, desires, and intentions, and likely also on the presence or absence of other people in the situation (Glock, 2006). If so, other types of explanations than direct efficient causal explanations should be considered – perhaps the reason-based explanations that we described earlier.

Abduction, or Inference to the Best Explanation

In the philosophy of science, the term *abduction* stands for what researchers typically do when they are faced with new and/or surprising data for which they have no explanation readily available. After looking closely at the data, and perhaps identifying suggestive patterns, the researcher searches for a hypothesis that would explain those patterns. The hypothesis that gets selected will be the one with the best resemblance between, on the one hand, the data, and, on the other hand, the consequences of the chosen hypothesis *if it were found to be true* (Uher, 2013). In brief: abduction is the practice of studying the data and, on that basis, proposing a hypothesis about the causes that had generated the data (Hubbard, Haig, & Parsa, 2019). The phrase "if it were found to be true," above, is obviously critical – and it is typically the most difficult precondition to achieve for credible abduction (see below).

Researchers tend to use abduction as an explanatory strategy when it is not possible to study a topic in an experiment that could elucidate the steps of a causal explanation (Goldman, 2021). This is what makes abduction popular: it allows researchers to suggest possible explanatory entities that have not yet been observed or that may be unobservable. Not surprisingly, explanation by abduction has been characterized as comparable to making a differential diagnosis in medicine (Mason et al., 2018), as well as to the decision processes in clinical psychology and psychotherapy (Ward, Clack, & Haig, 2016).

In real life, as well as in research, it is often unknown whether a hypothesis that has been suggested will fulfill the conditions for being true. Sometimes this is unknowable. This uncertainty is typically dealt with in this way: If a researcher has developed an explanatory hypothesis and can find no competing hypotheses that explain the same data equally well or better, the researcher will conclude that the chosen hypothesis is *probably* true (Grice, 2015; Michell, 2012). It is easy to see that this is a potentially risky strategy, because its soundness depends on the quality of the competing hypotheses that the researcher had discarded after comparing them with the chosen hypothesis. If the discarded competing hypotheses were of low quality, the researcher runs the risk of settling for an explanation (i.e., a hypothesis) that is *"the best of a bad lot"* (van Fraassen, 1989, p. 143).

As can be seen from our earlier descriptions, an abductive explanation is not conclusive. In principle, it is always possible to develop a new hypothesis that may be better than the chosen one. Philosophers of science therefore disagree about the value of explanations built on abduction. Should the fact that an explanation (a hypothesis) is the best available at a particular moment be enough to make one accept that particular explanation as *true*? Probably not. A more decisive criterion is needed to make it possible to judge the truth (or falsity) of the explanation (Fiedler, 2017). However, philosophers and psychologists also argue for the usefulness of abduction, especially in the early phases of research. Abductive explanations should be seen as tools to *begin* developing feasible, though probably temporary, explanations of "early" facts that do not lend themselves to conventional explanatory strategies (Hubbard, Haig, & Parsa, 2019; Uher, 2013). However, even while arguing for the usefulness of abduction, Hubbard, Uher, and many other psychologists recommend caution about their use. Abductive explanations call for constant reconsideration and reconstruction and should never be proposed as the conclusion of a study.

Determinism and Psychology

The term "determinism" usually refers to the idea that all events that occur are caused by earlier events, predictably and in accordance with the laws of nature (Tafreshi & Slaney, 2024). Questions about determinism, and therefore also about free will, are among the "big," and unresolved, questions that have been debated for as long as anything like philosophy has existed. Outside philosophy, though, determinism is often assumed, usually without much debate. This is true, for example, in large parts of the natural sciences and in parts of the behavioral sciences. We therefore take a brief look at how determinism features in psychological explanations, while also considering whether there might be anything problematic about psychological determinism.

To consider determinist claims in psychology, we can think of several of the types of psychological explanations that we have described in this chapter. We noted earlier that psychological research often searches for efficient causal explanations. Such explanations are by definition determinist, because if one applies a cause that is both sufficient and necessary, the effect *has* to follow.

How do efficient causal explanations (and thereby determinism) fare in psychological research? One indication that there may be problems is the notorious difficulty of achieving full proof of causality in psychological research, that is, of being able to pinpoint a sufficient *and* necessary cause of a particular behavior. If determinism were common, one would expect to find proof of efficient causality fairly regularly in psychological research and, on that basis, also stable and replicable research results. But as we discussed in Chapter 9, many psychological research findings have proven difficult to replicate.

We also need to ask what an assumption of determinism would tell us about psychologists' views of the people whose behaviors they aim to explain (here we can think about Ruth Leys's scrutiny of priming research that we referred to earlier). On the assumption of determinism, there is no room for free will. It is likely that only a few people would be comfortable with such a view. If a person's behavior can be causally explained (if one finds a cause that is both sufficient and necessary), then the person clearly had no choice but to behave in that way. One would therefore have to exempt the person from guilt or responsibility for that behavior. Such exemptions have been vigorously debated through history, especially in the fields of law and mental health.

In Conclusion

As will have been obvious when reading this chapter, we favor explanations that take into account peoples' interpretations of their experiences and actions. We prefer such explanations, because they are built on the assumption that people inevitably experience and interpret their own and other's actions, capacities, and biological functions through the lenses provided by their cultural context. In the two following chapters, we build further on this approach. In Chapter 13, we describe how someone who is new to psychology can scrutinize the discipline using the strategies we have described in this book. In Chapter 14, the final chapter, we describe some of the ways in which researchers who work from this stance go about their research.

Being a Discerning Reader of Psychology

This chapter concerns ways of thinking about and scrutinizing the discipline of psychology – its history as well as its contemporary workings – with the aim of identifying those practices and theories that work well, and those that are problematic. Throughout the history of the psychology discipline, there have been periods of especially intense scrutiny, the most recent example being the efforts to resolve the replication crisis, which we described in Chapter 9. Such efforts often have limitations, though. In the case of the replication crisis, observers have pointed out that many proposed remedies have been "more of the same" and have therefore failed to challenge conventional practices and assumptions that may have precipitated the crisis. That is, many suggestions stayed within the original thought collectives' thinking styles, confirming Ludwik Fleck's observation (see Chapter 2) that remaining committed to one thinking style will limit the kinds of problems one can identify, and also the solutions one can suggest.

Why have many reform efforts remained committed to the original thinking style? Some critics have argued that part of the explanation is that many psychologists *"are virtually unpracticed when it comes to critiquing the fundamental logic of method itself"* (Slife, O'Grady, & Kosits, 2017, p. 44). Other critics have argued that the psychology discipline lacks a framework for discussing quality in psychological research that is not based on the predominant thinking styles (Flis, 2019). And, to use terms that Ludwik Fleck might have used, such a lack would leave psychologists with little ability to move outside their usual thinking style. This interpretation is in line with one of the premises of this book: to really know psychology, it is not enough to master the teachings and research findings of the discipline; one also needs to acquire skills that enable one to reflect *on* the discipline.

Reflecting on the discipline requires that one observe psychology from a vantage point that differs from the ones typically available "inside" the discipline. If most of the scrutiny comes from the inside of the discipline, and if the scrutinizers are not accustomed to questioning the main assumptions of the discipline, it is likely that they will never ask critical questions emanating from outside the dominant thinking style. Such "outside" questions will simply not appear to the inside scrutinizers. This is a well-known phenomenon, commonly observed in scholarly work (see, e.g., Gradmann, 2004; and Binney, 2016a, for examples from medical research).

In this chapter, we suggest some ways to observe psychology from the outside as well as from the inside of the discipline. In the first section, we describe conceptual analysis, the close scrutiny of psychologists' uses of words and concepts. In the second section, we suggest a number of specific questions, based on conceptual analysis, to ask when reading and scrutinizing a psychology book, article, or research report, or when planning a study or a research report.

Conceptual Analysis: Taking Psychological Words and Concepts Seriously

Our scrutiny of psychology in this book can be seen as an instance of *conceptual analysis*; that is, we scrutinize the conceptual bases of psychological theory and practice. The methods and purposes of conceptual analysis originated in the discipline of philosophy, which is often concerned with elucidating concepts and concept use. This means that the methods and purposes of conceptual analysis are quite different than are those of empirical scientific investigations and analyses. Conceptual analysis of a body of scholarly work is concerned with identifying what does and what does not make sense in a text or an argument. It is also concerned with resolving the conceptual confusions that result from uses of words and concepts that do not make sense (Machado & Silva, 2007; Racine, 2015; Slaney & Racine, 2011). For, as Max Bennett and Peter Hacker have pointed out, researchers must be careful about how they use words:

> Language, and the concepts expressed in our languages, are the medium of scientific thought. If one ties knots in the web of words, one can get nothing right, save per accidens – and even should one be so fortunate, one will not understand what one has discovered. (Bennett & Hacker, 2022, p. 13)

The Australian psychologist Simon Boag is among the increasing number of psychologists who argue strongly for the importance of conceptual analysis. In his words, "*. . .critically evaluating theoretical premises using the tools of logical and conceptual analysis is a vital component of maintaining psychology as a rigorous scientific discipline*" (2011, p. 235). We agree.

Conceptual analysis is the study of the words, terms, and concepts in psychologists' theories and texts, with special attention to how psychologists *use* these words, terms, and concepts. The goals of conceptual analysis are to determine what psychologists mean by their terms when they use them, whether some term uses are obscure, illogical, or in other ways confused or unclear, and if some uses of a term could have unintended consequences that threaten the soundness of the theory or research (Racine, 2015).

Resolving *conceptual* questions, such as the ones above, should always precede the empirical phase in research. This is so because, while the methods used to perform scientific research are well-suited to answer *empirical* questions and resolve *empirical* uncertainties, these methods are neither suited to, nor designed to, resolve conceptual questions and confusions, such as problematic uses of central terms and concepts. Resolving such questions requires conceptual analysis.

Conceptual confusions and mistakes have very real negative consequences, in research as well as in practical applications of psychology. This is so because the ways that psychologists understand and use concepts will unavoidably guide their practice. This necessarily means that it is only after conceptual confusions and uncertainties have been resolved that a psychologist is ready to start empirical work (Bennett & Hacker, 2022). Conceptual analysis helps one to identify what does and what does not make sense in one's use of words and concepts, and to resolve conceptual confusions that result from uses that do not make sense. The work of Nachev & Hacker (2014), which we referred to in Chapter 5, provides an example. Their conceptual analysis tested the coherence of word use, and thereby of research hypotheses, in cognitive neuroscience.

Conceptual analysis is helpful not just for researchers, it is also key to enabling a reader to gain a full understanding of scholarly texts. Conceptual analysis can proceed in different ways, depending on what is being analyzed and what the analyzer's purpose is. We have identified three general steps in the kind of conceptual analysis suited to the scrutiny of scholarly texts such as articles in scientific journals. We offer abbreviated descriptions of the steps; for more details, see for instance Racine (2015).

The *first* step is to locate the most significant words and concepts in an article – those that describe and denote what the article "is about." The *second* step is to examine how the significant words and concepts are used in the text; that is, with what meanings. The purpose is to decide whether some of those uses are problematic. For instance, are they incoherent or used inconsistently? Here are some aspects to examine in this second step:

Meanings and Confusions

One purpose of the second step is to see if any terms are given inconsistent meanings. In other words, is the same term used with several meanings at different points in the text? And is this done without comment or discussion? If so, some conceptual confusion in what is written often results. To give an example, it is not unusual for the word "gender" to be used with several meanings in the same text. It may be used as a synonym for the human sex categories (meaning "the genders"), but it may also be used to denote the societal practices of treating people in different sex categories differently (meaning "the gender system").

Conceptual Fields

Look at the two different uses of the word "gender" in the previous paragraph. They originated in different parts of the scholarly world: the first use is grammatical, and the second use comes from feminist and queer theories. This observation is a reminder that the scholarly setting, or the *conceptual field*, in which a word is used often shapes a particular meaning of the word. The same word can therefore mean quite different things in different academic disciplines, and sometimes even in different sub-disciplines within a discipline. Further, a particular word or concept can be more (or less) at home in different cultural and historical contexts. The context of a word's use, therefore, needs to be considered when analyzing how it is used.

Meanings and Controversies

In the second step one needs to identify words and word uses about which there are controversies. For instance, in the chapters about minds and about brains, we noted that researchers disagree about what words like "mind" and "cognition" should be taken to mean, and therefore how they should be used. A body of work, or a conceptual field, that is built on one use of such a word may well be disregarded or rejected by a reader who is committed to a different use of the word. How one is able to resolve such controversies will vary depending on the rigidity (or flexibility) of the thinking style(s) in the fields in question.

Meanings That Do Not Make Sense

One should also look for passages in a text in which words are used in ways that do not make sense. This is not about whether one gives the *wrong* or *right* meaning to a particular word. It is about whether one has given a meaning to a word that the word *could not have*; that is, a meaning that would be senseless to ascribe to that word. In Chapter 7, about language, we illustrated this kind of senselessness in our discussion about why psychological words do not name the kinds of things to which one can ascribe colors. We should note that an individual instance of this type of analysis is often not universally applicable, because each instance relies on the rules that a particular language community has developed for using a certain word or concept. Knowing these local rules helps one to see if a particular text uses a word with a meaning that does not make sense in that language community. For example, consider the discussion in Chapter 5, about brains, and the disagreements about what kinds of actions can be ascribed to brains. Many popular writers, and some scientists, are happy to ascribe actions like deciding, seeing, falling in love, and judging beauty to people's brains. Other scientists, and many philosophers, reserve active verbs like these for the persons whose brains are being talked about or studied. These latter scientists and philosophers argue that the first group of scientists and popular writers are committing a category mistake; that is, it is wrong to apply these actions to the category "brains." The critics argue that brains are not in the category of "things" which can be said to, for instance, judge, see, and decide. According to the critics, using such active verbs about brains breaks the rules for how these verbs can be used; therefore, such word use makes no sense.

The *third* step in conceptual analysis aims to find ways to resolve the conceptual problems that have been identified. The details of this step vary depending on the conceptual issues at stake and the disciplinary fields or texts under scrutiny. The resolution may consist, for instance, of a change of term use in the text to make the meaning clearer in a text. Or it may consist of changing how the identified words are used, such that they can make sense. And sometimes it may consist of changes in theory or thinking style.

Which words, concepts, and word uses should psychologists be especially eager to subject to conceptual analysis? Obvious candidates are those that, because of unclear definitions or great discrepancies in their uses, may be particularly likely to cause confusion or conflict in the practice of empirical research, or in practical applications of psychology. We can think especially about words that are used with different meanings in different thinking styles and by different thought collectives. Other equally important candidates are those concepts that are taken for granted by those who share one's thinking style. Because these concepts are hardly ever brought into focus, there is always a risk that they, and any conceptual confusions connected with them, may pass under what we can call *the conceptual radar*.

Here are some suggestions for words and concepts that psychologists might submit to conceptual analysis in the texts they encounter: attitude, attribute, brain, cognition, cognitive schema, consciousness, context, culture, emotion, explanation, gender, individual, intelligence, measurement, memory, mental representation, method, mind, motivation, person, personality, psychopathology, sex, sexuality, trait, trauma, variable.

A psychologist who performs a conceptual analysis of a psychological article scrutinizes how the psychological concepts that are used have been defined, and how they are measured. The purpose is to decide whether the meanings they were given make sense in the setting of the research or the theoretical ideas brought forward. This kind of analysis provides *conceptual* knowledge, in contrast to empirical knowledge. It is necessary for researchers to achieve conceptual knowledge and thereby achieve conceptual clarification about the uses and meanings of concepts before beginning to gather empirical data and knowledge. This is so because research designs, arguments, and discussions of research results that are based on confused and inconsistent uses of words and concepts cannot make scientific sense. This is the case even if the researcher has used the most sophisticated and up-to-date research methods available. There can be no empirical clarity without conceptual clarity!

For more details about conceptual analysis by psychologists, see, for example, LaVine & Tissaw (2015), Machado & Silva (2007), and Racine (2015). For a detailed example of conceptual analysis of the uses of psychiatric diagnoses and of the changes over time in the breadth of how such diagnoses are defined, see Haslam (2016).

In the next section we provide a set of questions that can be useful when carrying out conceptual analysis of an article or a book, and also when planning one's own work.

Questions and Suggestions for the Discerning Reader

The questions and suggestions in this section are meant to be helpful while you acquaint yourself with a particular psychological theory and the research connected with the theory, or with a particular psychotherapeutic school or other application of psychology. The questions can also be useful when designing a study of your own. Further, the questions can be used as aids when carrying out conceptual analysis. The questions we suggest here invite (and, we hope, enable) the reader to adopt the "outside" perspective on psychology that we mentioned in the introduction to this chapter. It is a perspective that we have applied in many parts of this book. We encourage such reflection from the outside, because it enables one to find out and learn important things about psychology that one cannot learn while remaining "inside."

It is a good idea to summarize your thoughts and reflections about these questions in a notebook while you are reflecting on them. Having such a written record can enable you to see significant patterns of assumptions and meanings that characterize the literature you have read.

(1) **What foundational views (or "active assumptions") about humans shape the theory, research project, or psychotherapeutic school that you are considering?** For instance, are the people under study being portrayed as persons who are culturally and socially situated in a specific historical setting? Or are people more generically portrayed as instances of universal humans from which the researcher can generalize to all or most of humanity, and across culture and history? Or are they not actually "portrayed" at all, such that the reader is left to form their own conclusions about the writer's image of humans, as it were, backwards from the data collections methods and strategies for data analysis that are used? See Chapter 2 for more about the kinds of assumptions at stake here.

  – In several of this book's chapters, we have discussed the consequences in specific psychological subfields of working from either of the sets of assumptions we just mentioned. But psychology covers much more ground than we have covered in this book. It is, therefore, a good idea to consider what the possible consequences of choosing different sets of assumptions about humans could be for some other psychological subfields besides the ones we have discussed.

  – If you are reading to learn about a field of research or practice that is new to you, consider whether there seems to be one overarching view of humans (for instance, as persons or as universal humans) that is shared by researchers in the field. If not, can you discern competing views of humans within the field? If there are competing views, consider which view is most consonant with your own vision of persons.

 – If you are designing a study of your own, consider how your own assumptions about humans might shape both your search of the literature and your reading of it. When you begin designing your study, consider whether your ideas for a research design are compatible with your view of humans.

(2) **What kinds of explanations are used in the theories or research projects that you are reading about?** For instance, are the arguments and conclusions phrased in terms of causal explanations, therefore explicitly assuming determinism? Or do the conclusions, while not explicitly stated as causal, nonetheless seem to imply causality, thereby leaving the question of determinism undecided? Or are arguments and conclusions phrased as interpretative explanations, therefore explicitly disavowing determinism? Is the explanatory traffic assumed to move in one direction only, or in more than one direction (see the section *Psychological Explanations* in Chapter 12). For suggestions of additional details to look for, review Chapter 12.

 – Consequences: consider whether the explanations that you find in particular theoretical writings or research publications are consonant with your own worldview and your vision of what guides people's decisions and choices in their everyday lives. Also, consider connections between your answers to this question and the question posed in (1) about the view of humans held by the researchers whose work you are reading.

(3) **What kinds of definitions are given priority in the literature you are reading?** The discipline of psychology has a long tradition of relying on operational definitions rather than on theoretical definitions. Each type of definition has advantages and disadvantages. If operational definitions are used, the defined concepts are easily amenable to empirical study. However, there will be drawbacks, such as limited generalizability across studies that define concepts by different operations. On the other hand, if a researcher relies on a theoretically derived definition, concepts may be widely applicable, but there may be disagreements about the best ways to study them. Whether you are approaching a new field of psychology, or planning a study of your own, you should look closely at the definitions used for the most important concepts in the field. Consider what choice of definition might work best for your own studies.

(4) **Are the properties that are studied assumed to have a quantitative structure, or not?**
This question is seldom explicitly addressed in research reports
written by psychologists. However, the answer usually can be
inferred from the researcher's data-gathering methods, as they are
described in the text. In studies that rely on quantitative data-
gathering methods, the researcher assumes – explicitly or implicitly –
that the properties being studied have a quantitative structure. In
a study in which quantitative data-gathering methods are not used,
no assumptions about the structure of the properties studied are
necessary.

  – If the study or theory relies on quantitative measurements,
    consider whether the authors are justified in assuming that the
    properties that are studied have a quantitative structure. Do the
    authors offer any argument to justify that assumption, or does it
    appear that they take it for granted?
  – If you doubt that the assumption of quantitative structure is
    warranted in a particular study, reflect on what the consequences
    might be if the assumption is unjustified. Is there a risk of
    drawing false conclusions from such research?
  – If you are planning a study of your own, consider what structure
    the properties you plan to study have – quantitative or non-
    quantitative. Your decision will determine the data-gathering
    and analytic methods that you should use.

(5) **Can you discern any imperative(s) about assumptions, theories,
or methods in your institutional setting?** Assessing this is the
same as investigating the kind(s) of thinking style(s) that prevails
in your setting. If you identify a predominant imperative, you
might want to consider its impact on the possible options
regarding topics, methods of data gathering and analysis,
research settings, and so on in your setting. You can get
a picture of the stringency of the imperative by making a brief
assessment of the variety of research methods that are used in
your disciplinary surroundings. You might also consider the
kind of work that most commonly appears on course syllabi. If
you find a sizable number of researchers who use different kinds
of methods, this may be an indication of tolerance for methodological diversity.

> - If you identify a powerful imperative, consider whether there are signs of the existence of resisters or dissenters in the local setting. Also consider whether dissent is tolerated, or if the dissenters have paid a price, either professionally or personally, for resisting or dissenting.

(6) **As you read research studies, theories, or clinical case reports, look for evidence of the ideology that infuses the study or theory under scrutiny.** We use the word "ideology" in a broad sense here to refer to a belief system. It can be of many kinds, from religious to political to ethnic, and more. Keep in mind that complete *neutrality* in research and theory is impossible.

If you are reading a research article or textbook, take stock of the most frequently cited and most praised works, and consider the ideological standpoints expressed or implied in them. If you are planning a study of your own, consider the ideological standpoints expressed or implied in the books and articles you read while planning. Which ones are compatible with your own ideological standpoints?

Also, attend to statements that authors whose work you read make about themselves, and whether these statements indicate an awareness of how their own ideas might have been shaped by their life experiences and social status.

(7) **Consider the thinking styles in the literature you are reading.** Remind yourself of Ludwik Fleck's ideas about thinking styles and their *active assumptions* and *passive* elements, and make sure to note the differences between them. Then, select a central part of the book or article you are scrutinizing. Look for indications of the decisions and choices that, in your judgment, were *actively* made, either by the present author or earlier by those referred to by that author. Next, look for the *passive* elements – that is, those that follow self-evidently or automatically because a certain active choice had been made. Remember that the passive elements are usually not seen as, nor described as, choices at all. Instead they are typically seen as necessary and natural, as "just the way we do things here."

> - Then consider: Does your identification of the active assumptions of the thinking style that informs a publication influence your judgment of the quality of the research or theory presented there? Are there certain assumptions that you especially appreciate as well-grounded? And are there other assumptions that you judge to be particularly questionable?

– If you are planning a study of your own, look closely at the *passive* elements of the thinking styles evinced in the research literature that you are reading. Methodological choices would be likely examples. Do you agree with the authors that the passive (e.g., methodological) elements you have identified are so self-evident that they do not have to be explicitly considered and discussed? Can they be taken for granted? If you do not agree with the authors, then try to work your way back to the *active* choices (assumptions) made earlier that underlie the passive elements (even if they only inform that writing indirectly). Then consider whether you find these choices acceptable.

(8) **If the assumptions of a thinking style appear illogical or misdirected, consider what needs to be changed.** Thinking styles are not hewn in stone but are, in fact, constantly changing, often because of changes in a discipline's scientific and cultural surroundings.

– Imagine that you are planning a study of your own, and that your reading of the research literature has convinced you that some divergence from a dominant thinking style is necessary for your study to do what you want it to do. Begin by carefully thinking through which assumptions and elements are most in need of change. And consider what will be possible for you to change at this point: theoretical statements (that are based on certain active assumptions) or methodological conventions (i.e., passive elements). The answer to the question of what can be changed is closely connected to the next question.

(9) **Thought collectives – strict or lenient?** Remember how Ludwik Fleck described the nature of the thought collectives that scientific disciplines and therapeutic schools tend to create. They vary along several dimensions: they can be more or less stringent about keeping to a particular thinking style; they can be more or less hierarchically organized; they can be more or less prepared to give voice to newcomers or their younger members; and they can be more or less inclined to stay in contact with other thought collectives, and so on.

– If one reads only one book or one research article in a field, it will likely be difficult to discern the characteristics of the thought collective to which the authors belong. However, reading several articles in a field, and especially reading critical texts, is likely to help one identify some characteristics. One way to identify the characteristics typical of a scientific thought collective is to scan the main scientific journals in its field of study. Do the journals publish articles based on a variety of theories and research methods, or is the variety of methods and theories kept within strict bounds? Do the journals make space for critical reflections, articles that challenge methodological or disciplinary conventions, and essays that offer syntheses? Or do the journals solely contain compilations of empirical studies?

— If you are a student planning a study of your own, you are likely to be doing this in an institutional setting such as a psychology department. The department may be characterized by one or several thought collectives, depending on its size and the diversity of its sub-disciplines. As a student, you will likely be among the newest and youngest members. For you, it may therefore be important whether there is a heavy emphasis on adherence to a dominant thinking style. If there is, consider finding sources of knowledge and support in other parts of the discipline, or outside the discipline in cross-disciplinary collaborations.

(10) **Conventions about what counts as "psychological."** Do the theoretical and methodological conventions in your department, subfield, or discipline define only certain kinds of psychological questions as worthy of study? Can you identify other kinds of psychological questions that you find interesting, but which are deemed to be "not psychology" in the setting where you work? If so, consider what changes in thinking styles might be necessary for such questions to be accepted as "psychological."

Some Final Words about the Questions

After you have worked through the questions, it is a good idea to consider what your notes about them can tell you about your own views of *psychology* and of *persons*. Further, the questions, your notes, and your conclusions from them could perhaps also form material for seminar discussions, or for conversations with fellow students.

Naturally, some of the questions in our list may be irrelevant to your work or studies. And, of course, the questions we have listed before are not exhaustive. You can probably come up with several more questions that would be meaningful to ask. Do so!

CHAPTER 14

Studying the Psychology of Persons: Methods, Assumptions, and Commitments

This book contains many references to psychological approaches and research studies that take human beings to be socially and culturally situated *persons*. This chapter describes some of the ways of doing research that were used in these studies, in the hope that the descriptions will inspire readers to learn more about such methods. To refresh readers' memory, we briefly revisit some of the descriptions and examples here.

In the book, we describe how a recognition of the importance of cultural contexts has inspired researchers' methods for studying persons in their everyday life (e.g., Chapter 3). We cite psychologists who have shown that psychological concepts often do not have universal validity, and that the meanings of such concepts are often shaped by cultural norms and institutions (Chapter 9). This means that it is not possible to reduce a concept – or a research finding – to a context-independent core meaning, because removing context removes part of the meaning of the concept. We also discuss the types of psychological explanations are best suited for explaining a person's choices and actions in everyday life (Chapter 12). We argue for a psychology of human individuals that goes beyond a focus on the "inside" of the mind and instead takes the capacities of the whole person in context into account (Chapter 4). When we describe ways of conceiving of human brains that include the person, we draw on the work of thinkers who warn that a decontextualized, "brain-centric" image of the human brain may lead psychologists, including clinical practitioners, to lose sight of the person (Chapter 5). We also describe psychological approaches that take thinking to be part of an interactive and dynamic system – approaches often called situated cognition (Chapter 6). We describe the action tradition in psychological studies of language, with its emphasis on language use as a joint and contextualized communicative activity among speakers (Chapter 7). We describe major shifts in psychodiagnostic systems over the years, and we discuss some long-running problems. We point to attempts to reform diagnostic systems to take social context and cultural difference into account (Chapter 8).

An increasing number of psychologists are taking considerations such as the ones we just mentioned into account in their research and practical work. We devote the next part of this chapter to describing common features of the research approaches adopted by these psychologists. There are several such approaches, which are based on a range of theoretical understandings and assumptions. Our discussion of them, therefore, offers a general characterization; the details of the approaches vary. Our aim is not to teach any method in detail, but to inspire readers to learn more about these approaches.

After reading the descriptions of these research approaches, some readers may find that beginning to do such research is very different from what they have been taught, or what they have practiced until now. Trying these methods may even require that one tries on a new thinking style! We therefore end the book with a short reflection on what moving between thinking styles can be like, and whether there are ways to facilitate such moves.

Doing Interpretative Research

The research approaches we summarize here have been called by different names, none of which characterizes all of them. Perhaps the most common term is "qualitative methods." This is an unfortunate choice of name, however, for a number of reasons. First, it seems to imply a restriction on the kinds of data that can be gathered and used in this kind of research (i.e., only "qualitative" data). Second, the name may lead readers to conclude that all research that does not use quantitative measures is more or less identical, a conclusion that is very far from the truth. Third, the name may be misunderstood to indicate that only researchers who use "qualitative" methods make qualitative judgments. In fact, all researchers must continually make, and do make, qualitative judgments.

To forestall misunderstandings such as these, we prefer the term *interpretative methods*. This term does not contain indications of the kinds of data that are being collected. Moreover, it highlights the interpretative nature of human understanding and experiences, and the kinds of explanations sought in this research (see Chapter 12). Moreover, the term highlights the importance of interpretation for the understandings that researchers strive to achieve in their work.

In what follows, we provide close descriptions of many typical steps in interpretative research projects. But remember that the descriptions are not exhaustive. We illustrate the steps with examples from several research projects. We provide these descriptions because we expect many readers to be unfamiliar with the methods in question. Following the descriptions, we summarize the assumptions and commitments which these methods entail.

Developing a Knowledge Interest

The impetus for a research project often originates with some issue or "trouble" that claims the researcher's attention. It may be an issue observed in daily life or an issue that stands out in the scholarly literature. Based on this "trouble," the researcher formulates a general *knowledge interest*. This is the overarching topic, problem, or question that the researcher wants to learn about. It is not unusual for a researcher's knowledge interest to originate in personal concerns, experiences, or commitments, or in the experiences of a social group with which the researcher is familiar.

In one example, Lars-Christer Hydén (2014, p. 115), a Swedish psychologist who had long experience of research about dementia, had become interested in how, as he expressed it, *"persons with dementia do things together with others, either with persons without dementia – such as other family members or professional staff – or with other persons with dementia."* He had observed that very little research had been directed toward such persons' interactions with people in their surroundings.

In another example, one of us (EM) was intrigued by the fact that, although practically everybody in the Nordic countries claimed to be in favor of gender equality, national statistics showed that, in practice, many heterosexual couples organized their daily lives in quite unequal ways. The knowledge interest that EM formulated was this: What were couples' own explanations of the discrepancy between their joint professed ideology of equality, and their unequal lived practice (Magnusson, 2008)?

While formulating their knowledge interests, researchers search the existing literature for studies of the topic or "trouble" in question. They also talk to knowledgeable people about their knowledge interest. Knowledgeable people might include one's research supervisor or other researchers, as well as people in the settings one is interested in studying. These people can probably offer advice about whether a project based on the knowledge interest is feasible (for instance, within the researcher's time frame, financial resources, likelihood of recruiting participants, and so on). These conversations often lead to the next step.

Familiarization

In this step, the researcher seeks to become familiar with the social settings and normative practices of those who are likely to take part in the study. One might, for instance, converse informally with people in those settings. Topics might include their experiences and interactions with others in the setting, as well as important social relations, such as kin relations or workplace hierarchies. The researcher makes notes about those conversations and observations. These notes will serve as aids for deciding which kinds of people to seek out as participants.

In one example, Kristiina Tyni (see Tyni, Wurm, & Bratt, 2024), a Swedish clinical psychologist who studied young children who identify as transgender or gender-diverse, participated in conferences of trans organizations that focused on young people before she began to collect data. She had conversations with conference participants about what they saw as the most important issues to study. She also assembled a reference group of five persons with different kinds of experiences of trans life. The members of this group contributed much practical knowledge throughout the project. This included, for example, recommendations for the wording of the advertisements that Tyni used to invite potential participants in the study. Further, Tyni participated in a meeting of a group of parents raising trans children and took part in several informal meetings with parents and their trans children.

From Knowledge Interest to Researchable Questions

In parallel with gaining knowledge about possible settings and participants for their projects, researchers begin to transform their initial knowledge interest into a set of researchable questions. This is necessary because a general knowledge interest rarely lends itself to direct study. We use the expression *researchable* questions to underscore that these questions serve to specify the researcher's knowledge interest in enough detail to make it possible to design a study. Because interpretative researchers are interested in learning about meaning-making, that is, about people's ways of understanding and making sense of the world and themselves, the researchable questions typically focus on particulars, such as a specific historic time, a geographic place, a social context, and particular people. Beyond these characteristics, researchable questions can vary considerably. And, because of the focus on the local and the specific, as well as on people's narratives and sense-making, the researchable questions likely will develop and be refined in the course of a project as the researcher learns more and more about the people being studied. In this kind of research, therefore, the researchable questions are not limited to the initial formulation of hypotheses, as in hypothesis-testing research. We should note here that the *researchable* questions are not the questions that the researcher puts directly to research participants. Those questions are developed later in the research process (see a later section).

In one example, based on their general knowledge interest in what enabled or hindered children with disabilities from becoming well integrated when they begin school, the Norwegian researcher Bjørg Fallang and her colleagues (2017) developed these researchable questions: "*How do processes of exclusion evolve in school activities involving children with disabilities, their peers and professionals? How do children with disabilities experience these processes when starting school? How are interactions carried out between the child and professionals, peers and the physical environment and how do processes of exclusion evolve?*" (p. 272).

In another example, Lars-Christer Hydén (see above, and 2014) developed his general knowledge interest into a researchable question formulated as a wish to understand the performance of everyday activities by persons with dementia as part of a cognitive and communicative ecosystem, not only in terms of individual cognitive abilities. He further specified this question as the aim to find out what was special when carrying out joint activities (see Chapter 7 here) that involve persons with dementia. Hydén was especially interested in the "scaffolding" work that carers and family members need to perform to enable the person with dementia to carry on a conversation or a work task such as cooking or baking.

Selecting Participants and Composing a Group for Study

When a researcher is confident that they have developed a set of workable, researchable questions, it is time to begin making detailed decisions about the research participants. The aim is to compose a study group that is suited to help the researcher address the researchable questions. This means identifying categories of people who are likely to have had the kinds of experiences that the researcher is interested in. The research literature is usually a good source of knowledge at this stage. Of course, the ways of locating potentially suitable participants vary substantially, as do the possible difficulties involved in locating them. Recruiting potential participants as actual participants is usually not difficult, but in some situations or circumstances, there may be obstacles. Let us give a few examples. Some categories of potential participants may be so small that it is difficult to find a large enough number to study. Also, if a category has only a very small number of members, it may not be impossible to safeguard the anonymity of participants. Further, individuals in some categories may be hidden (e.g., living under assumed identities or in secret shelters) and therefore not possible to find. And individuals in some categories may be unwilling to disclose, even anonymously, events or conditions in their lives that they see as stigmatizing.

A psychologist who thinks of people as culturally and socially situated will purposefully select participants with as wide a range as possible of the experiences or characteristics that the psychologist wants to study. This means that random sampling is not relevant. A random sample of a population might give an indication of the prevalence of certain experiences. This, however, is not the focus of interest in this kind of research. Here, the interest is directed toward learning about the breadth of understanding and meaning-making among people who have had the experiences of interest. Therefore, the researcher aims first to locate people who have had the experiences in question. The researcher then needs to ensure that there is a wide variety of experiences among the people studied.

In one example, Aina Olsvold, a Norwegian psychologist, and her colleagues (2019) were interested in how middle-class and working-class fathers of boys who had recently been diagnosed with ADHD perceived their sons and their sons' diagnoses. The researchers recruited participants through four outpatient clinics for child and adolescent psychiatry. In the recruitment, they assessed the range of social class backgrounds of the fathers they selected for interview by gathering data about their educational background and type of occupation.

In another example, Elizabeth Rahilly (2022), a US sociologist, was interested in the stories and experiences of parents who were raising their children in what she termed a gender-open way. This meant that from birth onward, the parents rejected sex/gender designation of their child, and that they used neutral pronouns for them. Rahilly was able to locate a private discussion group of such "gender-open" parents on social media. Because the group was private, Rahilly was prohibited from addressing the group directly or taking part in the group's discussions. However, the moderator of the group distributed Rahilly's invitation to take part in the study to the members of the group. A sufficient number of the group participants, with a sufficient variety of experiences, responded to her invitation and took part in the study.

Constructing an Interview Guide

Many interpretative researchers use semi-structured interviews to gather the data for their studies. An important benefit of such interviews is that participants will try to, and are expected to, explain their experiences to the interviewer, who is inevitably an outsider to the participants' personal experiences. The researchable questions form the basis for developing an interview guide. The guide serves as a memory aid for the interviewer during the interview to ensure that every topic gets covered, with all the relevant details that the researcher is interested in. Having a detailed interview guide is crucial if there is more than one interviewer in a project. It can also be crucial to provide carefully considered language to enable the interviewer to address issues that might be sensitive or potentially offensive to the participants. Long experience has taught us that it always pays to spend substantial time working through and refining the interview questions.

Many of the "questions" in the guide will be in the form of open invitations to talk about a topic or an experience, not actual questions. The aim of this kind of research is to encourage participants to tell about their experiences in their own ways and in their own words. Researchers, therefore, ask the participants about concrete experiences and their reflections on those experiences. Researchers also take care that the wording in the interview guide does not impose the researcher's own classifications or categorizations on the participant.

In one example, Kristiina Tyni and her colleagues (mentioned earlier), who interviewed children, had to think especially carefully about the wording of questions and to adjust their vocabulary to the children's capacities. Besides doing this, they took special care with questions that dealt with sensitive topics, such that the questions were neutral and nonjudgmental. The interview guide opened with "easy" and nonsensitive questions; the questions that were likely to be most sensitive came in the next-to-last part of the interview. The interview guide closed with another set of nonsensitive questions.

Test Interviews

A necessary step at this stage is what is called test interviews or pilot interviews. That is, a researcher carries out a small set of test interviews in order to get feedback about how the questions work. This feedback can be of two kinds. The first kind is feedback on how the questions "function." Is the wording clear enough that it will be understood by the interviewees? This feedback can usually be given by colleagues. The second kind is feedback on whether the items tap into issues and themes that are important to the intended participants. This feedback should be gathered from people in the pool of informants or those very similar to them. During and after the test interviews, researchers have the chance to observe and adjust their own demeanor in the interviews, and thereby improve their skills as interviewers. Researchers often make a habit of regularly reflecting on their own behavior during the "real" interviews as well: what worked well, what worked less well, and so on.

Participant Observation Research and Ethnographic Studies

For researchers whose goal is to learn about the patterns of meanings shared by members of a cultural group – an interpretive community – ethnography offers a useful strategy. Remember that "patterns of shared meaning" is what the term interpretive communities refers to (see Chapter 3). The word ethnography derives from two Greek words: ethnos, meaning "folk," and grapho, meaning "writing." The heart of an ethnographer's work, however, is not writing, but close and experience-near observations, usually over an extended period. Usually, researchers engage in the mundane lives of the members of the social community or workplace that they wish to study. During this period of immersion, the researcher keeps copious daily notes. These notes may include observations of interactions, activities, and informal conversations, as well as the researcher's reactions to and interpretations of what she or he is observing. This immersion can lead to a deep understanding of the range of assumptions, moral visions, and reasoning processes among members of the social group. The frames of meaning that guide everyday behavior and relationships often are so taken for granted by those in the social group that they are not readily verbalized (Quinn, 2005). Very often, the insights gleaned from immersion in a community setting lead researchers to revise or expand the questions that guide their research. And it may well lead them to alter or augment other aspects of their research plan as well.

In one example, Talia Weiner (2011), a psychotherapist and clinical ethnographer in the US, carried out two years of fieldwork exploring a treatment model labeled "self-management." Weiner took part in meetings of an ongoing support group of people who had been diagnosed with bipolar disorder. In the meetings, group members recounted their day-to-day struggles. Weiner came to see that, although the self-management model was intended to develop greater personal responsibility, this goal could not be reached unless social and economic disparities were addressed.

In another example, Bambi Chapin (2014), a US anthropologist, studied norms and practices related to child-rearing, family life, and kin relations in rural Sri Lanka. With her husband and her 3 ½-year-old son, Chapin lived in a rural village for two years. Living alongside families with young children, Chapin had many opportunities for close observations of her neighbors' family life and childrearing, and for informal conversations about the goals and reasons that shaped their everyday choices. These experiences served as a window into local norms, moral values, and beliefs.

Doing Interviews

Research interviewing is a craft, and as with any other craft, it takes time and work to become proficient as an interviewer. For details about interviewing, see, for instance, Magnusson and Marecek (2015, chapter 6). A research interview is always an asymmetrical conversation: the participants are expected to share information about themselves, as well as judgments and personal experiences; the interviewer is not. The participants are the experts on the topics about which they are being interviewed, and the interviewer should therefore be open and nonjudgmental about the participant's responses. Besides asking questions and providing invitations to speak, the interviewer's task is to ensure that the conversation flows smoothly and that the participant feels comfortable. The interviewer, therefore, uses informal language and adjusts to the conversational style of the participant. The intent is to create good conditions for all participants, regardless of their educational and other background factors. Such adjustment is seen as the way to make the material obtained in the interviews comparable across participants. Note that this strategy is different from that used in survey research, in which it is important to use the same words and expressions with all participants.

To begin the interview, the interviewer describes the project in such a way that the purpose of participating in the study becomes clear to the participant. The interviewer then informs the participant about the rules regarding privacy and anonymity, the right to withdraw from the study, and the right to decline to answer particular questions. This is followed by an overview of the topics and the kinds of information the interviewer hopes to learn from the participant. By and large, interviews are audio recorded, a procedure that requires the participant's consent. The interviewee is usually asked to sign a written consent form. When interviewing children, the researcher needs the children's parents to sign such a form.

The interviewer's task is to invite the participant to talk about the interview topics in their own words, and to make sure that all topics are covered. Often the topics are not taken up in the order in which they appear in the interview guide. This is one consequence of encouraging participants to talk freely about experiences and reflections. It is not a problem as long as the interviewer can be sure that all the topics have been covered. Ending the interview is seldom a problem. Usually both interviewer and participant know when all the scheduled topics have been satisfactorily covered and will cooperate in closing the session in a way that feels comfortable to both.

Analysis

The *preparations* for analysis will depend on the nature of the data the researcher has collected. The analysis of interview materials typically begins with transcribing recorded interviews. Researchers typically aim to get the transcription done as soon as possible after each interview. This enables them to add notes about significant details of the interview, such as the emotional tenor of the interview, moments of tension, and so on. Several schemes for transcribing exist; they vary in how much detail, such as pauses and nonverbal sounds, they record. Which one to choose depends on the kind of analysis one has planned to do.

The analysis phase requires researchers to work closely with their participants' words. A crucial feature of such analyses is that they go well beyond simply sorting similar words or phrases into "buckets." (Sometimes, novice researchers mistakenly label these buckets "themes.") Such sorting can be a useful first step, but sorting should not be confused with analysis. It is meaning-making, that is, the ways in which the participants understand what is being talked about, which is in focus in the analysis phase. Finding out about the participants' meaning-making requires a deeper engagement with their narratives than does sorting. Researchers are also usually interested in each participant's context, and the participant's intentions in relation to that context. Therefore, social, historical, and cultural aspects are of prime importance in these kinds of analyses. Several kinds of analysis that focus on meaning-making exist today. Researchers with different theoretical backgrounds have developed detailed analytical frameworks and procedures that enable the researcher to focus on different aspects of the interview material.

Assumptions and Commitments in Interpretative Research

As we emphasized earlier, our descriptions of the procedures involved in interpretative research do not cover all varieties of such research. Nor would all the different approaches to interpretative research be informed by a single thinking style, to use Ludwik Fleck's term. Despite the variety among these approaches, though, doing interpretative research will inevitably mean a change of thinking style for a psychologist trained in more conventional, quantitative psychological research methods. In this section, we describe some assumptions and commitments that form the basis of much interpretative research today.

To begin, interpretative researchers think of the people they study as *persons* who experience and interpret their abilities, actions, capacities, and biological functions through the lenses provided by their cultural contexts. Further, these researchers assume that relations and interactions among people form the basic conditions for human psychological life to develop and be sustained. Consequently, the researchers share a conviction that it is in contextualized interactions that one will find the origins and the maintenance of human self-understanding, morality, and reasoned agency. Further, interpretative researchers assume that people are capable of reflecting on their own and other people's experiences and actions. These researchers also assume that their research participants are willing to share these reflections with others. This assumption is usually confirmed in research practice, but researchers cannot always take this for granted. There are situations and contexts in which it is not self-evident that sharing experiences is without risk to the research participant. Such situations sometimes entail difficult ethical considerations that need to be carefully thought through before a project is begun.

Another assumption made by interpretative researchers is that knowledge about the breadth and variety of people's experiences is of prime value, more so than learning about distributions of responses in a population. In the section about selecting participants to study, we noted that interpretative researchers, therefore, often seek to identify the range of the experiences that are of interest, and then locate participants who can tell them about as wide a range as possible of those experiences.

All told, such assumptions and convictions lead to the interest in learning about what is specific and contextualized in human life, an interest that is typical of interpretative researchers. These assumptions are also the origins of the context-focused knowledge interests and researchable questions that are typical of interpretative research.

Most interpretative researchers assume that people primarily make meaning through language use, and that this meaning-making very often happens in the course of interactions among people. This assumption has led to interpretative researchers' interest in how people use words to make sense of their own experiences as well as of people in their surroundings, and of those people's experiences. This interest in words as the vehicle for meaning-making is the reason for the use of open-ended questions that invite spontaneous, rich talk, and of recordings of spontaneous speech in other kinds of interpretative research. Further, interpretative researchers are typically interested in people's narratives and meaning-making about their own and others' *acting*, in the sense of their planned-intentional actions (see Schnepf & Groeben, 2024, to whom we referred in Chapter 9). The focus on planned-intentional actions typically leads interpretative researchers to be interested in the *reasons* people give for their own and others' behavior.

Many interpretative researchers argue that it is not enough to take into account only the local context and local interactions in one's research. To gain an adequate understanding of the people being studied, the researcher must also become knowledgeable about the larger social and cultural aspects of people's lives. This demand leads to an interest among many interpretative researchers in integrating knowledge about the cultural norms and social and political hierarchies that may determine the conditions for local interactions with their analyses of people's narratives.

Changing Thinking Styles

In this section, we briefly discuss how changes in researchers' thinking styles can come about and be experienced. We should first observe that thinking styles are not hewn in stone. Even the most ingrained assumptions and ways of thinking and working will eventually change in one way or another as successive cohorts of practitioners or researchers enter established thought collectives. The new members will bring with them experiences of growing up in, and studying in, other cultural settings than the seniors who embody the established thinking style. These experiences may lead the new members to ask other kinds of questions than their seniors do. The new members may also look for research methods based on thinking styles other than those of their seniors. Established researchers and clinicians often welcome such outward-looking questions and interests, but sometimes they do not. As we noted in Chapter 2, it is not unusual for resistance to change to be built into the lives of thought collectives. And it is not unusual for this resistance to persist even when change would be beneficial. According to Ludwik Fleck, such resistance is based on what he called ingrained and taken-for-granted "active assumptions" that can make it difficult for seniors to discern problems in their approach. Movement toward other thinking styles therefore often first occurs among new members of a thought collective, or members who have affiliation to more than one thought collective. Such double memberships may reflect a preparedness to expose one's work to ideas from more than one thinking style. For the individual, the move from one thinking style to another is often experienced as a dramatic shift in perspective. This means that after having made the move between thinking styles, one looks in new ways at previously self-evident truths.

Moves between thinking styles never appear out of nowhere. Such a move is always prefigured by a period of preparation and of getting used to trying new ways of thinking and working. It is often preceded by contacts and exchanges with members of other thought collectives. There may also be an increasing sense of skepticism toward some of one's collective's accepted practices. The increasing skepticism may lead to a "directed readiness" for change in a member (Liliequist, 2003, p. 69). And it can also, according to Ludwik Fleck, lead to a tendency to (at least temporarily) put hitherto taken-for-granted assumptions in one's collective on hold. For psychologists, this directed readiness and the putting of assumptions on hold may involve questioning one's collective's ideas, first, about what kind of object is being studied (what we, for short, could call their image of the person: the *ontological level*); second, about the appropriate kinds of research questions (what it is the researcher wants to know: the *epistemological level*); and third, about the best ways to study these research questions (the *methodological level*).

Those who engage in critical scrutiny of these three aspects of their collective's thinking style from the perspective of another thinking style may find that many established concepts and habits lose their previous status as self-evident. This is all to the good, according to Fleck, because it forces the scrutinizers to begin thinking what he calls *incomplete thoughts*. This is exactly what is needed: to go through a period of open-minded searching among unfamiliar ways of thinking and working. Such open-minded searching will not be possible if one clings to the old thinking style, for, as Fleck emphasizes, with its finished concepts, one cannot express new and incomplete thoughts (1935, p. 87). Therefore, what is needed is exposure to ideas and ways of doing things other than those one is used to.

Can a single individual in a collective move to a different thinking style? Certainly. But if the individual is a member of thought collective that is very tightly held together, such a move may be uncomfortable. We recommend anyone who wants to try the thinking and methods of thought collectives other than their own to seek out conversation partners who have similar interests. Sometimes one may find such conversation partners in one's thought collective, but often one does not. If not, the best choice is to seek them outside one's usual professional surroundings. That is what we did.

We have both had the experience of moving outside our original thought collectives to try out new ways of thinking about and "doing" psychology. We were inspired to make this move by cross-disciplinary collaborations with other social scientists, especially in the settings of women's and gender studies. Those settings were organized around a commitment to social justice and a focus on social issues and social problems. The scholars in those settings were not wedded to particular stances on the three "levels" that we mentioned earlier: the ontological, epistemological, and methodological levels.

When a Thought Collective Decides That Change Is Necessary

Sometimes a situation arises in which a thought collective is beset by many problems and critiques, and decides to do something about its approach. As a possible example of such a situation, think about the "replication crisis" in psychology that we described in Chapter 9. As we saw, the crisis led to many efforts at reform and even some soul-searching among psychologists about what had been done wrongly. We also saw that some of the suggestions for change that resulted stayed within the bounds of the established methods and the established thinking style, while other suggestions involved a move away from the contemporary thinking styles.

How might the established members of a thought collective act if they want to promote some rethinking of their thinking style, or even a move to another style? Here are a few suggestions, taken from the writings of Ludwik Fleck and of the Swedish philosopher Bengt Liliequist (1997), who has engaged especially with these aspects of Fleck's works.

Initiating, and then maintaining, contacts with other thought collectives is a prime way to encourage curiosity and a readiness to change. Encouraging the exchange of ideas between members of different thought collectives, and also providing real opportunities for such exchanges, may enable members to question and unsettle parts of their thinking style and try to think – in Fleck's words – "incomplete thoughts."

Identifying and engaging the most change-prone members of one's thought collective is a good idea. As we mentioned earlier, one such category consists of those who are members of more than one thought collective. Such dual alliances may reflect a preparedness to expose oneself, and thereby one's ideas, to influences from more than one thinking style. Also, because of their double memberships, these members can serve as links between different thought collectives. Another category of members that may be particularly change-prone are those who do not have a long history with the collective. However, they are usually also the ones with the lowest formal status in the collective, and this may limit their sense of freedom to move outside the usual boundaries.

Those who want to encourage change in their thought collective need to pay serious attention to how the collective handles status issues. In a hierarchical organization, where high-status members dominate meetings and decision-making processes, it may be risky for juniors to suggest new and untried ways of thinking and working. This is likely to discourage all members, not just the juniors, from thinking about change. In such a situation, more general changes in the working climate – not just in thinking styles – will be necessary. Fleck and Liliequist advise collective members, especially seniors, to search for ways to dislodge internal hierarchies that prevent what they call "a free traffic of thoughts." One suggestion is to create forms of socializing and working in the collective that give junior members space and security to try "style-external" ways of thinking and working. This can be one way of creating safe opportunities for members to temporarily let go of, or at least unsettle, some of the taken-for-granted ontological and epistemological assumptions and habits of their thinking style.

In Conclusion

In this book, we have many times noted the value of taking a step back to look "from the outside" at one's own ideas, as well as at one's discipline more broadly. One advantage of trying to see from an outsider's perspective is that it can make visible what has become invisible because of its familiarity. Looking from the outside also may enable one to identify, and learn more about, one's own and one's collective's thinking style. We have focused especially on assumptions connected to the images of persons that pervade different thinking styles. These assumptions are usually so ingrained that they are more or less automatic. They may, therefore, not be visible while one is "inside" one's habitual ways of working and thinking. One needs to stand in another place, as it were, and look in from that other place. This is the kind of looking that we have tried to do throughout this book.

We have investigated several arenas, subfields, and topics in psychology, though many more remain to be investigated as well. We have also scrutinized several investigate methods. Many of the topics we have addressed hark back to the earliest days of psychology – such as measurement, methodological commitments, and epistemology. They remain matters of contemporary debate.

We have taken up several contentious issues and questions, especially questions that concern persons. Our intention has been to discern and then describe how some approaches to psychological questions enable psychologists to take the social and cultural situatedness of human beings – that is, *persons* – into account, while some approaches do not.

We hope readers will take away these overarching messages from our book: First, we hope that our travels into fields and issues in psychology may inspire readers to undertake further explorations of these and other fields and issues. We further hope that readers have become interested in exploring the approaches to psychology that we have put forward, which are compatible with a *persons* view of psychology. And finally, we hope the approach we have adopted in this book – that of gazing critically at the discipline of psychology from the outside – may inspire readers to set out on their own voyages of scrutiny and discovery.

References

Abeyasekera, A. L. (2021). *Making the right choice: Narratives of marriage in Sri Lanka*. Rutgers University Press.

Abi-Rached, J. & Rose, N. (2010). The birth of the neuromolecular gaze. *History of the Human Sciences*, Vol. 23, pp. 11–36.

Adams, F. & Aizawa, K. (2010a). Defending the bounds of cognition. In R. Menary (ed.) *The extended mind*. MIT Press.

Adams, F. & Aizawa, K. (2010b). The value of cognitivism in thinking about extended cognition. *Phenomenology and the Cognitive Sciences*, Vol. 9, pp. 579–603.

Ainsworth, M. D. S., Blehar, M. C., Waters, E., & Wall, S. (1978). *Patterns of attachment: A psychological study of the strange situation*. Lawrence Erlbaum.

Alvarez, M. (2018). Reasons for action, acting for reasons, and rationality. *Synthese*, Vol. 195, pp. 3293–3310.

American Psychiatric Association. (2013). *Diagnostic and statistical manual of mental disorders*, 5th ed.

Anderson, M. L. & Champion, H. (2022). Some dilemmas for an account of neural representation: A reply to Poldrack. *Synthese*, Vol. 200, pp. 1–13.

Angell, M. (2009). Drug companies and doctors. *New York Review of Books*, Vol. 56 (1).

Angell, M. (2011). The illusions of psychiatry. *New York Review of Books*, Vol. 58 (1).

APA, American Psychological Association (2024). Operational definitions. *Online Dictionary of Psychology*. Retrieved on July 21, 2024. https://dictionary.apa.org/operational-definition

Apicella, C., Norenzayan, A., & Henrich, J. (2020). Beyond WEIRD: A review of the last decade and a look ahead to the global laboratory of the future. *Evolution and Human Behavior*, Vol. 41, pp. 319–329.

Aunger R., Deterding S., Zhao X., & Baxter W. (2024). Applying the Barker School concept of "behaviour settings" to virtual contexts. *Philosophical Transactions of the Royal Society B: Biological Sciences*, Vol. 379, 20230291.

Baggs, E., Raja, V. & Anderson, M. (2019). Culture in the world shapes culture in the head (and vice versa). *Behavioral and Brain Sciences*, 42, E172.

Baggs, E. & Sanches de Oliveira, G. (2024). Rewilding psychology. *Philosophical transactions of the Royal Society of London. Series B: Biological Sciences*, Vol. 379, p. 20230287.

Baier, A. (1985). *Postures of the mind: Essays on mind and morals*. University of Minnesota Press.

Bakan, D. (1971). Adolescence in America: From idea to social fact. *Daedalus*, Vol. 100, pp. 979–995.

Baranova, J. & Dingemanse, M. (2016). Reasons for requests. *Discourse Studies*, Vol. 18, pp. 641–675.

Bayne, T., Cleeremans, A., & Wilken, P. (eds.) (2009). *The Oxford companion to consciousness*. Oxford University Press.

Bechtel, W. (2016). Investigating neural representations: The tale of place cells. *Synthese*, Vol. 193, pp. 1287–1321.

Bennett, M. & Hacker, P. (2022). *Philosophical foundations of neuroscience*, 2nd ed. John Wiley & Sons.

Berwick, R. C. & Chomsky, N. (2016). *Why only us? Language & evolution*. MIT Press.

Bhatia, S., Long, W., Pickren, W., & Rutherford, A. (2024). Engaging with decoloniality, decolonization, and histories of psychology otherwise. In L. Comas-Díaz, H. Y. Adames, & N. Y. Chavez-Dueñas (eds.), *Decolonial psychology: Toward anticolonial theories, research, training, and practice*. American Psychological Association.

Billig, M. (1996). *Arguing and thinking: A rhetorical approach to social psychology*. Cmabridge University Press.

Binney, N. (2016a). *On the historical contingency of medical knowledge: An integrated historical and philosophical investigation into the development and epistemic status of knowledge about heart failure*. Doctoral dissertation, University of Exeter.

Binney, N. (2016b). Ludwik Fleck's "active" and "passive" elements of knowledge revisited: Circular arguments in the medical literature on inflicted head injury in the light of Fleck's epistemology. *Transversal: International Journal for the Historiography of Science*, Vol. 1, pp. 101–115.

Binney, N. (2023). Ludwik Fleck's reasonable relativism about science. *Synthese*, Vol. 201, p. 40.

Birns, B. (1999). Attachment Theory revisited: Challenging conceptual and methodological sacred cows. *Feminism & Psychology*, Vol. 9, pp. 10–21.

Boag, S. (2011). Explanation in personality psychology: "Verbal magic" and the five-factor model. *Philosophical Psychology*, Vol. 24, pp. 223–243.

Boag, S. (2018). Personality dynamics, motivation, and the logic of explanation. *Review of General Psychology*, Vol. 22, pp. 427–436.

Bohan, J. (ed.) (1992). *Seldom seen, rarely heard: Women's place in psychology*. Westview Press.

Bongard, J. & Levin, M. (2021). Living things are not (20th century) machines: Updating mechanism metaphors in light of the modern science of machine behavior. *Frontiers in Ecology and Evolution*, Vol. 9, 650726.

Bonilla, S., Lamb, S., & Anantharam (2025). "Triggered": The depth and breadth of a psychological construct. *Philosophy, Psychiatry, & Psychology*, Vol. 32, E1–E14.

Bookwala, J. & Newton, N. (eds.). (2022). *Reflections of pioneering women in psychology.* Cambridge University Press.

Bordo, S. (1993). *Unbearable weight: Feminism, western culture, and the body.* University of California Press.

Bowlby, J. (1951). *Maternal care and mental health.* World Health Organization Monograph.

Bowlby, J. (1988). *A secure base: Parent-child attachment and healthy human development.* Basic Books.

Brette, R. (2019). Neural coding: The bureaucratic model of the brain. *Behavioral and Brain Sciences,* Vol. 42, e243.

Brette, R. (2022). Brains as computers: Metaphor, analogy, theory or fact? *Frontiers in Ecology and Evolution,* Vol. 10, 878729.

Brette, R. (2024). Review of Farid Zahnoun, *"The embodiment of meaning"* New York: Routledge, 2024. *Phenomenology and the Cognitive Sciences.* doi .org/10.1007/11097-024-09998-3

Brette, R. (in press 2026). *The brain, in theory.* Princeton University Press.

Brick, C., Hood, B., Ekroll, V., & de-Wit, L. (2022). Illusory essences: A bias holding back theorizing in psychological science. *Perspectives on Psychological Science,* Vol. 17, pp. 491–506.

Brinkmann, S. (2018). *Persons and their minds: Towards an integrative theory of the mediated mind.* Routledge.

Brinkmann, S. (2024). What are mental disorders? Exploring the role of culture in the harmful dysfunction approach. *Integrative Psychological and Behavioral Science,* Vol. 58, pp. 1048–1063.

Byrne, B. M. & van de Vijver, F. (2010). Testing for measurement and structural equivalence in large-scale cross-cultural studies. *International Journal of Testing,* Vol. 10, pp. 170–186.

Cahalan, S. (2019). *The great pretender: The undercover mission that changed our understanding of madness.* Grand Central.

Carlat, D. (2010). *Unhinged: The trouble with psychiatry.* Simon and Schuster.

Cash, M. (2009). Normativity is the mother of intention: Wittgenstein, normative practices and neurological representations. *New Ideas in Psychology* (Special Issue on Wittgenstein's relevance for psychology), Vol. 27, pp. 133–147.

Cash, M. (2013). Cognition without borders: "Third wave" socially distributed cognition and relational autonomy. *Cognitive Systems Research,* Vol. 25–26, pp. 61–71.

Casper, M.-O. & Artese, F. G. (2022). Maintaining coherence in the situated cognition debate: What computationalism cannot offer to a future post-cognitivist science. *Adaptive Behavior,* Vol. 30, pp. 3–17.

Cassidy, S., Dimova, R., Giguère, B., Spence, J., & Stanley, D. (2019). Failing grade: 89% of introduction-to-psychology textbooks that define or explain statistical significance do so incorrectly. *Advances in Methods and Practices in Psychological Science,* Vol. 2, pp. 233–239.

Cattell, J. M. (1893). Mental measurement. *Philosophical Review,* Vol. 2, pp. 316–332.

Chalmers, D. (ed.) (2021). *Philosophy of mind: Classical and contemporary readings*, 2nd ed. Oxford University Press.

Chapin, B. L. (2014). *Childhood in a Sri Lankan village: Shaping hierarchy and desire*. Rutgers University Press.

Charles, D. (2021). *The undivided self: Aristotle and the "mind–body problem."* Oxford University Press.

Chater, N. & Christiansen, M. (2018). Language acquisition as skill learning. *Current Opinion in Behavioral Sciences*, Vol. 21, pp. 205–208.

Chater, N. & Christiansen, M. (2023). From the pragmatics of charades to the creation of language. *The Behavioral and Brain Sciences*, Vol. 46, pp. e7–e7, Article e7.

Chater, N., McCauley, S., & Christiansen, M. (2016). Language as skill: Intertwining comprehension and production. *Journal of Memory and Language*, Vol. 89, pp. 244–254.

Chater, N., Zeitoun, H., & Melkonyan, T. (2022). The paradox of social interaction: Shared intentionality, we-reasoning, and virtual bargaining. *Psychological Review*, Vol. 129, pp. 415–437.

Chernin, K. (1981). *The obsession: Reflections on the tyranny of slenderness*. Harper & Row.

Chesler, P. (1972). *Women and madness*. Doubleday.

Chiao, J. Y. & Blizinsky, K. D. (2019). Cultural neuroscience. In D. R. Matsumoto & H. S. Hwang (eds.), *The handbook of culture and psychology*. Oxford Academic.

Chirimuuta, M. (2024). *The brain abstracted: Simplification in the history and philosophy of neuroscience*. The MIT Press.

Chomsky, N. (2000). *New horizons in the study of language and mind*. Cambridge University Press.

Chomsky, N. (2006). *Language and mind*. Cambridge University Press.

Christensen Allesøe, B. (2023). Lifespan development seen through Niche construction theory. *Integrative Psychological and Behavioral Science*, Vol. 57, pp. 1158–1171.

Christensen Allesøe, B., Mathiesen, M., & Birk, R. et al. (2025). Special issue: Situated psychology. *Integrative Psychological and Behavioral Science*, Vol. 59, article 46.

Christiansen, M. & Chater, N. (2009). The myth of language universals and the myth of universal grammar. *Behavioral and Brain Sciences*,Vol. 32, pp. 452–453.

Christiansen, M. & Chater, N. (2018). *Creating language. Integrating evolution, acquisition, and processing*. MIT Press.

Christiansen, M. & Chater, N. (2022). *The language game: How improvisation created language and changed the world*. Bantam Press.

Christopher, J. C., Wendt, D. C., Marecek, J., & Goodman, D. M. (2014). Critical cultural awareness: Contributions to a globalizing psychology. *American Psychologist*, Vol. 69 (7), pp. 645–655.

Cisek, P. (2022). The brain is a control system. In Kelty-Stephen, D. G., Cisek, P. E., De Bari, B., et al. In search for an alternative to the computer metaphor of the mind and brain. *ArXiv*: 2206.04603

Cisek, P. & Green, A. (2024). Toward a neuroscience of natural behavior. *Current Opinion in Neurobiology*, Vol. 86, 102859.

Cisek, P. & Hayden, B. Y. (2021). Neuroscience needs evolution. *Philosophical Transactions of the Royal Society, B*, Vol. 377, 20200518.

Clark, A. (2010a). Memento's revenge: The extended mind. In R. Menary (ed.), *The extended mind*. MIT Press.

Clark, A. (2010b). Coupling, constitution, and the cognitive kind: A reply to Adams and Aizawa. In R. Menary (ed.), *The extended mind*. MIT Press.

Clark, A. & Chalmers, D. (1998). The extended mind. *Analysis*, Vol. 58, pp. 7–19.

Clark, A. & Chalmers, D. (2010). The extended mind. In R. Menary (ed.), *The Extended Mind*. MIT Press.

Clark, H. H. (1996). *Using language*. Cambridge University Press.

Clark, H. H. (1998). Communal lexicons. In K. Malmkjær & J. Williams (eds.), *Context in language learning and language understanding*. Cambridge University Press.

Clark, H. H. (2006). Social actions, social commitments. In S. C. Levinson & N. J. Enfield, (eds.), *Roots of human sociality: Culture, cognition and interaction*. Routledge.

Cobb, M. (2020). *The idea of the brain: A history*. Profile Books.

Cobb, M. (2021). A brief history of wires in the brain. *Frontiers in Ecology and Evolution*, Vol. 9, pp. 760269.

Cohen, J. (1994). The earth is round (p<0.05). *American Psychologist*, Vol. 49, pp. 997–1003.

Costall, A. (2023). "Cognition" – Let's forget it? *Rivista Internazionale Di Filosofia E Psicologia*, Vol. 14, pp. 135–141.

Craffert, P. F. (2024). You are (not) your brain: Incompatible images of human beings in the neurosciences. *Phronimon*, 2024–02.

Crawford, M. & Marecek, J. (1989). Psychology reconstructs the female: 1968–1988. *Psychology of Women Quarterly*, Vol. 13, pp. 147–165.

Crenshaw, K. (1989). Demarginalizing the intersection of race and sex: A Black feminist critique of antidiscrimination doctrine, feminist theory, and antiracist politics. *University of Chicago Legal Forum*, Vol. 14, pp. 538–554.

Cromby, J. (2022). Meaning in the Power Threat Meaning framework. *Journal of Constructivist Psychology*, Vol. 35, pp. 41–53.

Cromby, J., Harper, D., & Reavey, P. (2013). *Psychology, mental health and distress*. Palgrave Macmillan.

Cumming, G. (2014). The new statistics: Why and how. *Psychological Science*, Vol. 25, pp. 7–29.

Cuthbert, B. N. (2020). The role of RDoC in future classification of mental disorders. *Dialogues in Clinical Neuroscience*, Vol. 22, pp. 81–85.

Dabrowska, E. (2015). What exactly is Universal Grammar, and has anyone seen it? *Frontiers of Psychology*, Vol. 6: 852.

Danielson, M. L., Claussen A. H., Bitsko, R. H., et al. (2024). ADHD prevalence among U.S. children and adolescents in 2022: Diagnosis, severity, co-occurring disorders, and treatment. *Journal of Clinical Child Adolescent Psychology*, Vol. 53, pp. 343–360.

Danziger, K. (1985). The methodological imperative. *Philosophy of Social Science*, Vol. 15, pp. 1–13.

Danziger, K. (1997). *Naming the mind: How psychology found its language*. Sage.

Danziger, K. (2003). Prospects of a historical psychology. *History and Philosophy of Psychology Bulletin*, Vol. 15, pp. 4–10.

Danziger, K. (2006). Comment: Special issue on indigenous psychologies. *International Journal of Psychology*, Vol. 41, pp. 269–275.

Danziger, K. (2006). Universalism and indigenization in the history of modern psychology. In A. Brock (ed.), *Internationalizing the history of psychology*. New York University Press.

Danziger, K. & Dzinas, K. (1997). How psychology got its variables. *Canadian Psychology/Psychologie canadienne*, Vol. 38, pp. 43–48.

Daston, L. (2008). On scientific observation. *Isis*, Vol. 99, pp. 97–110.

Davidson, L. (2016). The Recovery Movement: Implications for mental health care and enabling people to participate fully in life. *Health Affairs*, Vol. 35, pp. 1091–1097.

Davidson, L., Tondora, J., Lawless, M. S., O'Connell, M. J., & Rowe, M. (2008). *A practical guide to recovery-oriented practice: Tools for transforming mental health care*. Oxford University Press.

Davies, J. (2014). *Cracked: Why psychiatry is doing more harm than good*. Simon and Schuster.

De Bari, B. & Dixon, J. (2022). Dissipative structures as an alternative to the machine metaphor of the mind and brain. In Kelty-Stephen, D. G., Cisek, P. E., De Bari, B., et al. In search for an alternative to the computer metaphor of the mind and brain. *ArXiv*: 2206.04603.

de Boer, B., Thompson, B., Ravignani, A., & Boeckx, C. (2020). Evolutionary dynamics do not motivate a single-mutant theory of human language. *Scientific reports*, Vol. 10, Article 451.

Debrouwere, S. & Rosseel, Y. (2021). The conceptual, cunning, and conclusive experiment in psychology. *Perspectives on Psychological Science*, Vol. 17, pp. 852–862.

De Jaegher, H., Pieper, B., Clénin, D., & Fuchs, T. (2017). Grasping intersubjectivity: An invitation to embody social interaction research. *Phenomenology and the Cognitive Sciences*, Vol. 16, pp. 491–523.

de-Wit, L., Alexander, D., Ekroll, V., & Wagemans, J. (2016). Is neuroimaging measuring information in the brain? *Psychon. Bulletin Review*, Vol. 23, pp. 1415–1428.

Di Rienzo G., Myin, E., & van Dijk, L. (2024). Navigating the normativity of behaviour settings: an observational case study. *Philosophical Transactions of the Royal Society B: Biological Sciences*, Vol. 379, 20230295.

Dicker, G. (2013). *Descartes: An analytical and historical introduction*. Oxford University Press.

Dideriksen, C., Christiansen, M., Tylén, K., Dingemanse, M., & Fusaroli, R. (2023). Quantifying the interplay of conversational devices in building mutual understanding. *Journal of Experimental Psychology, General*, Vol. 152, pp. 864–889.

Dingemanse, M. (2020a). Resource-rationality beyond individual minds: The case of interactive language use. *The Behavioral and Brain Sciences*, Vol. 43, pp. e9–e9, Article e9.

Dingemanse, M. (2020b). Between sound and speech: Liminal signs in interaction. *Research on Language and Social Interaction*, Vol. 53, pp. 188–196.

Dingemanse, M. (2024). Interjections at the heart of language. *Annual Review of Linguistics*. Vol. 10, pp. 257–277.

Dingemanse, M. & Enfield, N. J. (2024). Interactive repair and the foundations of language. *Trends in Cognitive Sciences*, Vol. 28, pp. 30–42.

Dingemanse, M., Liesenfeld, A., Rasenberg, M., et al. (2023). Beyond single-mindedness: A figure-ground reversal for the cognitive sciences. *Cognitive Science*, Vol. 47, e13230.

Dołęga, K., Roelofs, L., & Schlicht, T. (2018). Introduction to the Special Issue "Enactivism, representationalism, and predictive processing." *Philosophical Explorations*, Vol. 21, pp. 179–186.

Donald, M. (1993). *Origins of the modern mind: Three stages in the evolution of culture and cognition*. Harvard University Press.

Donald, M. (2009). The sapient paradox: Can cognitive neuroscience solve it? Book review. *Brain*, Vol. 132, pp. 820–824.

Doyen, S., Klein, O., Pichon, C. L., & Cleeremans, A. (2012). Behavioral priming: It's all in the mind, but whose mind? *PLoS ONE*, Vol. 7, e29081.

Drescher, J. (2015). Out of the DSM: Depathologizing homosexuality. *Behavioral Sciences*, Vol. 4, pp. 565–575.

Dutilh Novaes, C. (2013). A dialogical account of deductive reasoning as a case study for how culture shapes cognition. *Journal of Cognition and Culture*, Vol. 13, pp. 459–482.

Dutilh Novaes, C. (2021). *The dialogical roots of deduction: Historical, cognitive, and philosophical perspectives on reasoning*. Cambridge University Press.

Edley, N. (2001). Analysing masculinity: Interpretative repertoires, ideological dilemmas, and subject positions. In M. Wetherell, S. Taylor, & S. Yates (eds.), *Discourse as data: A guide for analysis*. Sage.

Edley, N. & Wetherell, M. (1997). Jockeying for position: The construction of masculine identities. *Discourse & Society*, Vol. 8, pp. 203–217.

Edwards, D. (1991). Categories are for talking: On the cognitive and discursive bases of categorization. *Theory & Psychology*, Vol. 1, pp. 515–542.

Edwards, D. (1997). *Discourse and cognition*. Sage.

Edwards, D. (2006). Discourse, cognition and social practices: The rich surface of language and social interaction. *Discourse Studies*, Vol. 8, pp. 41–49.

Edwards, D. (2012). Discursive and scientific psychology. *British Journal of Social Psychology*, Vol. 51, pp. 425–435.

Eagleman, D. (2020). Livewired: The inside story of the ever-changing brain. Canongate Books.

Enfield, N. J. (2022). Enchrony. *Wires Cognitive Science*, Vol. 13, p. E1597.

Enfield, N. J. & Sidnell, J. (2017). *The concept of action.* Cambridge University Press.

Enfield, N. J. & Sidnell, J. (2022). *Consequences of language: From primary to enhanced intersubjectivity.* MIT Press.

Engel, A., Friston, K., & Kragic, D. (eds.) (2016). *The pragmatic turn: Toward action-oriented views in cognitive science.* MIT Press.

Erikson, E. H. (1968). *Identity, youth and crisis.* W. W. Norton.

Eysenck, M. & Brysbaert, M. (2018). *Fundamentals of cognition, 3rd ed.* Routledge.

Fabry, R. (2018). Betwixt and between: The enculturated predictive processing approach to cognition. *Synthese*, Vol. 195, pp. 2483–2518.

Fabry, R. & Pantsar, M. (2021). A fresh look at research strategies in computational cognitive science: The case of enculturated mathematical problem solving. *Synthese*, Vol. 198, pp. 3221–3263.

Fallang, B., Øien, I., Østensjø, S., & Gulbrandsen, L. M. (2017). Microprocesses in social and learning activities at school generate exclusions for children with disabilities. *Scandinavian Journal of Disability Research*, Vol. 19, pp. 269–280.

Faulconer, J. E. & Williams, R. N. (1985). Temporality in human action: An alternative to positivism and historicism. *American Psychologist*, Vol. 40, pp. 1179–1188.

Favela, L. (2022). Complexity: Understanding brains and minds on their own terms. In Kelty-Stephen, D. G., Cisek, P. E., De Bari, B., et al. (2022). *In search for an alternative to the computer metaphor of the mind and brain.* ArXiv: 2206.04603.

Favela, L. H. & Machery, E. (2025). The concept of representation in the brain sciences: The current status and ways forward. *Mind & Language.* Vol. 40, pp. 215–225.

Favela, L. H., Amon, M. J., Lobo, L., Chemero, A. (2021). Empirical evidence for extended cognitive systems. *Cognitive Science*, Vol. 45, e13060.

Feest, U. (2005). Operationism in psychology: What the debate is about, what the debate should be about. *Journal of the History of the Behavioral Sciences*, Vol. 41, pp. 131–149.

Feest, U. (2017). Phenomena and objects of research in the cognitive and behavioral sciences. *Philosophy of science*, Vol. 84, pp. 1165–1176.

Ferree, M. M. & Martin, P. Y. (eds.) (1995). *Feminist organizations: Harvest of the new women's movement.* Temple University Press.

Fiedler, K. (2014). From intrapsychic to ecological theories in social psychology: Outlines of a functional theory approach. *European Journal of Social Psychology*, Vol. 44, pp. 657–670.

Fiedler, K. (2017). What constitutes strong psychological science? The (neglected) role of diagnosticity and a priori theorizing. *Perspectives on Psychological Science*, Vol. 12, pp. 46–61.

Fisher, A. J., Medaglia, J. D., & Jeronimus, B. F. (2018). Lack of group-to-individual generalizability is a threat to human subjects research. *Proceedings of the National Academy of Sciences, USA*, Vol. 115, E6106–E6115.

Fleck, L. (1935/1979). *Genesis and development of a scientific fact*. [Entstehung und Entwicklung einer wissenschaftlichen Tatsache. Entführung in die Lehre von Denkstil und Denkkollektiv]. Benno Schwabe & Co./University of Chicago Press.

Fleck, L. (1936/1986). The problem of epistemology. In R. Cohen & T. Schnelle (eds.), *Cognition and fact: Materials on Ludwik Fleck*. D. Reidel.

Flis, I. (2019). Psychologists psychologizing scientific psychology: An epistemological reading of the replication crisis. *Theory & Psychology*, Vol. 29, pp. 158–181.

Flis, I. & Eck, N. (2018). Framing psychology as a discipline (1950–1999): A large-scale term co-occurrence analysis of scientific literature in psychology. *History of Psychology*, Vol. 21, pp. 334–362.

Fraiberg, S. (1978). *Every child's birthright: In defense of mothering*. Bantam Books.

Frances, A. (2013). *Saving Normal: An insider's revolt against out-of-control psychiatric diagnosis, DSM-5, Big Pharma, and the medicalization of ordinary life*. William Morrow.

Franz. D. (2022a). "Are psychological attributes quantitative?" is not an empirical question: Conceptual confusions in the measurement debate. *Theory & Psychology*, Vol. 32, pp. 131–150.

Franz. D. (2022b). Psychological measurement is highly questionable but the details remain controversial: A response to Tafreshi, Michell, and Trendler. *Theory & Psychology*, Vol. 32, pp. 171–177.

Friedan, B. (1963). *The feminine mystique*. Norton.

Frisch, S. (2016). Are mental disorders brain diseases, and what does this mean? A clinical-neuropsychological perspective. *Psychopathology*, Vol. 49, pp. 135–142.

Frisch, S. (2022). The tangled knots of neuroscientific experimentation. *Integrative Psychological and Behavioral Science*, Vol. 56, pp. 910–929.

Fuchs, T. (2018). *Ecology of the brain: The phenomenology and biology of the embodied mind*. Oxford University Press.

Fuchs, T. (2021). *In defense of the human being: Foundational questions of an embodied anthropology*. Oxford University Press.

Fuchs, T. (2023). Understanding as explaining: How motives can become causes. *Phenomenology and the Cognitive Sciences*, Vol. 22, pp. 701–717.

Galton, F. (1879). Psychometric experiments. *Brain*, Vol. 2, pp. 149–162.

Garcini, L. M., Barrita, A., Cadenas, G. A. et al. (2025). A decolonial and liberation lens to social justice research: Upholding promises for diverse, inclusive, and equitable psychological science. *The American psychologist*, Vol. 80, pp. 1–14.

Gastelum-Vargas, M., Chemero, A., & Raja, V. (2024). Places for reasoning. *Philosophical Transactions of the Royal Society B: Biological Sciences*, Vol. 379, 20230294.

Geertz, C. (1973). *The interpretation of cultures*. Basic Books.

Gergen, K. (1973). Social psychology as history. *Journal of Personality and Social Psychology*, Vol. 26, pp. 309–320.

Gibson, E. & Pick, A. (2023). *An ecological approach to perceptual learning and development*. Oxford University Press.

Gibson, J. J. (1979). *The ecological approach to visual perception*. Houghton Mifflin.

Gigerenzer, G. (1991). From tools to theories: A heuristic of discovery in cognitive psychology. *Psychological Review*, Vol. 98, pp. 254–226.

Gigerenzer, G. (2004). Mindless statistics. *The Journal of Socio-Economics*, Vol. 33, pp. 587–606.

Gigerenzer, G. (2018). Statistical rituals: The replication delusion and how we got there. *Advances in Methods and Practices in Psychological Science*, Vol. 1, pp. 198–218.

Gilhooly, K., Lyddy, F., Pollick, F., & Buratti, S. (2022). *Cognitive psychology, 2nd ed.* McGraw-Hill.

Gillett, A. J. (2022). Development, resilience engineering, degeneracy, and cognitive practices. *Review of Philosophy and Psychology*, Vol. 13, pp. 645–664.

Glenberg, A., Witt, J., & Metcalfe, J. (2013). From the revolution to embodiment: 25 years of cognitive psychology. *Perspectives on Psychological Science*, Vol. 8, pp. 573–585.

Glock, H.-J. (2006). Thought, language and animals. *Grazer Philosophische Studien*, Vol. 71, pp. 139–160.

Glock, H.-J. (2009). Concepts: Where subjectivism goes wrong. *Philosophy*, Vol. 84, pp. 5–29.

Glock, H.-J. (2010). Concepts, abilities and propositions. *Grazer Philosophische Studien*, Vol. 81, pp. 115–134.

Glock, H.-J. (2015). Propositional attitudes, intentional contents and other representationalist myths. In A. Coliva, D. Moyal-Sharrock, & V. Munz (eds.), *Mind, language and action. Proceedings of the 36th international Wittgenstein symposium*. De Gruyter.

Glock. H.-J. (2020). Minds, brains, and capacities: Situated cognition and neo-Aristotelianism. *Frontiers in Psychology*, Vol. 11, 566385.

Goldman, S. (2021). *Science wars: The battle over knowledge and reality*. Oxford Academic.

Gradmann, C. (2004). A harmony of illusions: Clinical and experimental testing of Robert Koch's tuberculin 1890–1900. *Studies in the History and Philosophy of Biology & Biomedical Sciences*. Vol. 35, pp. 465–481.

Graffi, G. (2019). Between linguistics and philosophy of language: The debate on Chomsky's notion of "Knowledge of Language." *Cahiers de l'ILSL*, Vol. 53, pp. 39–58.

Graziano, A. & Raulin, M. (2014). *Research methods: A process of inquiry*. 8th ed. Pearson International.

Green, C. (1992). Of immortal psychological beasts: Operationism in psychology. *Theory & Psychology*, Vol. 2, pp. 291–320.

Green, C. (2001). Operationism again: What did Bridgman say? What did Bridgman need? *Theory & Psychology*, Vol. 11, pp. 45–51.

Green, C. (2021). Perhaps psychology's replication crisis is a theoretical crisis that is only masquerading as a statistical one. *International Review of Theoretical Psychologies*, Vol. 1, pp. 178–192.

Greenberg, G. (2013). *The book of woe: The DSM and the unmaking of psychiatry.* Blue Rider Press.

Greenspan, M. (1983/1999). *A new approach to women and therapy.* McGraw-Hill.

Grice, J. (2015). From means and variances to persons and patterns. *Frontiers of Psychology*, Vol. 6, p. 1007.

Grice, J. W., Medellin, E., Jones, I., et al (2020). Persons as effect sizes. *Advances in Methods and Practices in Psychological Science*, Vol. 3, pp. 443–455.

Grills, S. & Prus, R. (2008). The myth of the independent variable: Reconceptualizing class, gender, race, and age as subcultural processes. *American Sociologist*, Vol. 39, pp. 19–37.

Hacker, P. (2001). *Wittgenstein: Connections and controveries.* Clarendon Press.

Hacker, P. (2007). *Human nature: The categorial framework.* John Wiley & Sons.

Hacker, P. (2012). The brain and consciousness. In R. Harré & F. Moghaddam (eds.), *Psychology for the third millenium.* Sage.

Hacker, P. (2013a). Before the mereological fallacy: A rejoinder to Rom Harré. *Philosophy*, Vol. 88, pp. 141–148.

Hacker, P. (2013b). *The intellectual powers: A study of human nature.* John Wiley & Sons.

Hacker, P. (2016). Philosophy and scientism: What cognitive neuroscience can, and what it cannot, explain. In R. N. Williams & D. N. Robinson (eds.), *Scientism: The new orthodoxy.* Bloomsbury.

Hacking, I. (1983). *Representing and intervening: Introductory topics in the philosophy of natural science.* Cambridge University Press.

Hacking, I. (1995). *Rewriting the soul: Multiple personality and the sciences of memory.* Princeton University Press.

Hacking, I. (1998). *Mad travelers: Reflections on the reality of transient mental illnesses.* University of Virginia Press.

Hacking, I. (1999). *The social construction of what?* Harvard University Press.

Hacking, I. (2004). Minding the brain. *The New York Review of Books*, Vol. 51, p. 3.

Hacking, I. (2007a). Natural kinds: Rosy dawn, scholastic twilight. *Royal Institute of Philosophy Supplement*, Vol. 61, pp. 203–239.

Hacking, I. (2007b). Kinds of people: Moving targets. *Proceedings of the British Academy*, Vol. 151, pp. 285–318.

Hagerty, S. L. (2023). Toward precision characterization and treatment of psychopathology: A path forward and integrative framework of the hierarchical taxonomy of psychopathology and the Research Domain Criteria. *Perspectives on Psychological Science*, Vol. 18, pp. 91–109.

Hagoort, P. (ed.) (2019). *Human language: From genes to brains to behavior.* MIT Press.

Hanisch, C. (1970). The personal is political. In S. Firestone & A. Koedt (eds.) *Notes from the second year: Women's Liberation.* https://find.library.duke.edu/c atalog/DUKE002362942.

Harper, D. & Cromby, J. (2022). From "What's wrong with you?" to "What's happened to you?": An introduction to the Special Issue on the Power Threat Meaning Framework. *Journal of Constructivist Psychology*, Vol. 35, pp. 1–6.

Harre, R. & Secord, P. F. (1972). *The explanation of social behaviour.* Rowman & Littlefield.

Haslam, N. (2016). Looping effects and the expanding concept of mental disorder. *Journal of Psychopathology*, Vol. 22, pp. 4–9.

Haslanger, S. (2019). Cognition as a social skill. *Australasian Philosophical Review*, Vol. 3, pp. 5–25.

Hasselman, F. (2022). Radical embodied computation: Emergence of meaning through the reproduction of similarity by analogy. In Kelty-Stephen, D. et al (2022). *In search for an alternative to the computer metaphor of the mind and brain. ArXiv:* 2206.04603.

Hawkins, R. X. D., Goodman, N., & Goldstone, R. (2019). The emergence of social norms and conventions. *Trends in Cognitive Sciences*, Vol. 23, pp. 158–169.

Heintz, C. & Scott-Phillips, T. (2023). Expression unleashed: The evolutionary and cognitive foundations of human communication. *Behavioral and Brain Sciences*, Vol. 46, e1: pp. 1–53.

Henrich, J. & Muthukrishna, M. (2021). The origins and psychology of human cooperation. *Annual Review of Psychology*, Vol. 72, pp. 207–240.

Henrich, J., Heine, S., & Norenzayan, A. (2010). The weirdest people in the world. *Behavioral and Brain Sciences*, Vol. 33, pp. 61–135.

Heyes, C. (2018). *Cognitive gadgets: The cultural evolution of thinking.* The Belknap Press of Harvard University.

Heyes, C. (2019). Précis of cognitive gadgets: The cultural evolution of thinking. *Behavioral and Brain Sciences*, Vol. 42, p. e169.

Heyes, C. (2024). Rethinking norm psychology. *Perspectives on Psychological Science*, Vol. 19, pp. 12–38.

Heyes, C., Bang, D., Shea, N., Frith, C., & Fleming, S. (2020). Knowing ourselves together: The cultural origins of metacognition. *Trends in Cognitive Science* Vol. 24, pp. 349–362

Heyes, C. & Moore, R. (2023). Henrich, Heyes, and Tomasello on the cognitive foundations of cultural evolution. In R. Kendal, J. Tehrani, & J. Kendal (eds.), *The Oxford Handbook of Cultural Evolution.* Oxford University Press.

Hibberd, F. (2019). What is scientific definition? *The Journal of Mind and Behavior*, Vol. 40, pp. 29–52.

Hoffman, P. (2009). *Essays on Descartes.* Oxford University Press.

Holler, J. & Levinson, S. (2019). Multimodal language processing in human communication. *Trends in Cognitive Sciences*, Vol. 23, pp. 639–652.

Hook, D. (2025). *Fanon, psychoanalysis, and critical decolonial psychology: The mind of Apartheid.* Routledge.

Hopper, K., Harrison, G., Janca, A., & Sartorius, N., (eds.) (2007). *Recovery from schizophrenia*. Oxford University Press.

Hornstein, G. (1988). Quantifying psychological phenomena: Debates, dilemmas, and implications. In J. Morawski (ed.), *The rise of experimentation in American psychology*. Yale University Press.

Hornstein, G. & Star, S. (1990). Universality biases: How theories about human nature succeed. *Philosophy of the Social Sciences*, Vol. 20, pp. 421–436.

Hornstein, G. A., Putnam, E. R., & Branitsky, A. (2020). How do hearing voices peer-support groups work? A three-phase model of transformation. *Psychosis: Psychological, Social and Integrative Approaches*, Vol. 12, pp. 201–211.

Horton-Salway, M. (2001). The construction of M.E.: The discursive action model. In M. Wetherell, S. Taylor, & S. Yates (eds.), *Discourse as data: A guide for analysis*. Sage.

Hubbard, R. (2019). Will the ASA's efforts to improve statistical practice be successful? Some evidence to the contrary. *The American Statistician*, Vol. 73 (suppl. 1), pp. 31–35.

Hubbard, R., Haig, B. D., & Parsa, R. A. (2019). The limited role of formal statistical inference in scientific inference. *The American Statistician*, Vol. 73 (suppl. 1), pp. 91–98.

Hutchins, E. (1995). *Cognition in the wild*. MIT Press.

Hutmacher, F. & Franz, D. J. (2024). Approaching psychology's current crises by exploring the vagueness of psychological concepts: Recommendations for advancing the discipline. *American Psychologist*, Vol. 80, pp. 220–231.

Hydén, L. C. (2014). Cutting Brussels sprouts: Collaboration involving persons with dementia. *Journal of Aging Studies*, Vol. 29, pp. 115–123.

Hydén, L. C. (2017). *Entangled lives: Collaborative storytelling and the re-imagining of dementia*. Oxford University Press.

Hyman, S. E. (2010). The diagnosis of mental disorders: The problem of reification. *Annual Review of Clinical Psychology*, Vol. 6, pp. 155–179.

Hyman, S. E. (2021). Psychiatric disorders: Grounded in human biology but not natural kinds. *Perspectives in Biology and Medicine*, Vol. 64, pp. 6–28.

Ibañez, A. (2022). The mind's golden cage and cognition in the wild. *Trends in Cognitive Sciences*, Vol. 26, pp. 1031–1034.

Ibáñez, A. & Cosmelli, D. (2008). Moving beyond computational cognitivism: Understanding intentionality, intersubjectivity and ecology of mind. *Integrative Psychological and Behavioral Science*, Vol. 42, pp. 129–136.

Isbilen, E. S. & Christiansen, M. H. (2020). Chunk-based memory constraints on the cultural evolution of language. *Topics in Cognitive Science*, Vol. 12, pp. 713–726.

Jacklin, C. N. (1981). Methodological issues in the study of sex-related differences. *Developmental Review*, Vol. 1, pp. 266–273.

Jaeger, J., Riedl, A., Djedovic, A., Vervaeke, J., & Walsh, D. (2024). Naturalizing relevance realization: Why agency and cognition are fundamentally not computational. *Frontiers in Psychology*, Vol. 15, 1362658.

Joel, D., Hänggi, J., & Pool, J. (2016). Why differences between brains of females and brains of males do not "add up" to create two types of brains. *PNAS*, Vol. 113, p. 1972.

Johnson, D. M., & Erneling, C. E. (eds.) (1997). *The future of the cognitive revolution*. Oxford University Press.

Johnstone, L. & Boyle, M. with Cromby, J., Dillon, J., Harper, D., et al. (2018). *The Power Threat Meaning framework: Overview*. British Psychological Society.

Jungert, M. (2017). Neurophilosophy or philosophy of neuroscience? What neuroscience and philosophy can and cannot do for each other. In J. Leefmann & E. Hildt (eds.) *The human sciences after the decade of the brain*. Elsevier.

Kagan, J. (1998). *Three seductive ideas*. Harvard University Press.

Kalis A., Pascoe J., & Segundo Ortin, M. (2024). Running away from the marshmallow: The relevance of behaviour settings for a situated science of self-control. *Philosophical Transactions of the Royal Society B: Biological Sciences*, Vol. 379, 20230289.

Keijzer, F. (2022). Tunnel vision, tunnel action, tunnel mind: Just get out. In Kelty-Stephen, D. G., Cisek, P. E., De Bari, B., et al. *In search for an alternative to the computer metaphor of the mind and brain. ArXiv*: 2206.04603.

Keijzer, F. (2025). Full naturalism: The objectivity of subjective points of view. *Biological Theory*, Online first publ. doi.org/10.1007/s13752-025-00493-9.

Keller, E. F. (2010). *The mirage of a space between nature and nurture*. Duke University Press.

Kelty-Stephen, D. G., Cisek, P. E., De Bari, B., et al. (2022). *In search for an alternative to the computer metaphor of the mind and brain. ArXiv*: 2206.04603. doi.org/10.48550/arXiv.2206. 04603.

Kendal, J., Tehrani, J., & Odling-Smee, J. (2011). Human niche construction in interdisciplinary focus. *Philosophical transactions of the Royal Society of London. Series B. Biological sciences*, Vol. 366, pp. 785–792.

Kendler, H. (1981). The reality of operationism: A rejoinder. *The Journal of Mind and Behavior*, Vol. 2, pp. 331–341.

Kendler, H. (1983). Operationism: A recipe for reducing confusion and ambiguity. *The Journal of Mind and Behavior*, Vol. 4, pp. 91–97.

Kendler, K. (2016). The phenomenology of Major Depression and the representativeness and nature of DSM criteria. *American Journal of Psychiatry*, Vol. 173, pp. 771–780.

Kendler, K. (2017). DSM disorders and their criteria: How should they inter-relate? *Psychological Medicine*, Vol. 47, pp. 2054–2060.

Kenny, A. (1992). *The metaphysics of mind*. Oxford University Press.

Kessler, S. & McKenna, W. (1978). *Gender: An ethnomethodological approach*. University of Chicago Press.

Kind, A. (2020). *Philosophy of mind: The basics*. Taylor & Francis.

Kirsch, I. (2011). *The Emperor's new drugs: Exploding the antidepressant myth*. Basic Books.

Kleinman, A. (1988). *The illness narratives: Suffering, healing, and the human condition*. Basic Books.

Kline, R. B. (2009). *Becoming a behavioural science researcher: A guide to producing research that matters*. Guilford Press.

Koch, S. (ed.) (1959). *Psychology: a study of a science*. Study 1, Conceptual and systematic, Vol. 3, Formulations of the person and the social context. McGraw-Hill.

Kostic, D. & Halffman, W. (2023). Mapping explanatory language in neuroscience. *Synthese*, Vol. 202, art. 112.

Kravetz, D. (2004). *Tales from the trenches: Politics and practice in feminist service organizations*. University Press of America.

Kroeber, A. L. & Kluckhohn, C. (1952). *Culture: A critical review of concepts and definitions. Papers. Peabody Museum of Archaeology & Ethnology*. Harvard University, Vol. 47, p. 223.

Lamiell, J. (2019). *Psychology's misuse of statistics and persistent dismissal of its critics*. Palgrave studies in the theory and history of psychology. Palgrave.

Lamiell, J. (2021). On the systemic misuse of statistical methods within mainstream psychology. In J. T. Lamiell & K. L. Slaney (eds.) *Problematic research practices and inertia in scientific psychology: History, sources, and recommended solutions*. Routledge.

LaVine, M. & Tissaw, M. (2015). Philosophical anthropology. In J. Martin, J. Sugarman, & K. L. Slaney (eds.), *The Wiley handbook of theoretical and philosophical psychology: Methods, approaches, and new directions for social sciences*. John Wiley.

Le Texier, T. & Kazak, A. E. (2019). Debunking the Stanford prison experiment. *American Psychologist*, Vol. 74, pp. 823–839.

Leahey, T. (1980). The myth of operationism. *The Journal of Mind and Behavior*, Vol. 1, pp. 127–143.

Leahey, T. (1981). Operationism still isn't real: A temporary reply to Kendler. *The Journal of Mind and Behavior*, Vol. 2, pp. 343–348.

Leahey, T. (1983). Operationism and ideology: Reply to Kendler. *The Journal of Mind and Behavior*, Vol. 4, pp. 81–89.

Leahey, T. (2001). Back to Bridgman?! *Theory and Psychology*, Vol. 11, pp. 53–58.

Levinson, S. C. & Evans, N. (2010). Time for a sea-change in linguistics: Response to comments on "The Myth of Language Universals." *Lingua*, Vol. 120, pp. 2733–2758.

Levinson, S. C. (2023). Gesture, spatial cognition and the evolution of language. *Philosophical transactions of the Royal Society of London. Series B. Biological sciences*, Vol. 378 (1875), Article 20210481.

Lewin, M. (ed.) (1984). *In the shadow of the past: Psychology portrays the sexes*. Columbia University Press.

Leys, R. (2017). *The ascent of affect: Genealogy and critique*. University of Chicago Press.

Leys, R. (2024). *Anatomy of a train wreck: The rise and fall of priming research*. University of Chicago Press.

Lilienfeld, S. & Strother, A. (2020). Psychological measurement and the replication crisis: Four sacred cows. *Canadian Psychology*, Vol. 61, pp. 281–288.

Lilienfield, S., Aslinger, E., Marshall, J., & Satel, S. (2017). Neurohype: A field guide to exaggerated brain-based claims. In S. Johnson & K. Rommelfanger (eds.), *The Routledge Handbook of Neuroethics*. Routledge.

Liliequist, B. (2003). *Ludwik Flecks jämförande kunskapsteori*. [Ludwik Fleck's comparative epistemology]. Umeå Studies in Philosophy, No. 6.

Lowe, J. (2009). Dualism. In T. Bayne, A. Cleeremans, & P. Wilken (eds.), *The Oxford companion to consciousness*. Oxford University Press.

Luhrmann, T. M., Padmavati, R., Tharoor, H., & Osei, A. (2015). Differences in voice-hearing experiences of people with psychosis in the USA, India and Ghana: Interview-based study. *The British Journal of Psychiatry*, Vol. 206, pp. 41–44.

Luhrmann, T. M., and Marrow, J. (2016). *Our most troubling madness: Case studies in schizophrenia across cultures*. University of California Press.

Lutz, C. (1982). The domain of emotion words in Ifaluk. *American Ethnologist*, Vol. 9, pp. 113–128.

Lutz, C. (1988). *Unnatural emotions: Everyday sentiments on a Micronesian atoll and their challenge to Western theory*. University of Chicago Press.

Lyon, P., Keijzer, F., Arendt, D., & Levin, M. (2021). Reframing cognition: Getting down to biological basics. *Philosophical Transactions of the Royal Society B: Biological Sciences*, Vol. 376 (1820), p. 20190750.

Maccoby, E. E. & Jacklin, C. N. (1974). *The psychology of sex differences*. Stanford University Press.

Machado, A. & Silva, F. J. (2007). Toward a richer view of the scientific method: The role of conceptual analysis. *American Psychologist*, Vol. 62, pp. 671–681.

Machery, E. (2009). *Doing without concepts*. Oxford University Press.

MacMartin, C. & Winston, A. (1990). The rhetoric of experimental social psychology, 1930–1960: From caution to enthusiasm. *Journal of the History of the Behavioral Sciences*, Vol. 36, pp. 349–364.

Magnusson, E. (2008). The rhetoric of inequality: Nordic women and men argue against gender equality. *NORA: Nordic Journal of Feminist and Gender Research*, Vol 16, pp. 79–95.

Magnusson, E., & Marecek, J. (2012). *Gender and culture in psychology: Theories and practices*. Cambridge University Press.

Magnusson, E. & Marecek, J. (2015). *Doing interview-based qualitative research: A learner's guide*. Cambridge University Press.

Maiers, W. (2022). Just another instance of the replication of crises in psychology? Historical retrospections and theoretical-psychological assessments. *Review of general psychology*, Vol. 26, pp. 250–260.

Malkiel, N. W (2016). *"Keep the damned women out": The struggle for coeducation*. Princeton University Press.

Mangalam, M., Fragaszy, D., Wagman, J., et al. (2022). On the psychological origins of tool use. *Neuroscience and Biobehavioral Reviews*, Vol. 134, pp.104521–104521, Article 104521.

Maraun, M. & Peters, J. (2005). What does it mean that an issue is conceptual in nature? *Journal of Personality Assessment*, Vol. 85, pp. 128–133.

Marecek, J. (2020). Abortion in context. In J. M. Ussher, J. C. Chrisler, & J. Perz (eds.), *Routledge international handbook of women's sexual and reproductive health*. Routledge.

Marraffa, M. & Paternoster, A. (2012). Functions, levels, and mechanisms: Explanation in cognitive science and its problems. *Theory & Psychology*, Vol. 23, pp. 22–45.

Martin, E. (1991). The egg and the sperm: How science has constructed a romance based on stereotypical male-female roles. *Signs*, Vol. 16, pp. 485–501.

Martin, E. (2004). Talking back to neuro-reductionism. In H. Thomas, & J. Ahmed, (eds.), *Cultural bodies*. John Wiley & Sons.

Martin, J. & Bickhard, M. (2013). Introducing persons and the psychology of personhood. In J. Martin & M. Bickhard (eds.), *The psychology of personhood: Philosophical, historical, social-developmental, and narrative perspectives*. Cambridge University Press.

Martin, J., Sugarman, J. H., & Hickinbottom, S. (2009) *Persons: Understanding psychological selfhood and agency*. Springer.

Maselli, A., Gordon, J., Eluchans, M., et al. (2023). Beyond simple laboratory studies: Developing sophisticated models to study rich behavior. *Physics of Life Reviews*, Vol. 46, pp. 220–244.

Mason, W. A., Cogua-Lopez, J., Fleming, C. B., & Scheier, L. M. (2018). Challenges facing evidence-based prevention: Incorporating an abductive theory of method. *Evaluation & the Health Professions*, Vol. 41, pp. 155–182.

Matassi, G. & Martinez, P. (2023). The brain-computer analogy: A special issue. *Frontiers in Ecology and Evolution*, Vol. 10, 1099253.

Mayrhofer, R., Büchner, I., & Hevesi, J. (2024). The quantitative paradigm and the nature of the human mind: The replication crisis as an epistemological crisis of quantitative psychology in view of the ontic nature of the psyche. *Frontiers in Psychology*, Vol. 15: 1390233.

Mayrhofer, R & Hutmacher, F. (2020). The principle of inversion: Why the quantitative-empirical paradigm cannot serve as a unifying basis for psychology as an academic discipline. *Frontiers in Psychology*, Vol. 11, 596425.

McCrae, R. R. & Costa, P. T., Jr. (1995). Trait explanations in personality psychology. *European Journal of Personality*, Vol. 9, pp. 231–252.

McGuire, W. J. (1973). The yin and yang of progress in social psychology: Seven koan. *Journal of Personality and Social Psychology*, Vol. 26, pp. 446–456.

Meehl P. E. (1978). Theoretical risks and tabular asterisks: Sir Karl, Sir Ronald, and the slow progress of soft psychology. *Journal of Consulting and Clinical Psychology*, Vol. 46, pp. 806–834.

Meerman te, S., Freedman, J. E., & Batstra, L. (2022). ADHD and reification: Four ways a psychiatric construct is portrayed as a disease. *Frontiers of Psychiatry*, Vol. 13, 1055328.

Menary, R. (2007). *Cognitive integration: Mind and cognition unbounded*. Palgrave Macmillan.

Menary, R. (2010a). Introduction to the special issue on 4E cognition. *Phenomenology and the Cognitive Sciences*, Vol. 9, pp. 459–463.

Menary, R. (2010b). Cognitive integration and the extended mind. In R. Menary (ed.), *The extended mind*. MIT Press.

Menary, R. (2010c). Introduction: The extended mind in focus. In R. Menary (ed.), *The extended mind*. MIT Press.

Menary, R. (2010d). Dimensions of mind. *Phenomenology and the Cognitive*, Vol. 9, pp. 561–578.

Menary, R. (2012). Cognitive practices and cognitive character. *Philosophical Explorations*, Vol. 15, pp. 147–164.

Menary, R. (2013). Cognitive integration, encultured cognition and the socially extended mind. *Cognitive Systems Research*, Vol. 25–26, pp. 26–34.

Menary, R. (2014). Neural plasticity, neuronal recycling and niche construction. *Mind and Language*, Vol. 29, pp. 286–303.

Menary, R. (2015). Pragmatism and the pragmatic turn in cognitive science. In D. Kragic, K. J. Friston, & A. K. Engel (eds.), *The pragmatic turn: Toward action-oriented views in cognitive science*. MIT Press.

Menary, R. & Gillett, A. J. (2017). Embodying culture: Integrated cognitive systems and cultural evolution In J. Kiverstein (ed.), *The Routledge handbook of philosophy of the social mind*. Routledge.

Menary, R. & Gillet, A. J. (2022). The tools of enculturation. *Topics in Cognitive Science*, Vol. 14, pp. 363–387.

Menary, R. & Kirchhoff, M. (2014). Cognitive transformations and extended expertise. *Educational Philosophy and Theory*, Vol. 46, pp. 610–623.

Michell, J. (1997). Quantitative science and the definition of measurement in psychology. *British Journal of Psychology*, Vol. 88, pp. 355–383.

Michell, J. (1999). *Measurement in psychology: A critical history of a methodological concept*. Cambridge University Press.

Michell, J. (2001). Teaching and misteaching measurement in psychology. *Australian Psychologist*, Vol. 36, pp. 211–217.

Michell, J. (2004). The place of qualitative research in psychology. *Qualitative Research in Psychology*, Vol. 1, pp. 307–319.

Michell, J. (2006). Psychophysics, intensive magnitudes, and the psychometricians' fallacy. *Studies in History and Philosophy of Biological and Biomedical Sciences*, Vol. 17, pp. 414–432.

Michell, J. (2012). "The constantly recurring argument": Inferring quantity from order. *Theory & Psychology*, Vol. 22, pp. 255–271.

Michell, J. (2022). "The art of imposing measurement upon the mind": Sir Francis Galton and the genesis of the psychometric paradigm. *Theory & Psychology*, Vol. 32, pp. 375–400.

Michell, J. (2023). "Professor Spearman has drawn over-hasty conclusions": Unravelling psychometrics' "Copernican Revolution." *Theory & Psychology*, Vol. 33, pp. 661–680.

Miłkowski, M. (2018a). Objections to computationalism: A survey. *Roczniki Filozoficzne*, Vol. LXVI (3), pp. 57–75.

Miłkowski, M. (2018b). From computer metaphor to computational modeling: The evolution of computationalism. *Minds and Machines*, Vol. 28, pp. 515–541.

Miłkowski, M., Clowes, R., & Rucinska, Z., et al. (2018). From wide cognition to mechanisms: A silent revolution. *Frontiers in Psychology*, Vol. 9, p. 2393.

Miller, G. (2010). Mistreating psychology in the decades of the brain. *Perspectives on Psychological Science.* Vol. 5, pp. 716–743.

Morawski, J. (2019). The replication crisis: How might philosophy and theory of psychology be of use? *Journal of Theoretical and Philosophical Psychology*, Vol. 39, pp. 218–238.

Morelli, G. A. & Henry, P. I. (2013). Cross-cultural challenges to Attachment Theory. In N. Quinn & J. M. Mageo (eds.), *Attachment reconsidered: Cultural perspectives on a Western theory.* Palgrave.

Morgan, B. (2017). Situated cognition and the study of culture: An introduction. *Poetics Today*, Vol. 38, pp. 213–233.

Morris, K. J. & Jacquette, D. (2018). The hard problem of understanding Descartes on consciousness. In Jacquette, D. (ed.), *The Bloomsbury companion to the philosophy of consciousness.* Bloomsbury.

Moynihan, R., Heath, I., & Henry, D. (2002). Selling sickness: The pharmaceutical industry and disease mongering. *BMJ (Online)*, Vol. 324 (7342), pp. 886–890.

Nachev, P., & Hacker, P. (2014). The neural antecedents to voluntary action: A conceptual analysis. *Cognitive Neuroscience*, Vol. 5, pp. 193–208.

Nastase, S., Goldstein, A., & Hasson, U. (2021). Keep it real: Rethinking the primacy of experimental control in cognitive neuroscience. *NeuroImage*, Vol. 222, Article 117254.

Nelson, K. & Fivush, R. (2020). The development of autobiographical memory, autobiographical narratives, and autobiographical consciousness. *Psychological Reports*, 123, pp. 71–96.

Nelson, L., Simmons, J., & Simonsohn, U. (2018). Psychology's renaissance. *Annual Review of Psychology*, Vol. 69, pp. 511–534.

Newen, A., De Bruin, L., & Gallagher, S. (eds.) (2018). *Oxford handbook of 4E cognition.* Oxford University Press.

Nichter, M. (1981). Idioms of distress: Alternatives in the expression of psychosocial distress: A case study from South India. *Culture, Medicine, And Psychiatry*, Vol. 5, pp. 379–408.

Nickerson, R. S. (2000). Null hypothesis significance testing: A review of an old and continuing controversy. *Psychological Methods*, Vol. 5, pp. 241–301.

Nordin, M. (2020). Ska vi sluta använda oss av statistisk signifikans? [Should we stop using statistical significance?]. *Ekonomisk debatt*, Vol. 48, pp. 38–47.

Normile, C. J., Bloesch, E. K., Davoli, et al. (2019). Introducing the new statistics in the classroom. *Scholarship of Teaching and Learning in Psychology*, Vol. 5, pp. 162–168.

Nosek, B. A., Hardwicke, T. E., Moshontz, H., et al. (2022). Replicability, robustness, and reproducibility in psychological Science. *Annual Review of Psychology*, Vol. 73, pp. 719–748.

Nosek, B. A. & Lakens, D. E. (2013). Call for proposals: special issue of *Social Psychology* on "replications of important results in social psychology." *Social Psychology*, Vol. 44, pp. 59–60.

Núñez, R., Semenuks, A., Allen, M., et al. (2019). What happened to cognitive science? *Nature-Human Behaviour*, Vol. 3, August, pp. 782–791.

Oberauer, K. & Lewandowsky, S. (2019). Addressing the theory crisis in psychology. *Psychonomic Bulletin & Review*, Vol. 26, pp. 1596–1618.

Olofsson, J. & Örestig, J. (2015). *Evolutionsteori och människans natur.* [Evolutionary theory and human nature]. Natur & Kultur.

Olsvold, A., Aarseth, H., & Bondevik, H. (2019). "I think my son is a wonderful chap": Working-class and middle-class fathers' narratives of their son's ADHD diagnosis and medication. *Families, Relationships and Societies*, Vol. 8, pp. 105–120.

Open Science Collaboration (2012). An open, large-scale, collaborative effort to estimate the reproducibility of psychological science. *Perspectives on Psychological Science*, Vol. 7, pp. 657–660.

Open Science Collaboration (2015). Estimating the reproducibility of psychological science. *Science*, Vol. 349 (6251), p.aac4716.

Pagel, R. (2019). The concept of (depth) cues: An exemplification of homuncular language in vision science. *Theory & Psychology*, Vol. 29, pp. 66–86.

Parlee, M. (1979). Psychology and women. *Signs: Journal of Women in Culture and Society*, Vol. 5, pp. 121–133.

Parsons, T. (1951). Illness and the role of the physician: A sociological perspective. *American Journal of Orthopsychiatry*, Vol. 21, pp. 452–460.

Paulus, M. (2022). Should infant psychology rely on the violation-of-expectation method? Not anymore. *Infant and Child Development*. Vol. 31, p. e2306.

Pessoa, L., Medina, L., & Desfilis, E. (2021). Refocusing neuroscience: Moving away from mental categories and towards complex behaviours. *Philosophical Transactions of the Royal Society*, B, Vol. 377, 20200534.

Pezzulo, G., Vosgerau, G., Frith, U., et al. (2015). Acting up: An approach to the study of cognitive development. In A. K. Engel, D. Kragic, & K. J. Friston (eds.), *The pragmatic turn: Toward action-oriented views in cognitive science.* MIT Press.

Piantadosi, S., Byar, D., & Green, S. (1988). The ecological fallacy. *American Journal of Epidemiology*, Vol. 127, pp. 893–904.

Pléh, C. (2019). The inspirational role of Chomsky in the cognitive turn of psychology. *Acta Linguistica Academica*, Vol. 66, pp. 397–428.

Pleyer, M. & Hartmann, S. (2019). Constructing a consensus on language evolution? Convergences and differences between biolinguistic and usage-based approaches. *Frontiers of Psychology*, Vol. 10, p. 2537.

Plotkin, H. (2004). *Evolutionary thought in psychology: A brief history.* John Wiley & Sons.

Plotkin, H. (2011). Human nature, cultural diversity, and evolutionary theory. *Philosophical transactions of the Royal Society of London. Series B. Biological sciences*, Vol. 366, pp. 454–463.

Poldrack, R. A. (2021). The physics of representation. *Synthese*, Vol. 199, pp. 1307–1325.

Poldrack, R. A., Baker, C. I., Durnez, J., et al. (2017). Scanning the horizon: Towards transparent and reproducible neuroimaging research. *Nature Reviews: Neuroscience*, Vol. 18, pp. 115–126.

Porter, T. M. (1995). *Trust in numbers: The pursuit of objectivity in science and public life.* Princeton University Press.

Potter, J. (2012). Re-reading "Discourse and social psychology": Transforming social psychology. *British Journal of Social Psychology*, Vol. 51, pp. 436–455.

Probst, B. (2014). The life and death of Axis IV: Caught in the quest for a theory of mental disorder. *Research on Social Work Practice*, Vol. 24, pp. 123–131.

Putnam, H. (1988). *Representation and reality.* MIT Press.

Quinn, N. (ed.) (2005). *Finding culture in talk: A collection of methods.* Palgrave Macmillan.

Quinn, N. & Mageo, J. M. (eds.) (2013). *Attachment reconsidered: Cultural perspectives on a Western theory.* Palgrave.

Racine, T. P. (2015). Conceptual Analysis. In J. Martin, J. Sugarman, & K. L. Slaney (eds.), *The Wiley handbook of theoretical and philosophical psychology: Methods, approaches, and new directions for social sciences.* John Wiley & Sons, Ltd.

Rączaszek-Leonardi, J., Tylen, K., Dingemanse, M. et al. (2023). Putting interaction center-stage for the study of knowledge structures and processes. In M. Goldwater, F. K. Anggoro, B. K. Hayes, & D. C. Ong (eds.), *Proceedings of the Annual Meeting of the Cognitive Science Society*, Vol. 45.

Rahilly, E. (2022). "Well duh, that's how you raise a kid": Gender-open parenting in a (non)binary world. *LGBTQ+ Family: An Interdisciplinary Journal*, Vol. 18, pp. 262–280.

Raja, V. (2022). Resonances in the brain. In Kelty-Stephen, D. G., Cisek, P. E., De Bari, B., et al. *In search for an alternative to the computer metaphor of the mind and brain.* ArXiv: 2206.04603.

Reddy, G. (2006). *With respect to sex: Negotiating Hijra identity in South India.* University of Chicago Press.

Reicher, S. D., Van Bavel, J. J., & Haslam, S. A. (2020). Debate around leadership in the Stanford Prison Experiment: Reply to Zimbardo and Haney (2020) and Chan et al. (2020). *American Psychologist*, Vol. 75, pp. 406–407.

Rey, G. (2010). Eliminitavism. In T. Bayne, A. Cleeremans, & P. Wilken (eds.), *The Oxford companion to consciousness.* Oxford University Press.

Richards, G. (1997). Psychology and "scientific racism" 1860–1910. In G. Richards, *Race, racism and Psychology: Towards a reflexive history.* Routledge.

Richards, G. & Stenner, P. (2023). *Putting psychology in its place: Critical historical perspectives.* 4th ed. Routledge.

Richters, J. E. (2021). Incredible utility: The lost causes and causal debris of psychological science. *Basic and Applied Social Psychology*, Vol. 43, pp. 366–405.

Ritchie, J., Lewis, J., McNaughton Nicholls, C., & Ormston, R. (2014). *Qualitative research practice: A guide for social science students and researchers.* SAGE.

Robbins, P. & Aydede, M. (eds.) (2009). *The Cambridge handbook of situated cognition.* Cambridge University Press.

Robinson, D. N. (1995). The logic of reductionist models. *New Ideas in Psychology,* Vol. 13, pp. 1–8.

Robinson, D. N. (2010). Consciousness: The first frontier. *Theory & Psychology,* Vol. 20, pp. 781–793.

Robinson, D. (2016). Explanation and the "brain sciences." *Theory & Psychology,* Vol. 26, pp. 324–332.

Rodriguez, S. B. (2014). *Female circumcision and clitoridectomy in the United States: A history of a medical treatment.* University of Rochester Press.

Rodríguez-Flores, T. C., Palomo-Briones, G. A., Robles, F., & Ramos, F. (2023). Proposal for a computational model of incentive memory. *Cognitive Systems Research,* Vol. 77, pp. 153–173.

Rogler, L. H. (1997). Making sense of historical changes in the *Diagnostic and Statistical Manual of Mental Disorders*: Five propositions. *Journal of Health and Social Behavior,* Vol. 38, pp. 9–20.

Rose, N. & Abi-Rached, J. (2013). *Neuro: The new brain sciences and the management of the mind.* Princeton University Press.

Rose, N., Birk, R., & Manning, N. (2021). Towards neuroecosociality: Mental health in adversity. *Theory, Culture & Society,* Vol. 39, pp. 121–144.

Rosenlicht, N. (2024). *My brother's keeper: The untold stories behind the business of mental health – and how to stop the abandonment of the mentally ill.* Simon & Schuster.

Rosenthal, R. (1968). Experimenter expectancy and the reassuring nature of the null hypothesis decision procedure. *Psychological Bulletin,* Vol. 70, pp. 30–47.

Roth, W. M. & Jornet, A. (2013). Overview: Situated cognition. *WIREs Cogn Sci,* Vol. 4, pp. 463–478.

Rowlands, M. (1999). *The body in mind: Understanding cognitive processes.* Cambridge University Press.

Rowlands, M. (2003). *Externalism: Putting mind and world together again.* Acumen.

Rowlands, M. (2010). *The new science of the mind: From extended mind to embodied phenomenology.* MIT Press.

Rowlands, M. (2015). Consciousness unbound. *Journal of Consciousness Studies,* Vol. 22, pp. 34–51.

Rowold, K. (ed.) (1996). *Gender and science: Late nineteenth century debates on the female mind and body.* Thoemmes Press.

Rupert, R. (2004). Challenges to the hypothesis of extended cognition. *Journal of Philosophy,* Vol. 101, pp. 389–428.

Rupert, R. (2009). *Cognitive systems and the extended mind.* Oxford University Press.

Rupert, R. (2010). Representation in extended cognitive systems: Does the scaffolding of language extend the mind? In R. Menary (ed.), *The extended mind.* MIT Press.

Rychlak, J. (1983). Operationism and the source of meaning in bridging the theory/method bifurcation. *The Journal of Mind and Behavior*, Vol. 4, pp. 99–119.

Sanches de Oliveira, G. (2021). Representationalism is a dead end. *Synthese*, Vol. 198, pp. 209–235.

Sanches de Oliveira, G. & Chemero, A. (2015). Against smallism and localism. *Studies In Logic, Grammar and Rhetoric*, Vol. 41, pp. 9–23.

Sanches de Oliveira, G. & Baggs, E. (2023). *Psychology's WEIRD Problems.* Cambridge University Press.

Scarborough, E. & Furumoto, L. (1987). *Untold lives: The first generation of American women psychologists.* Columbia University Press.

Schatzberg, A., Scully, J., Kupfer, D., & Regier, D. (2009). Setting the record straight: A response to Dr. France's commentary on DSM 5. *Psychiatric Times*, Vol. 26, p. 1.

Schechter, S. (1982). *Women and male violence: The visions and struggles of the battered women's movement.* South End Press.

Schechtman, M. (2014). *Staying alive: Personal identity, practical concerns, and the unity of a life.* Oxford University Press.

Schleim, S. (2018). Subjective experience, heterophenomenology, or neuroimaging? A perspective on the meaning and application of mental disorder terms, in particular major depressive disorder. *Frontiers in Psychology*, Vol. 9, p. 702.

Schleim, S. (2020). To overcome psychiatric patients' mind–brain dualism, reifying the mind won't help. *Frontiers in Psychiatry*, Vol. 11, p. 605.

Schleim, S. (2022). Why mental disorders are brain disorders: And why they are not: ADHD and the challenges of heterogeneity and reification. *Frontiers of Psychiatry*, Vol. 13, 943049.

Schnepf, J. & Groeben, N. (2024). The replication crisis as mere indicator of two fundamental misalignments: Methodological confirmation bias in hypothesis testing and anthropological oversimplification in theory-building. *New Ideas in Psychology*, Vol. 75, 101110.

Scull, A. (2009). *Hysteria: The biography.* Oxford University Press.

Scull, A. (January 2019). Rattled: The travails of social psychology. *Times Literary Supplement.*

Scull, A. (2022). *Desperate remedies: Psychiatry's turbulent quest to cure mental illness.* The Belknap Press.

Searle, J. (2007). Putting consciousness back in the brain. In M. Bennett, D. Dennett, P. Hacker, & J. Searle (eds.), *Neuroscience and philosophy: Brain, mind, and language.* Columbia University Press.

Sestir, M., Kennedy, L., Peszka, J., & Bartley, J. (2023). New statistics, old schools: An overview of current introductory undergraduate and graduate statistics pedagogy practices. *Teaching of Psychology*, Vol. 50, pp. 211–221.

Shadish, W. R., Cook, T. D., & Campbell, D. T. (2002). *Experimental and quasi-experimental designs for generalized causal inference*. Houghton Mifflin.

Shapin, S. (2010). *Never pure: Historical studies of science as if it was produced by people with bodies, situated in time, space, culture, and society, and struggling for credibility and authority*. Johns Hopkins University Press.

Sharp, P. & Miller, G. (2019). Reduction and autonomy in psychology and neuroscience: A call for pragmatism. *Journal of Theoretical and Philosophical Psychology*, Vol. 39, pp. 18–31.

Shields, S. (1975). Functionalism, Darwinism, and the psychology of women. *American Psychologist*, Vol. 30, pp. 739–754.

Shweder, R. A. & Beldo, L. (2015). Culture: Contemporary views. In J. D. Wright (ed.), *International Encyclopedia of Social and Behavioral Sciences*, 2nd ed. Elsevier.

Simmons, J. P., Nelson, L. D., & Simonsohn, U. (2011). False-positive psychology: Undisclosed flexibility in data collection and analysis allows presenting anything as significant. *Psychological Science*, Vol. 22, pp. 1359–1366.

Slaney, K. (2023). Why force a square peg into a round hole? The ongoing (pseudo-)problem of psychological measurement: Invited comment. *Theory & Psychology*, Vol. 33, pp. 138–144.

Slaney, K., Graham, M., Dhillon, R., & Hohn, R. (2024). Rhetoric of psychological measurement theory and practice. *Frontiers of Psychology*, Vol. 15, 1374330.

Slaney, K. & Maraun, M. (2007). There are no "specific correct" usages of concepts, only correct usages: Linguistic rules and the bounds of sense. *Journal of Theoretical and Philosophical Psychology*, Vol. 27, pp. 105–112.

Slaney, K. & Racine, T. (2011). On the ambiguity of concept use in psychology: Is the concept "concept" a useful concept? *Journal of Theoretical and Philosophical Psychology*, Vol. 31, pp. 73–89.

Slife, B., Burchfield, C., & Hedges, D. (2010). Interpreting the "biologization" of psychology. *The Journal of Mind and Behavior*, Vol. 31, pp. 165–178.

Slife, B., O'Grady, K., & Kosits, R. D. (2017). *The hidden worldviews of psychology's theory, research, and practice*. Taylor & Francis.

Slife, B. & Williams, R. (1995). *What's behind the research? Discovering hidden assumptions in the behavioral sciences*. Sage.

Slife, B. D., Wright, C. D., & Yanchar, S. C. (2016). Using operational definitions in research: A best-practices approach. *The Journal of Mind and Behavior*, Vol. 37, pp. 119–139.

Smit, H. (2021). How to resolve Comte's challenge: The answer of cognitive neuroscience and the neo-Aristotelian alternative. *Philosophia*, Vol. 49, pp. 1201–1217.

Smit, H. (2023). An overarching framework for understanding and explaining human nature. *Biological Theory*, Vol. 18, pp. 63–75.

Smit, H. & Hacker, P. (2014). Seven misconceptions about the mereological fallacy: A compilation for the perplexed. *Erkenntnis*, Vol. 79, pp. 1077–1097.

Smit, H. & Hacker, P. (2020). Two conceptions of consciousness and why only the neo-Aristotelian one enables us to construct evolutionary explanations. *Humanities and Social Sciences Communications*, Vol. 7, pp. 1–10.

Smith, K. (2020). How culture and biology interact to shape language and the language faculty. *Topics in Cognitive Science*, Vol. 12, pp. 690–712.

Smith, R. (2005). The history of psychological categories. *Studies in History and Philosophy of Biological and Biomedical Sciences*, Vol. 36, pp. 55–94.

Smith, R. (2007). *Being human: Historical knowledge and the creation of human nature*. Columbia University Press.

Smith, R. (2013). *Between mind and nature: A history of psychology*. Reaktion Books.

Smortchkova, J., Dołęga, K., & Schlicht, T. (2021). Introduction. In J. Smortchkova, K. Dołęga, & T. Schlicht (eds.) *What are mental representations?* Oxford University Press.

Spackman, J. & Yanchar, S. (2013). Embodied cognition, representationalism, and mechanism: A review and analysis. *Journal for the Theory of Social Behaviour*, Vol. 44, pp. 46–79.

Speelman, C. & McGann, M. (2016). Editorial: Challenges to mean-based analysis in psychology: The contrast between individual people and general science. *Frontiers in Psychology*, Vol. 7, p. 1234.

Spence, J. R. & Stanley, D. J. (2018). Concise, simple, and not wrong: In search of a short-hand interpretation of statistical significance. *Frontiers in Psychology*, Vol. 9, p. 2185.

Spence, J. T., Helmreich, R., & Stapp, J. (1973). A short version of the Attitudes Toward Women Scale (AWS). *Bulletin of the Psychonomic Society*, Vol. 2, pp. 219-220.

Spence, J. T. & Helmreich, R. L. (1978). *Masculinity and femininity: Their psychological dimensions, correlates, and antecedents*. University of Texas Press.

Spivey, M. J. (2023). Cognitive science progresses toward interactive frameworks. *Topics in Cognitive Science*, Vol. 15, pp. 219–254.

Sprague, E. (1999). *Persons and their minds: A philosophical investigation*. Routledge.

Stalnaker, R. C. (2002). Common ground. *Linguistics and Philosophy*, Vol. 25, pp. 701–721.

Stanovich, K. (2014). *How to think straight about psychology, 9th Ed*. Pearson International.

Steinberg, L. (2009). Adolescent development and juvenile justice. *Annual Review of Clinical Psychology*, Vol. 5, pp. 459–85.

Stevens, S. S. (1935). The operational definition of psychological concepts. *Psychological Review*, Vol. 42, pp. 517–527.

Stevens, S. S. (1946). On the theory of scales of measurement. *Science*, Vol. 103, pp. 667–680.

Stuckey, M., Heering, P., Mamlok-Naaman, R., Hofstein, A., & Eilks, I. (2015). The philosophical works of Ludwik Fleck and their potential meaning for teaching and learning science. *Science & Education*, Vol. 24, pp. 281–298.

Stunt, J., van Grootel, L., Bouter, L., et al. (2021). Why we habitually engage in null-hypothesis significance testing: A qualitative study. *PLoS ONE*, Vol. 16, p. e0258330.

Styron, T., Utter, L., & Davidson, L. (2017). The Hearing Voices Network: Initial lessons and future directions for mental health professionals and systems of care. *Psychiatric Quarterly*, Vol. 88, pp. 769–785.

Sugarman, J. (2009). Historical ontology and psychological description. *Journal of Theoretical and Philosophical Psychology*, Vol. 29, pp. 5–15.

Susswein, N. & Racine, T. (2008). Wittgenstein and not-just-in-the-head cognition. *New Ideas in Psychology*, Vol. 27, pp. 184–196.

Sutton, J., Harris, C. B., Keil, P. G., & Barnier, A. J. (2010). The psychology of memory, extended cognition, and socially distributed remembering. *Phenomenology and the Cognitive Sciences*, Vol. 9, pp. 521–560.

Tafreshi, D. (2022). Sense and nonsense in psychological measurement: A case of problem and method passing one another by. *Theory & Psychology*, Vol. 32, pp. 158–163.

Tafreshi, D. & Slaney, K. (2024). Science or not, conceptual problems remain: Seeking conceptual clarity around "psychology as a science" debates. *Theory & Psychology*, Vol. 34, pp. 377–391.

Tamariz, M. & Kirby, S. (2016). The cultural evolution of language. *Current Opinion in Psychology*, Vol. 8, pp. 37–43.

Tamariz, M. & Vance, B. (2020). A comparative evolutionary approach to the origins and evolution of cognition and of language. In B. Joseph & R. Janda (eds.), *The Handbook of historical linguistics*. Blackwell.

Tanney, J. (2013). *Rules, reason and self-knowledge*. Harvard University Press.

Tanney, J. (2022). *Meaning, mind, and action: Philosophical essays*. Anthem Press.

Taylor, D., Gönül, G., Cameron, A. et al. (2023). Reading minds or reading scripts? De-intellectualising theory of mind. *Biological Reviews of the Cambridge Philosophical Society*, Vol. 98, pp. 2028–2048.

Taylor, J. B. & Shuttleworth, S. (eds.) (1998). *Embodied selves: An anthology of psychological texts, 1830–1890*. Clarendon Press.

Terman, L. & Miles, C. F. (1936). *Sex and personality. Studies in masculinity and femininity*. McGraw-Hill.

Thompson, B., Kirby, S., & Smith, K. (2016). Culture shapes the evolution of cognition. *PNAS*, Vol. 113, pp. 4530–4535.

Tomasello, M. (2020). The adaptive origins of uniquely human sociality. *Philosophical Transactions of the Royal Society B*, Vol. 375(1803), 20190493.

Trafimow, D. (2019a). A frequentist alternative to significance testing, p-values, and confidence intervals. *Econometrics*, Vol. 7, pp. 1–14.

Trafimow, D. (2019b). Five nonobvious changes in editorial practice for editors and reviewers to consider when evaluating submissions in a post p<0.05 universe. *The American Statistician*, Vol. 73 (sup1), pp. 340–345.

Trendler, G. (2022). Is measurement in psychology an empirical or a conceptual issue? A comment on David Franz. *Theory & Psychology*, Vol. 32, pp. 164–117.

Trybulec, B. (2015). Extended cognitive system and epistemic subject. *Studies in Logic, Grammar and Rhetoric*, Vol. 40, pp. 111–128.

Turner, J. S. (2000). *The extended organism: The physiology of animal-built structures*. Harvard University Press.

Tyni, K., Wurm, M., & Bratt, A. S. (2024). A thematic analysis of the experiences of prepubertal transgender and gender-diverse children in Sweden. *Journal of LGBT Youth*, Vol. 22, pp. 1-24.

Uchiyama, R. & Muthukrishna, M. (2021). Cultural evolutionary neuroscience. In J. Y. Chiao, S.-C. Li, R. Turner, S. Y. Lee-Tauler, & B. Pringle (eds.), *Oxford Handbook of Cultural Neuroscience and Global Mental Health*. Oxford University Press.

Uher, J. (2013). Personality psychology: Lexical approaches, assessment methods, and trait concepts reveal only half of the story – why it is time for a paradigm shift. *Integrative Psychological and Behavioral Science*, Vol. 47, pp. 1–55.

Uher, J. (2021). Psychometrics is not measurement: Unraveling a fundamental misconception in quantitative psychology and the complex network of its underlying fallacies. *Journal of Theoretical and Philosophical Psychology*, Vol. 41, pp. 58–84.

Uher, J. (2022). Rating scales institutionalize a network of logical errors and conceptual problems in research practices: A rigorous analysis showing ways to tackle psychology's crises. *Frontiers of Psychology*, Vol. 13, p. 1009893.

van Fraassen, B. C. (1989). *Laws and symmetry*. Oxford University Press.

Vessonen, E. (2021). Respectful operationalism. *Theory & Psychology*, Vol. 31, pp. 84–105.

Vold, K. & Schlimm, D. (2020). Extended mathematical cognition: external representations with non-derived content. *Synthese*, Vol. 197, pp. 3757–3777.

Vygotsky, L. (1978). *Mind in society*. Harvard University Press.

Wagner, N.-F. (2019). Against cognitivism about personhood, *Erkenntnis*, Vol. 84, pp. 657–686.

Ward, T., Clack, S., & Haig, B. D. (2016). The abductive theory of method: Scientific inquiry and clinical practice. *Behaviour Change*, Vol. 33, pp. 212–231.

Waring, T. M. & Wood, Z. T. (2021). Long-term gene-culture coevolution and the human evolutionary transition. *Proceedings of the Royal Society. B, Biological sciences*, Vol. 288, p. 20210538.

Wasserstein, R. & Lazar, N. (2016). The ASA statement on p-values: Context, process, and purpose. *The American Statistician*, Vol. 70, pp. 129–133.

Wasserstein, R. L., Schirm, A. L., & Lazar, N. A. (2019). Moving to a world beyond "p < 0.05." *The American Statistician*, 73 (Suppl. 1), pp. 1–19.

Weiner, T. (2011). The (un)managed self: Paradoxical forms of agency in self-management of bipolar disorder. Culture, Medicine and Psychiatry, Vol.35, p.448-483.

West, C. & Zimmerman, D. (1987). Doing gender. *Gender & Society*, Vol. 1, pp. 125-151.

Wetherell, M. (2007). A step too far: Discursive psychology, linguistic ethnography and questions of identity. *Journal of Sociolinguistics*, Vol. 11, pp. 661–681.

Wetherell, M. (2012). *Affect and emotion. A new social science understanding*. Sage.

Wetherell, M. & Edley, N. (1999). Negotiating hegemonic masculinity. *Feminism & Psychology*, Vol. 9, pp. 335–356.

Wetherell, M., Taylor, S., & Yates, S. (2001) *Discourse as data: A guide for analysis*. Open University Press.

Whitaker, R. & Cosgrove, L. (2015). *Psychiatry under the influence: Institutional corruption, social injury, and prescriptions for reform*. Palgrave Macmillan.

White, P. & Gorard, S. (2017). Against inferential statistics: How and why current statistics teaching gets it wrong. *Statistics Education Research journal*, Vol. 16, pp. 55–65.

Wiggins, B. J. & Christopherson, C. D. (2019). The replication crisis in psychology: An overview for theoretical and philosophical psychology. *Journal of Theoretical and Philosophical Psychology*, Vol. 39, pp. 202–217.

Williams, R. & Gantt, E. (2022). Preserving agency as a human phenomenon. In B. Slife, S. Yanchar, & F. Richardson (eds.), *Routledge international handbook of theoretical and philosophical psychology. Critiques, problems, and alternatives to psychological ideas*. Routledge.

Wilson, M. (1993). DSM-III and the transformation of American psychiatry: A history. *American Journal of Psychiatry*, Vol. 150, pp. 399–410.

Wilson, R. (1995) *Cartesian psychology and physical minds: Individualism and the sciences of the mind*. Cambridge University Press.

Wilson, R. (2004). *Boundaries of the mind: The individual in the fragile sciences – cognition*. Cambridge University Press.

Wilson, R. (2010). Meaning-making and the mind of the externalist. In R. Menary (ed.), *The Extended Mind*. MIT Press.

Wilson, R. A. (2013). Ten questions concerning extended cognition. *Philosophical Psychology*, Vol. 27, pp. 19–33.

Wilson, R. A. & Clark, A. (2009). How to situate cognition: Letting nature take its course. In P. Robbins & M. Aydede (eds.), *The Cambridge handbook of situated cognition*. Cambridge University Press.

Witt, J. (2021). Tool use affects spatial cognition. *Topics in Cognitive Science*, Vol. 13, pp. 666–683.

Woolley, H. T. (1910). A review of recent literature on the psychology of sex. *Psychological Bulletin*, Vol. 7, pp. 335-342.

Zahnoun, F. (2020). Explaining the reified notion of representation from a linguistic perspective. *Phenomenology and the Cognitive Sciences*. Vol. 19, pp. 79–96.

Zittel, C. (2012). Ludwik Fleck and the concept of style in the natural sciences. *Studies in East European Thought*, Vol. 64, pp. 53–79.

Zittel, C. (2017). Fleck-fieber. *Zeitschrift für Ideengeschichte*. Heft XI/2 Sommer 2017, pp. 15–28.

Index

For EU product safety concerns, contact us at Calle de José Abascal, 56–1°,
28003 Madrid, Spain or eugpsr@cambridge.org.

www.ingramcontent.com/pod-product-compliance
Ingram Content Group UK Ltd.
Pitfield, Milton Keynes, MK11 3LW, UK
UKHW020109120526

470874UK00023B/597